LIGHTS ON IN THE HOUSE OF THE DEAD

Books by Daniel Berrigan

POETRY

TIME WITHOUT NUMBER
ENCOUNTERS
THE WORLD FOR WEDDING RING
NO ONE WALKS WATERS
FALSE GODS, REAL MEN
TRIAL POEMS (with Tom Lewis)
SELECTED AND NEW POEMS
PRISON POEMS

PROSE

THE BRIDE
THE BOW IN THE CLOUDS
THEY CALL US DEAD MEN
CONSEQUENCES: TRUTH AND . . .
LOVE, LOVE AT THE END
NIGHT FLIGHT TO HANOI
NO BARS TO MANHOOD
THE TRIAL OF THE CATONSVILLE NINE
THE GEOGRAPHY OF FAITH (with Robert Coles)
THE DARK NIGHT OF RESISTANCE
AMERICA IS HARD TO FIND
ABSURD CONVICTIONS, MODEST HOPES (with Lee Lockwood)
JESUS CHRIST (with Gregory and Deborah Harris)
LIGHTS ON IN THE HOUSE OF THE DEAD

Daniel Berrigan

LIGHTS ON IN THE HOUSE OF THE DEAD

A Prison Diary

DOUBLEDAY & COMPANY, INC.
GARDEN CITY, NEW YORK, 1974

ISBN: 0-385-03953-0
Library of Congress Catalog Card Number 73-16823
Copyright © 1974 by Daniel Berrigan
All Rights Reserved
Printed in the United States of America
First Edition

ACKNOWLEDGMENTS & DEDICATION, SORT OF

The following pages were contrived in the course of an eighteen-month Live-in Grant conferred on the author by the U.S. government. During the period August 1970–February 1972, I was a Federal Fellow at the Correctional Institute in Danbury, Connecticut.

Application for the fellowship was first made at the Knights of Columbus Hall in Catonsville, Maryland, in May of 1968. Processing began immediately. The author, along with several others, survived the various eliminations, and was invited to appear for a final oral presentation in the Federal Building, Baltimore, Maryland, in October of 1968. There the grant was conferred; the author was invited to begin serving his residency in April of 1970.

Ordinarily in accepting the grant, applicants are required to take up residence at Danbury on the agreed date. However, in this case, the April assignment was judged inconvenient and the author invoked epikeia from the common law, due to unfinished business. A vivid disagreement ensued, that wrestling which is the very soul of art. Finally, having consummated various unfinished businesses here and there, the author took up residence in the Connecticut hills in August of 1970.

The author's Live-in Grant was approved by the following public servants. To them, in gratitude, these pages are dedicated:

J. Edgar Hoover (d.), John Mitchell, H. R. Haldeman, J. Erlichman, R. Nixon, and many others.*

Several of the above public officials are presently on leave of absence from their onerous public duties. It is to be hoped that they, and others of equal merit, may also be awarded Grants in Residence at Danbury and elsewhere.

Such rewards of manifest virtue can only be called, in the words of the ancient liturgy, *dignum et justum.*

Truly, as the Buddha says, what goes around comes around.

* Well, not really. They're for you, Tom Buck and Bill Anderson, in love and gratitude.

CONTENTS

August 20, 1970

Notes on Socrates: gods of the state, the new gods

469 B.C.– soldier, sculptor
   came on a style through (1) personal poverty
                       (2) search for truth
                       (3) "Socratic" irony—personal ig-
                           norance confessed . . . "So
                           cratic" questions—method of
                           teaching—compared himself
                           to (a) gadfly (b) midwife
charges of the trial—(1) corrupter of youth
                     (2) atheist

Said: a man who is good for anything ought not calculate his chances of living or dying; he ought to consider only if he is doing good or evil . . . I know that injustice and disobedience whether to God or man is evil and dishonorable and I will never fear or avoid possible good rather than certain evil. I shall obey God rather than you though I honor and love you. Example of this: question— My friend, you who are a citizen of the great mighty and wise state of ——, why do you care so much about laying up the greatest possible money, repute, and honor—why do you care so little about wisdom, truth, and soul, which you never regard or heed at all! "No greater good has happened to the state than my service to God. If you kill me you will injure yourself more than me." "No one who wrestles with the unrighteousness and wrong worked by the state can hope to save his life."

[After death sentence] (My crime is that) I went about where I thought I could do the greatest good—trying to persuade each man to look to himself, to seek virtue and justice before his private interest: to look to the state before he looked to the interests of the state . . .

"Socrates, why don't you just disappear, and no one will harass you any longer or pursue you?" "If I say I can't because that would be to disobey a divine command, no one will take me seriously. If I say the greatest good possible to man is to talk about virtue and self-examination or that the unexamined life is not worth living—none of you will take me seriously." I have no regrets about my defense; I would rather speak as I did, and die for it, than speak as you did and live.

The difficulty is not how to escape the clutches of death; it is how to escape unrighteousness, which runs faster than death.

Socrates ⟶ I am old and move slowly; and the slower
death ⟶ runner, death has overtaken me;
accusers ⟶ My accusers are keen and quick; and
unrighteousness ⟶ the faster runner, unrighteousness, has
overtaken them . . .

When my sons are grown up—I ask you, my friends, to punish them, trouble them as I you; if they care about riches or anything else, more than virtue—if they pretend to be something when they are nothing . . .

The good citizen ought not to flee; he owes more to state than to father or ancestor.

Questions Socrates raises:

Can the just man survive in the state? Socrates: He ought not to care.

What can the just man do when falsely accused? Answer as best he can.
What can the just man do if falsely convicted? Pay the price.
What about his wife and family? Think of justice first.

August 22

Start of horror, a sense that I will die under the knouts here, with nothing accomplished. There is no answer I know of, except to live by faith day after day and let the future stand in the hands of God—a wager of Pascal or of Paul. This is the perennial refusal to let fear of the Man trick one into acting as he is meant officially to act—with fear as another god, a state god.

But how do I see my life? It is hard in middle age to be crushed between the two millstones of days and nights in captivity. Is it too hard to bear, or not yet hard enough to make a man? It would be easier if one could see some light on the horizon, some larger horizon opening before one which would allow the year to act as a mere interlude, a chastening of self toward a "normal" future in a civilized society. But the truth is something darker and more ominous. No dawn is in sight—in fact the night itself is deepening, to the point where one is constantly being pushed further to the edge of personal extinction, as the price of bringing any change at all.

There is this to be faced: that any action possible to us will bring little change worth mentioning. So one is reduced, not to impotence, but to something like a deeper gesture of fraternity with those who, here as elsewhere, are far more consistently and purposefully brutalized than I am.

Thus the refusal "to adore the gods of the state." Which would mean, in the context, refusing to place one's well-being, good time, good name, expectations (slight enough, God knows) of shortened imprisonment ahead of the iron course of injustice toward others. The gods of the state are, after all, the inflated ego of power, technology, money in their rake's progress, dragging all before into the abyss.

Socrates introduces other gods. A crime. If he believes in the true God, his crime is a capital one; thus the Grand Inquisitor indicts not only the Christian but Christ Himself. That ultimate crime being that He proposes not only strange gods for adoration, but Himself as very God—to dethrone all other gods, all principalities and powers, for all time. What were these "new gods" like, whose onset appeared to the state as such a mortal threat? Were they *like* men, or remote, distant, peerlessly above them? In what consisted their offensiveness to the established order?

The genius of both Socrates and Jesus, though apparently different, was to offer a vision of the godlike that was realizable—indeed immediately and palpably realized—in men themselves. This thirst for truth, this unassailable courage, this steadfast will toward the good: it was not only godlike, but it brought the new god(s) into the midst of men. It scorched human pusillanimity with the divine fire. It made idolatry a milksop venture which could never win truth to its side, making of men the prey of heroes, madmen—or godlike men.

Related to the charge: that of atheism. A crime against the state, note: since the state is specifically theistic, ruled by the gods of its own making, its own demented, inflated ego. To worship whom is to perish, inevitably.

"Socrates has other new divinities of his own." Their credentials will be this (in light also of Christ): that the "new divinities" behave in a way that is superior to the old. Simple as that. In casu, that the new divinities cling not at all to the parasitic life granted the older gods by the aging state. "He began to say to them that he must go up to Jerusalem, there be maltreated and die, and on the third day rise again." It was a pattern of life in the world which was admirably beyond the bumbling and bloodletting of the fascist gods of the fascist state. A new pattern of things. The new god (as in Socrates' case) commanded him in a voice both sovereign and unassailable to die for the truth. In the case of Jesus, a like destiny was announced as the Father's will. In both cases the new gods were, in the estimate of good men, winning out over the old; they had more chutzpa, we would say: they believed more strongly. Believed in whom, in what? We must say, if the new men are called to believe in the new gods, then these same gods validate themselves by believing in men. Just men move at their ease among the gods; the just gods are impassioned for the human scene.

August 25

Overheard in the yard: they're a paper tiger—they can hold me but they can't eat me . . .

If I can lighten the burden of one or another of the men; a simple exercise in the truth that "God is love." Thus one's life is simplified to the point that it may be worthy of God, worthy of man . . .

I lose heart so easily.

Long periods when I can only hang on, and hope—for the best against the worst.

This must be true of the majority here—especially of those terribly silent and broken men for whom prison is no mere interlude in a life that has gotten somewhere, but a dreary chapter in an infinitely dreary story—with more of the same ahead.

I am just beginning to learn to believe.

We are the silent third tier, on which I live like "the church of silence." We are beset with the basic fifty words of the lively group of homos below, who cluster and break again like skittish birds. Yell, sing, laugh, roar away like a surf at all hours. It is exhausting and without relief. One gives up privacy and the priceless gift of silence—except for what small measure he can create for himself. But at what cost!

Everything in scripture points beyond present distress—precisely by leading one deeper into hell and purgation—like Dante's merciless and compassionate guide. Lord, teach us to pray!

I am growing content to be silent, psychologically, to function at some 50 per cent of my native strength, without those passionate moments of insight and relief which elsewhere would issue in poetry. Nothing of this. The common prose, the filthy cramped enclosure which is the common life of man in the world. How exempt I have been from all this for a half century—the whole of my life up to now! I see here on all sides those who in one way or another worship the gods of the state—some are being punished for violating the rules—they worshiped too fervently, or fed off the gods' living, or took unseemly interest in the secular profits of the temple. But they never toppled official gods or declared themselves atheists in the heroic tradition of Jesus or Socrates . . . and they will return to the same old degraded service, mentally.

Then there are the official keepers of the shrine, vindicators of the gods' honor, judges, subalterns, foodbearers, paper shufflers, paymasters, masons, architects, lawyers, doctors—all the human mix required to keep something (big and lucrative) going—or to put it another way, to keep nothing going . . .

The whole making for a vast dervish dance, about the dollar, about the missile, about the President, about law and order, the Maypole dance of death. There is really nothing to be done to protest its emptiness—diabolism—except to refuse to join in it.

One of the tragic psychological outcomes—the dance as pacifier, totalizer. There was never a devotee of the true god to compare in noise or numbers with those harassed, ecstatic, feverish followers of Il Duce of whatever political leaning . . .

August 28

I daresay the native value of a good thing is only weakened by claims made on its behalf. An equally determined reaction sets in; this is especially true of religion today, when the most lucid evidence of holiness is quite lost in a clamor of conflicts and bickering. Even the saints are lost in the melee; their example no longer helps men grow thoughtful or achieve right thought. We are really at a time when it is necessary to keep silent and live as though the truth were its own vindication—as indeed it is, were we to stop getting in its way. Does Jesus, who was so reluctant to defend himself, need us to defend Him? It is not likely. Or at least, one had better begin living as though His "way" had attached to it some perennial value—even for us.

Hole: Guard: Noisy this A.M.! (It was: hellishly so.)
      Inmate: Wouldn't you be noisy too, locked up all day?
      Guard: Ah, I don't make the decisions here . . .

August 29

In midst of great turmoil and violence and the failure of nerve, the believer makes his way like a child, warned that new leaven is rising in the house. The mystery of life and love is so fragile that it risks "deadening" at a noisy blur, a reverberation, too loud a word. We are the careful household to whom is entrusted the new bread.

To keep conscious throughout the day of the mystery whose call first brought me here.

The "cloud of witnesses" to this travail, toward which my whole life has led, as a perfect lodestone—"God, my keeper and my Lord."

We are in good hands. I do believe. Lord help my unbelief.

The rigor of a faith that consents, not only to careful keeping, but also to constant testing on the cruelest of human scenes—prison, where every evil is rampant and in close conflict; there, for that reason, goodness may shine forth; a lightness in a northeaster on Block Island.

The drama has invaded the household. The inmates are shaken. It is a time when heroism, compassion, steadfastness are clearly scrutinized by a jealous Lord. On Calvary, it was not evil, but supreme goodness which met the hour, the powers of darkness.

In such a time, one is not heartened because he can remember this or that text, this consoling thought, that great saying or deed of God or man. Usually the mind is in such turmoil, or is so stupefied, that such an exercise is practically impossible. Nor is one commonly granted consolation because his life has made an impact on others. Beyond, beneath all this, the heart beats on. It would be true to this hour only—not demanding to be innately noble, imperishable, strong in resolve. A real test, a prolonged injustice, a stiff prison sentence, any of these suffices to bring muscle men to their knees—as I have so often seen. What then? The spirit of God is poured out upon us. In Him, our strength.

September 1

Most inmates dream of a return to the spoiled playground —the only moral and psychic landscape they have ever known. By a necessity that forever inhibits their imagination, the only one they will ever know. The believer is not attached to so ambiguous a reward for "good behavior." Do I not bear my reward and punishment within me, indeed decree, *even here*, whether I am to create heaven or hell as my natural endowment, my portion?

I look around the landscape of death, I smell death everywhere; and then Philip passes; and I take heart once more . . .

Philip and I have been, I would think, more than commonly conscious of the immanence of catastrophe that gathers force in the dark wings of consciousness. How to deal with so menacing an event, seemingly so inescapable, so dreaded, as though a man both battled and courted his own extinction. We have chosen one way it has brought us here. It simply involved us as imaginatively and concretely as was possible with the struggle for decency, justice, unity. A few friends, a law deliberately broken, punishment cheerfully borne. So it went. And here we are.

September 4

"A man . . . *ought not to consider his chance of living or dying; he ought only to consider on a given occasion whether he is doing right or wrong.*" (Socrates)

To allow such a principle to rule one's life, how many other considerations have to be swept aside; and how few are ready for such extraordinary detachment of heart. We think we are living—for God, for an ideal, for our brothers, for principle; and we end up at Mass on Sundays, as "warden of the wretched" for a livelihood—for our whole lives. And beget children, and love them, and keep our job, in despite of what we are doing in public . . . How cruelly such a life weaves its net—and how all the interstices cunningly join; an admirable life, after Gogol or Mauriac! A rabbi tells of the Catholics in Poland who ran an extermination camp near his home and bused to Mass on Sundays. The horrors that a single life can

"make sense of" are almost beyond belief, given the stupefy-
ing effect of habit, inheritance, routine.

To break through the net.

To be the occasion of a fresh start for man, because one
has made it for himself.

To stand with others even while he consciously walks a
few paces ahead of them.

The gift of Philip and of my family—that "gift of unhap-
piness" Socrates and Weil speak of, the supreme gift of grace,
habitually. We seem to be among the few who have had their
family with them on the exodus from slavery.

The "long haul" of patience, in the course of which one
not only prepares for the next stage of things, but actually
has it "revealed" to him—as did the Jews in the desert.

September 5

Sounds of gunfire outside the compound; ominous from
here, all day, for two days cold. Federal employees here
obliged to practice up once a year. Now I know what it feels
like to be in the gunsights of the law . . .

"If I were to desert my post through fear of death or any
other fear, . . . I might justly be charged in court with deny-
ing the existence of the gods. For I had disobeyed the oracle
in fear of death."

I find this a wonderfully concrete statement of morality.

It admits a mystical, non-verifiable basis for living in an
imperfect world; i.e., the "oracle" can no more be verified
than may the Divinity of Christ. Both are taken on the word
of the "interested party" in order to interest "other parties"
in the truth of existence. A wizened, rationalized, scientifi-
cally bedazzled culture always demands a sign—i.e., submit
before our criteria of proofs—come into our courts. But Jesus
and Socrates counter by offering a very different sort of sign—

the sign of death. This is their staggering, absurd act of faith and hope in man—that he will be able to read the sign.

The atheist is practically speaking the man who reneges on a genuine vocation. (*Sic* Socrates.) He has turned his back on the incarnate aspect of the *mystery*.

". . . the God who is with us is the God who forsakes us." (Bonhoeffer)

September 6

Jesus and His friends. Socrates and his friends. Two methods; in John's Gospel especially, the warmth, the human commingling, the passage from servanthood to friendship. That baring of the heart of God. Socrates is stern with the assimilated principle—the truth of life above the perdurance of life. He insists that the word of God to man is that man is called to be a man—in a plenary sense—at the hour of death; but also over the long haul of the dialogue, irony, riposte, in which the truth might emerge. It is a Greek mind at its quintessential, filtered through the lucid systematic prose of Plato; the old man dies supremely well, surpassing death by his calm assumption of immortality; the robbery of death's sting by the native virtue of manhood.

In Jesus: tenderness, majesty, and above all, personalism. The certainty of one who is not only familiar with the human scene and its range of experience, but with the transcendent life as well: "We testify to what we have seen. I give my life, as the Father commands me . . ." It is this double life, hypostatically joined, marrow, mind, fiber, heart—the infinite One, radiant and humiliated in our flesh. Prison is a new chance to test that faith: as one would seek, not added "evidence" of truth, but that apparent counter to truth which lends the truth substance in conflict . . .

They say so often here: it makes no difference whether he

is God or not, we find him a real man. One rejoins *sotto voce*, to his own spirit: it makes all the difference, as a clue leads to a hidden truth. Why this probed and approved manhood, whose stature even the worst sins of Christianity has been unable to diminish? Because He is God, he can command such constant historic respect, even from enemies, even from Christians.

I know for certain that deprived of this faith I could not for a single day endure the rigors of this jungle, keep myself from a destructive, exhausting, corrosive hatred. With Him, I endure. I believe, help my unbelief.

To Mars, not to us

An act of faith is uttered when everything seems to give the lie to faith. The truth would seem most nearly to approach the truth when a man could say: but I have natural hopes, friends, a future that will relieve this state of iron insanity into which I am locked. But these are subterfuges, as Socrates ironically reminds us, and Jesus also, and Gandhi. Alas, I am far from seeing my life in their way, drawing from the present its true meaning, which is to live in the present with all its pain, the pain of all those who have only the present to live for, whose future is the suppression of the breath of the spirit; far and wide to near and narrow—American existence in the '70s belongs—irretrievably?—to Mars, and therefore cannot belong to us.

A visit from Tom Buck, for his congressman. We are desperately trying to do something for the Vietnamese, the pris-

oners, ourselves. Against great odds. Buck toils on, with great
sorrow in his own family (which he did us the honor to share
with us also). The future is stubbornly unborn, the present
condemns us to its inhuman self-blinded measure. This is
true both of church and state. Good men are being wrung
dry, to the very heart. We are with them; we scarcely have
light to go by, let alone to share with others. How shall we
make, of so terrifying a life, a life for others? We must believe
in what we are doing, with its inevitable counterpoint of
renouncement of all that we cannot do.

September 12

It seems to me our presence here has to take into account
the suffering servanthood of Isaiah. Seriously into account.
Much of what that oracle speaks of is simply built into the
humiliating daily spectacle—I mean as it touches us, and
tests our fiber, and shears away so much of the cultural ac-
cretion that in life outside obscures the priesthood—or positively defaces it. We stand in the same garb, subject to the
same capricious discipline, as the other prisoners—live in
the same crowded, noisy conditions, feel the sharp file of the
days and hours scraping at our bones. From the majority of
the prisoners we receive the "institutionalized indifference"
which is the approved attitude—since men are advised to do
their time, mind their own business, make no friendships;
keep relationships at a distance which will forbid organization on "common fronts."

September 14

Philip is very restless with most of us, including himself.
I think he feels quite alone, in face of the immaturity and

childishness of most—and my own opaqueness and lack of drive. Truth told, I live so close to the edge of survival as to have almost no energy to spare, let alone spirit to undertake further risks and losses. This is the cruel course of the days' larceny. Things may grow better, I fervently hope they will, but they have not so far. I shall have to confide in him more fully. I have not yet been able to see my life as a seamless robe, inward, outward, as I venture he has. But I will have to be patient, and so will he. After all, he has almost a year's advantage of me, in prison time.

September 17

They are dancing in the cell block below because Ricky is going home tomorrow. He is one of the youngest and best of the motley company—a resister, finishing up some two years here. Not political in any hard-nosed sense. I will remember him banging his guitar on the long summer evenings. He was living with a thirty-five-year-old woman and her three children—they lived "as the birds do" and he is going back to her. Prison was simply an episode in his life—though all things considered, a highly noble one, which does him immense credit in the ledger of the living. Would that everyone could come to live as he will live from now on, a dropout in the still pool of some country place, hospitable, joyous, and free, fathering his instant family, keeping open house for the knights and ladies of the road.

September 20

I have been trying to understand the homosexuals who so grievously try the rest of us from their enclave on the first block. They natter, howl, shout, mime, preen for hours every night, while the rest of us are vainly trying to get some rest. No letup. But I find my reaction progressively less angry, more compassionate. What a double strike on one, to be black and gay! What legacy have they been born to, what lies ahead for them?

September 23

We were about our ordinary business in the dentist's office, peering like miners down someone's open gullet. Suddenly a scuffle broke out backstage in the lab. We rushed back. Our so normal clerks and aides were seriously mauling some poor shuffling stray from the medico center next door. For what, remained obscure; he had sneaked in, breathing yellow dog threats against our stout fellows. In spite of cleric and dentist, they chased him, cursing the while . . .

I was appalled, as a new boy always is at the natives' manners. Why the sudden violence, going up like a match flame in a storm—up and then out? I was to learn, as I have learned (largely from the goings on in my own skull), how the atmosphere keeps all but the most guarded (ha!), the best controlled, on edge. Edgy; almost over the edge. Noise, dislocation, off guard; the obvious and not so obvious threats imposed by the lockup, the lack of privacy and normal relationships, no free play of love . . .

September 24

"I caught my wife fucking on the living room couch. My two-year-old daughter sitting there. My son met me at the front door with the news: I was just out of jail, too. 'Daddy,' he said, 'Mommy has on the white pajamas you gave her.'

(They had three layers, I made her cut two away.) He and she came out when I knocked. He was in my slacks. I turned around, went to the kitchen, made a cup of coffee. She came down, asked me what I wanted. We started cursing. He came in, said, 'Freddy, you can't talk to her that way . . .'"

September 25

A long, ten-page flower-love-child letter read to me in toto in the yard, by J. An ecstatic camping trip through the western Rockies. What he hopes for, what keeps him going. His voice flares out, a deer in the clean wind. All he hopes for, as he reads.

September 26

Anyone who hasn't lived through a series of nights with the inmates of the "hole" doesn't know much about the cries, pounding catcalls, screams that issue from a painting by Bosch. What men come to. The simple bearing of the unbearable. Hell, but relieved by the concern of others, somewhat better off, who manage somehow to get cigarettes, reading, notes, passed in . . . The hole population is swelled by six young Jews, one in sympathy; the authorities refused to allow them to attend the holiday services. This in spite of the contrary decision, last Christmas, to allow Christians to attend Mass. How come, say the young? The old, white-collar Jews are astounded, there are frictions and divisions. Worship suddenly has something to do with the fate of the brethren? No one ever said so before . . . It is all boiling on, without the rabbi, who is busy with his local congregation . . . the consensus is that he would not be of much help anyway . . . But I marvel that such firecrackers are going off in the midst of all conventicles, the universal caucuses forming, as they usually do wherever two versions of the world collide . . .

October 2

An old man in the dental chair today—seventy years old. "I've been behind bars forty years. Going home to North Carolina. Oldest of nine, only one left. I helped build the inmates' church in Dannemora in '50. Told the chaplain, I'll be the stonemason but I won't take orders from any hack or *anybody*. Fell off the scaffolding seventy feet, live to tell it; chaplain ran up first; said, I saw you come down on wings!" Fitting him for plates; he said: "Look, I've got the heart and lungs of a man of fifty. Good clean living, no alcohol!"

October 3

An angel-faced pothead of twenty-two came in from the hole for an extraction. Took the needle, cold with fear. Fainted off, went into deep shock. Doctor was on him like the fastest falcon extant, started massage, pumping up and down on his chest, had him breathing again in forty-five seconds. WHEW! I went up to hospital ward an hour later, embraced the kid like Lazarus . . . son! He was walking around blithely again, combing his hair, cleaning up. Since restored to the compound, in full splendor and among friends. So it goes, the living live it up for the moment, make the best of a bad thing. The questions are for the graybeards like myself—what will become of this kid, what kind of future can he have?

October 5

The Mass we celebrate together—one makes his special effort at concentration, and knows how little it is he can offer; but there it is, out and on the table; the poor, the old, the war victims, the dead, the inmates, those in the hole; we come back week after week to the same refrain, patient as Quakers who have only their prayer, who go down praying— and know that was enough.

October 7

Reading the longer poems of Rexroth—that brutal meditation called "The Dragon and the Unicorn," on his trip to Italy, where his mind constantly oscillates between Italy the damned and U.S.A. the damned. He states in a way I find convincing and true, the way the world sits, the parrots' perch we sit on, tortured . . .

If jail is the great seizure of man by the death force of the state, then every assertion of life, goodness, cheerfulness, friendship is glue in the locks. No key may enter and claim.

If the state is a death mechanism, it is up to us to live here, and to give life, and to measure the passage of days, as well as our failure and growth, by the life we lead.

If "free men" make war, it is up to caged men to disclaim war, in their immediate dealings; and thus deal another hand.

Our sin is to parrot the state by our murderous treatment of one another, or to cherish like a death wish, a cancer in the bowels, our return to the "normalcy" of the state—which is to say, the society in which murder is the daily round of activity.

If religion is to be a leavening power, it is up to us to be religious—i.e., to give immediate palpable evidence that (1) we come here in conflict with the state, and (2) we so live here that the state suffers defeat at our hands—even though it is "winning" elsewhere, in its ordinary body counts.

Tale of a tall one

He is lithe and spirited, on a jail pilgrimage—Texas to New England has by no means dulled his edge. An ex-seminarian; has pedaled all the outer and inner space which the last six years have both opened and sucked us into, a giant vortex in nature and in us. Drugs, sex; still touchy about the religion he walked out of in shedding the mini-cassock of a high school boy. His father is a state trooper; what will his sons be like? He is intelligent, good-humored, endowed with a delightful coltish spirit that almost never fails him—a type of the new prisoner who is crowding the jails, thanks to the idiotic drug laws that slap the young so recurrently—two, three, even five years for possession of a common weed. But what I will remember most vividly about him is a kind of unassailable, unwavering innocence; it dwells, detached and free, in the other side of Blake's withered garden, the world. He has seen everything, tried some of it, with a fine, sensual, almost religious discrimination, and lives to tell it to the priest—not in the old way of confessional but in a newly found friendship, with an unspoiled spontaneity. He wants to go back to a farm commune he was snatched from to do time. There he will work the land, work at ceramics, and raise a family.

His dream is one with that of the nineteenth-century rebels who withstood the gargantuans, the slave traders and robber barons—Thoreau, Emerson, Whitman, Melville. "There's nothing else left. We have to work with our hands, give decent schooling to the kids, learn to live and work to-gether . . ." What will the church have to offer such a man? He finds one strain of foolishness in Phil's and my other-wise amiable characters; we still are seen at Sunday Mass, a spiritless affair dominated by a limp chaplain, a lamb in lamb's clothing. What for? A puzzlement and a touch of rancor.

What for indeed? We sit and stand and take communion with the old cons, most of whom are unafflicted with nau-sea when one of their company strikes up "Jesus, Jesus, come to me" in a winy falsetto: a pre-Vatican (he would say pre-Christian) performance. Our habits, indeed our powerless-ness, our submission before a local church which is more or less one with the local tyranny—he can stomach us six days a week. Sunday he turns away chilled.

We, on the other hand, believe. Even from such a priest, ignorant of the law, the prophets, the gospel, the lives of prisoners—a gift of life comes. We—older, wounded, bewil-dered, searching out a place to live or to die, existing here out of a decision that every hour exacts its price—we continue to believe. Which is almost to say—we need the Eucharist, even when the bread is stale to the point of rictus.

Dare we say we know, better than our friend, what is in man—that we have lived through a longer horror, fallen in a deeper pit?

One thing is certain—in multitudes of young people, like him, born in the church, nurtured in sacramental experience, schooled and shriven and instructed—the break is a clean one. For the present it may even be called final. They re-member the church in somewhat the way one remembers an aging grandparent who died in one's youth, whose vigor and best years went by too early to make any difference, who doddered about one's landscape and then petered out, one's memory of whom is tinged with pity, humor, and a dim anger against the clumsiness and moodiness of the senile.

"Let it die. You guys are giving a tribute to the dead, as though there was still some life in the old bones . . ." Perhaps, but then again perhaps not.

October 9

One is not commanded to be on the winning side, but to be in the right place—when the Lord returns.

Even to order one's immediate life in such a place as this, with some measure of sanity and compassion—*gratia efficax* . . .

The worst of men; there is no need to stigmatize the chaplains. They are stereotypes, turned out on the workbench of the working society. They think of themselves, confess and act out their role as religious arms of the secular body—hired to perform certain functions, magical gestures, to validate the inhuman regime, to induce a religious amnesia of submission; so that the will of Caesar may shine as the will of God.

Hidden in such unconscious perfidy, however, as I believe, is another gesture. It summons the unbelievably pure and vital presence of Christ, in his people. Thus the best may emerge—not so much from the "worst"—that baleful distinction is out of place here. But out of the average, formless, blurred, morally hesitant, fearful, tepid. Ourselves.

We go to Mass, our teeth are set on edge with another hour of endurance. We go; to confront ourselves. Also, in the power of Christ, if only for an hour or two by a power which

no man may ultimately snuff out; to surpass ourselves. O
gratia efficax! Renew in us, at each hour, the grace of Catonsville.

It is in your power whenever you choose, to retire into yourself . . .
. . . particularly when you hear within yourself thoughts that in-
        duce tranquillity,
which is to be thought of as the good ordering of the mind.
Constantly, then, return to this retreat, and renew yourself,
Let your principles be brief and fundamental; as soon as you recur
        to them
they will completely purify your soul,
and send you back free from all discontent.
For why are you discontented? With the evil of men?
Recall to mind that men exist for one another, that to endure
is a part of justice, that men do wrong involuntarily.
Consider how many men, after enmity, suspicion, hatred, fighting,
have fallen, reduced in death.
And so be quiet at last . . .
This remains: retire into your own terrain, do not distract or strain
        yourself,
but be free, look at things like a man, a citizen, a mortal.

                    (Marcus Aurelius: *Meditations*)

John Griffin's book on Merton came today. Set me thinking of that letter to Mexico in '67 when Griffin wrote he was
on his way to Rome and would protest my exile. My exile
went on nonetheless. Now Merton is dead an unbelievable
two years. And I am locked in an iron cage like the last man
or beast to walk the earth, fed and clothed and kept safe for
some outcome or other that escapes me (and I am sure,
others as well . . .). Nixon's face on the tube, Merton's face
on the book jacket under my arm. Two faces born in two
worlds: the one given to innocent and untimely death, the
other oozing out the latest platitudes of the latest peace
plan, which is to say, given the mad determinants, the latest
war plan. We shall simply have to live on, saying no, as Mer-

ton would have done, with unassailable courage. Calling on
him too, and living with the bitter fact, not only of his death,
but the death of so many good hopes that rode on his vision,
his realism, his vulgar and constant truthfulness. There is
not going to be much more going for us; we shall have to go
it alone, embodying his spirit as best we may . . .

There is so little toehold and real change here . . . I am
sure Philip feels despairing at times. One had to come to
this at least in the mind, each day; life calls us not merely to
live on, but to be ready to give ourselves to death. I put this
clumsily, feeling for the present that mere survival is about
all I can demand of myself for the present, and that to undertake more punishment or reprisal would be more of a death-
than a life-wish. To admit this requires a rueful humility,
evaluating as best one may the weight the wires can bear.

> The world is in a miserable state
> and just for spite we ought not to cry about it.
> If you want to know the truth
> that's the source of my perpetual good mood,
> my humor.
> Just for spite I'm not going to cry.
> Just to spite them, there's going to be laughter . . .
>
>   (S. Aleichem)

Things as they go here keep one very practical and concrete. The next meal, the nearest face, *things as they are*—
bad or good, but not much different. Morning to night, a
secular puritan discipline—the town stocks, the town jail, the
town gossip. The need of concrete patience, good will, lasting
out the day or hour—the discipline of humiliation, not per-
mitting oneself an unexamined self-pity.

October 10

"Just to spite them . . ."

He is admittedly "not programming." He is dismayed with himself, it shows in his eyes. What can be going wrong? He showed me the prospectus of his business outside; at twenty-seven he was "making it." Indeed, he need not have said so; the stench of success was on him. What else? He is finding that he cannot grab the ethos of the people he most admires here. So there is a kind of double trouble; the past is cut off—the present is not working. That cuteness and derring-do that made it on the electronics market (and the dope trade) are bad currency here. He chatters on about relatives, deals, sexual big time. But nothing quite adds up to the cubit of height he needs so badly. Mainly he wins so poor a thing as patience—stale bread indeed for a Big Boy . . .

In this novitiate for the not-yet-twice-reborn, one is slowly cut down, by a parallel discipline, whose faint memory stirs in every corner. Segregation, limits on mail and visitors, common table, common food and drink, "progress reports"—are we making it (as Jesuits?) as men? It is that desert recommended to neophytes by the Fathers, where the spirit springs higher—or is quenched.

Dear ones everywhere, whom I can neither see, face to dear face, nor write to, nor touch hands with—believe me, I am not quenched. Nor is Philip. Nor, I dare assert, shall we be!

October 11

Hard hit by casual news from Cornell—"Announce your job was liquidated . . ."

If the news had arrived, say, in course of a visit from someone I loved there, or even directly in a letter from Jack or John . . . I am trying to understand how this can spell a new kind of freedom, allowing the future to form itself, having no anchor ropes out to this or that. Easier said than done. I seem to know my deepest loves only in the loss of them. Thus again: life, the high wire act between allowing the heart its legitimacy and, on the other hand, not being ruled by a heart on the rampage.

It is quite possibly good for me to be forgotten for a while by the world at large. Though I confess the burden of people was at times very heavy on me, something like the millstones of Margaret Clitherow . . .

Many of us here, myself included, do not "come together" in our misery and loss. We accept our condemnation to hell and then go about ensuring its existence, by playing out a theater of cruelty toward one another. I marvel at how sweetly and strongly Philip resists all this in his sunny, courageous cheerfulness, no matter what the provocation. This, from a man who has consistently borne the heaviest burden of war resistance in the past years, and has the most savage sentence of all lying upon him.

Nero was an artist, a lyric and dramatic artist, a passionate lover of the ideal, a worshiper of ancient times, a collector of

medals, a traveler, a poet, an orator, a swordsman, a Don
Juan, a Lovelace, a nobleman full of wit, fancy, and fellow
feeling, overflowing with life and love of pleasure. That is why
he was Nero.

(Proudhon)

October 12

I heard today that the whole first section of these notes is
apparently lost. Another lifeline cut. I am learning hard, but
still learning, the price of Catonsville. We will continue to
pay. What we are paying for and the cost itself are often
strangely mixed—to help broken men, including ourselves,
survive. To work, to expand the contracting circle of allowed
life. To back up the brothers. To make it less certain that
others must perish—in the spirit, first of all, in the body after.

What if a request such as this were to be formulated in
the months ahead?—(1) That the sheet on the furloughs be
activated by us in the form of an educational program that
would release Phil and me for recruiting disaffected profs for
prison work? (2) That gradually ten or fifteen of the younger
prisoners be assembled for three or four hours outside prison
each week for informal classes—this to be expanded until
we spent most of the time outside. Growing into a living situation together—toward a kind of halfway university where
men would take courses, have competent therapy, and thus
prepare for "life outside."

How about this? I would like to approach Judge Thomson
on this . . .

October 13

The fact of death remains inert until it is rigorously faced each day—with its little deaths. One does not wish to be sentimental or self-centered about all this. Many, especially many other prisoners, are faced with much more of this day after day, than we. A "living death" is the old cliché, exasperation, despair, fury: this versus a "death in life" into which men enter by choice, unsure as men always are of the brute implications of such a choice.

A boy of twenty-two, arrested repeatedly on drug charges; in the background a drunken father infused with hatred of life, hatred of the sons of the family, the mother keeping an uneasy peace.

"I've given up on the Mass here. I'll go to Quaker meeting. That's it." The old story of the young—for whom the indifference, cowardice, laziness of institutionalized religion spells the end of the affair . . .

The Quakers here today. One does not know whether silence at "meeting" comes of bewilderment at being here, a condition not yet wiped clean from the mind; or from a genuine respect for the *massif* of silence built up minute by minute at these solemn assemblies. One thing seems clear, we are still far from the unity and strength of will which bring us to the point of effecting social change.

What are our resources in comparison to those of the Vietnamese? We shall have to be humiliated, we shall have to lose more, we shall have to allow a lesser heresy drive out the greater; quietism in place of activism. I do not know how else anything is to come to pass . . . but nothing so shakes the ego and its intemperate ways and means as the poverty evident when we really shut up and put up; i.e., empty our pockets in silence, before one another . . .

J. just called out good night; for him it's goodbye. Transfer tomorrow after two weeks in segregation . . . twenty-one years old, third transfer, for reasons variously described as "inflammatory action," "troublemaking." "Tell everyone not to be discouraged . . . We're on our way." We promise to keep in touch through his wife, a promise that will cost . . . but a case must be made if any change is to come in the practice of bundling prisoners off without legal foundation or excuse or recourse to outside.

October 14

Rieux: What pushes you into taking a hand in all this?
Tarron: I don't know, my ethic perhaps.
Rieux: And what's that?
Tarron: Understanding.

(Camus: *The Plague*)

October 15

"The reconciliation of man to God." A small number of the prisoners undergo a change of heart here. One is tempted to call the change a political one, in the highest sense of the word . . . i.e., they pass out of the shadow and slavery of criminality, by the state's definition, under threat of the state's life and death power. To return to God, which means in the simplest terms, to the embodiment of His hope—the community of the hopeless. This is often to take on a new "reborn" heart, which is, according to the state, a criminal existence. The difference between Jesus and Barabbas—or between Judas and Barabbas; the betrayal of man, versus fidelity unto death.

October 16

From the records (borrowed by a friend) under BERRI-GAN—"Two priests who took the law into their own hands. They might be rehabilitated, if the program offered were an intelligent one!" No comment.

October 17

To pass from the smaller power of death to the small powerlessness of life. Men who take up guns to protect their turf—the money game. Still the death game. From the daily mead of news to the lives of most prisoners—one thread of intent and method.

We do not have to be good politicians—*pace* R. Reuther and Garry Wills. We are only called to be men and Christians. A simpler game, which in the long run will be found to have included the former one as well.

October 20

That what we do, that what we endure, will have meaning for others.

That our lives are not wasted, in the measure in which we give them.

That the giving of our lives is a concrete, simple task; at center eye, the men we live with and suffer among and strive to serve.

That life in jail, in proportion to one's awareness, has

powerful analogies with "life outside" to the inquiring mind and the contemplative heart.

That to be fools for Christ's sake is a responsible political position, given the rampant death society, its irresponsibility and horror of life.

That we are called, as prisoners, to be disciplined, prayerful, constant, vigilant over sense and appetite, cheerful and of good heart.

That relief of inequity, inhumanity, and injustice are present and pressing tasks. The struggle goes on here too.

That powerlessness is a way which offers solidarity and concurrent action with all those who struggle and endure in the world.

That in prison we are in communion not only with suffering men and women of our world, but with the communion of saints in every time and place.

That our jailers also lie under the scrutiny as well as the saving will of God, and stand in great need of our compassion and our courtesy—especially the large number of Catholics among them.

That we are called to live the mystery of the cross and to sweat through the mystery of the resurrection.

That we accept first, in body and spirit, our conviction that human conditions must worsen, that there is more to be endured than we have so far endured, before amelioration comes.

That good humor and riding easy are the saving salt of our condition. We may win big, we may win small, we may lose everything. We can take whichever outcome. Important: stand where you must stand, be human there.

I traced this on my cell wall:

שלום Shalom   נוה Neve

(Oasis of Peace)

October 24

Born winners, born losers

There was once a country in which, willy-nilly, no one knowing quite how, everyone was divided into prisoners and wardens.

That was the name of the game: prisoners and wardens. Economics, religion, education, law as well as trade, building, selling, cobbling, from the smartest trades to the crudest, that was how it went.

It was not merely that some lost and some won.

Some were (in time, in fact) born losers, literally. I.e., they were born with a sort of second umbilical, joining their right hand to their left. This was invariably excised. There was a feeling on the part of those in power that in this instance genetics was playing a bad joke and ought to be cut back.

The stroke of midnight marked a change of roles. Prisoners became wardens, wardens prisoners; losers winners, winners losers.

Rich men became poor men, poor men took over chairs and boards and stock markets and bishops' miters and generals' stars and uniforms. Everyone was what he was for a day only, everyone played the game like mad, knowing he had only twenty-four hours in which to prove what he wanted to prove, or get over with what he had had to submit to. If he was down, he would be up and heard from again shortly; and he knew it.

Only it didn't last.

No one knew who first got the idea that winners ought, permanently and by rights, to be what they had been on occasion, that the game didn't have to go on the way it had always gone.

The medics especially were conscious of something strange; every child born in a twenty-four-hour period when his parents were on the top side of the law was born with free hands, clutching redly at the indistinct light and air; but every child born on the other side was tied by the strong cord of skin; bound hands tight. Then the idea started in someone's head, went around unformulated, unspoken as such words always are. What if the cord were left intact, the rules of the game changed, the time of the game extended?

The first step was only publicly revealed later. One baby, two babies, three were quietly removed to a sequestered ward of a lying-in hospital, out of public sight. The parents were told of the need of special care and sequestering, of mysterious symptoms, observation. They agreed, they were down anyway, losers, and had no objection they cared to voice . . .

It was observed that the natural manacle did no harm to the infants over the next twenty-four-hour period, then over the next. Meantime the parents exchanged roles as usual.

The results of the test were evident. The children, dangling both hands in unison, tracing right and left the same vague hieroglyphics in the air, were found normal in every respect, perfectly adapted to the slight alteration which nature had introduced in their bodies. A great light dawned, the news was leaked to a small number of people then in power. Nature was demanding an alteration in the rules of the immemorial game; she was declaring herself on the side of those who could read the signs—the rest, as someone declared to a select and secret gathering, "was up to us."

The moment was electric with danger. The intent faces around the table flashed like a two-headed coin spun in the air: danger and opportunity—in a remote conference room of the central committee—they savored the moment like an elixir. What to do?

They knew what to do. The knowledge passed from eye to eye to eye. They breathed deep the air of the unrepeatable moment, a moment alighting in their midst like a miraculous cockatoo, a bird of the spirit, a Holy Ghost, a god arrayed like an immortal bird.

Decisions followed quickly. The borders of the country were fortified. The game was frozen; constituencies of prisoners and wardens held firm. The winners declared themselves wardens in perpetuum. They composed a prayer to be recited on a day of national thanksgiving, "for the preservation of the civilized from the depredations, toils, conspiracies, and latent ambushes so recently and miraculously uncovered, laid bare, and foiled by the responsible powers."

God save the wary and wise, they intoned at the high altar next day. A thrill of delicious fear ran through the collective cortex of the massed citizens.

At the climax of the service the keys of the national dungeon, which since time immemorial had changed hands at the stroke of midnight, were brought forward, plunged in the sacred brazier before the altar, and fused into a white-hot pool of scrap. White-hot, then red, then warm, then solid, then cold. The dungeon was sealed, permanently. The prisoners and their generations of prisoners; bad seed, polluted sources.

When I was a child, intoned the preacher the following Sunday from the imperial pulpit, I played games. Now that I am a man, I have put away the things of a child . . .

Notes for a study group; apt for ignominy and glory

1) What seems chiefly to draw young minds to Christ in every generation is his example as a model of humanity; i.e., he is marked by the suppleness, freedom, and conviction which enable him to live for others in the world, in a culture, in a family—and thus to die. "If I am lifted up, I will draw all men to myself." In a true sense, it was not his enemies who lifted him up—rather it was the height and grandeur of his moral virtue which made him apt for both ignominy and glory. These same qualities which marked him for greatness marked him for a tragic death. Death, one must admit, is the natural outcome, the reward of the world conferred on the great of heart. Christ "asked for it"—his nonviolent life excited fury and violence in exact proportion to his restraint, consistency, and self possession.

2) At the same time, one must admit a difficulty in approaching this man. He has been transformed (inevitably?) from a *human and divine* one (the primitive data about him is clear) to a "religious" being. Now he is made subject to ideologies, which are huckstered in his name, as though with his blessing. So a strict mystery becomes subject to mystifi-

cation. In the process, both human and divine reality are obscured. The mystery becomes a "problem"—so everything about him becomes problematic. A man who was a source of unending truth, beauty, and love becomes a patron of causes; faith in him is degraded to a loyalty oath, blood is shed, wars are fought. Some people "enlist" because "the faith" offers a secure code of conduct. Others walk off, fed up with hypocrisy, cruelty, and narrow-mindedness. Both, I suggest, miss the point, an invitation to walk toward humanness, freedom, contemplation, responsible action in the world. An act of faith that is *lived*, as it was first lived by the one who issued the invitation.

3) I think the false solutions ("staying," "walking out") are false because they are less than fully conscious acts. They walk out on wrong, they stay with wrong. What then is right? An invitation to listen, learn, grow in one's humanity. An invitation issued by one who walked the human road, presented his credentials in human fashion, offered others a workable "style"—a way of being man among men—in his work, play, friendship, trust, self-giving, suffering, personal conviction, and courage—finally, in death itself. An invitation, with the freedom implied in the invitation: some would love and accept him, some would withdraw, worse than before, some would act as prosecutors and executioners.

One is reminded of the words the old man Simeon spoke as he took the child Christ in his arms and told of the bitter future that awaited Him. He was to be a "sign of contradiction." A crossroads, at which others would have to choose, a "crucial" man, a man who would induce choices merely by being around, by standing for something, standing by his word. He was in the old line of Hebrew prophets, who conceived the word as a substance, an emanation, a part of the person—a movement outward, creating space which the speaker was literally to occupy; a space of life, and where necessary, a space of death. Let one stand where his words take him. Let him refuse to lie, compromise, double-deal or wheel, temporize.

It is this peaceful, courageous balance between word and quality of life that keeps men and women hanging around Christ, in spite of the deformations worked on him. There are so few who serve in bad times, whose light and life are not extinguished or dimmed out. We grow sick of words that issue from plastic bladders, we grow equally sick of the defeatism that bids us endure like animals. We want to be human in a time when being human may be a literally criminal act. We want to be human in a way we ourselves have come on, with our own brain and heart, step by step. We want room even for mistakes, we want the freedom even to be wrong. We want to be free to go at our own pace, deaf to the mad lock step of both right and left, alert to the cry of human need, free to answer, succor, commune. We want a task; a life that is serious and still offers occasions—events—joys —spontaneous happenings, something to celebrate.

What we don't want is prison, slavery, exploitation, fear, hatred, dread of change, hunter and hunted. The U.S.A.? We want it different, or not at all.

One looks in vain in the New Testament for any of the following: (1) a political program for the ideal state; (2) an infallible blueprint for settling human differences; (3) a formula for successful living; (4) a faith that takes one out of this world or assures one of success within it; (5) a blessing on power, money, good repute, war, nationalism, pride of place; (6) a curse on the alien, the stranger, the unbeliever, the sinner.

What then to look for? The "minority position" of God; his preference for the underdog, the reject, the deviant, the outcasts, the unacceptables of a given culture or religion.

A curse on the works of man when these pretend to grab, own, huckster God's salvation or the conferring of His life and grace.

The smashing of idols as a religious act.

A distrust of "religious" life and observance.

A distrust of the powers, methods, weapons of this world, as presuming to win God's favor, to work human change, to turn things around.

A blessing on the "holy man"—who is generally unrecognized, despised by his own.

4) To be a disciple implies that one is poor and powerless before the world (before the church as well). He is either born to this (and therefore apt to hear the word) or he deliberately makes himself so. In the latter case, an adult convert rigorously and explicitly renounces this world. Practically speaking, such a one is forbidden to be a soldier or a rich man. He is "called from" this world. His calling is dramatized in the nakedness with which he enters the baptismal waters, and in the laying down of his sword.

Note too the suspicion with which primitive Christians regarded civil authority and its claims over them, or the holding of civil office.

5) Thus a conflict was soon set up within the church itself. On the one hand, a tendency toward moral purity, sectarianism; on the other, a tendency toward compromise for the sake of universality. The church witnessed to Christ by standing apart, the church witnessed by standing within.

The conflict was quickly joined, in Rome, certainly by the year 80. It was also rather quickly settled, at least from the point of view of authority. Perhaps by the time of Constantine. But the baptism of the emperor and the "establishment" of religion hardly settled anything. It only dramatized the conflict publicly, all the while making inevitable men and movements like Savonarola, the Cathari, the Beguines, Luther.

The cross followed the sword, or vice versa; but the two standards became signs, not of faith, but of a bloody ideology. In times of conflict, the church entered, not to forbid war, but to bless it. Now there could be holy wars, crusades, a tragic history, a tragic betrayal of Christ.

The nuclear age brought a new phase to the struggle of assimilation versus primitive purity. A qualitatively new violence demands a renewed "no" to violence, not merely a no to the use of such weapons, but to their stockpiling. Further, the issue is clarified by the destitution of the world's people—largely ignored while the world's goods, services, and brains were being consecrated to wars, hot or cold; in such an age, the word "peace" being simply another term for "war." The world powers have paid lip service to human need through their front organizations at the UN, while continuing to widen the gap between affluence and poverty, and to develop even more effective technologies and tools of death. So the situation created at Hiroshima is extended into the '70s.

6) The Christian pacifist has a clear option in a world where the great powers and the lackey churches have reached agreements on nationalistic frenzies and policies. Indeed his moral position is only clarified by the mad drift of events. He is now called more strongly than ever to renounce any part in modern war.

The just war theory, evolved at a time when wars were limitable, no longer applies—to say the least. (It is difficult, of course, to see how the theory ever in fact applied in any "conventional" war ever waged.) How such a theory could apply today, in Vietnam, Israel, or in Pentagon—Kremlin nuclear gymnastics, is at least equally unclear. The times are such as to demand action, practical resistance on the part of a Christian, in the following ways, among others:

a) He cannot consent to be drafted—either for war or for government alternative service. "If a man is doing worthwhile work, why should the government be allowed to displace him for projects of its own choosing? And if he is not already working for human welfare, how can such a man consider himself a Christian?" (A. J. Muste)

b) He can in no way approve or attempt to legitimate capital punishment or any personal injury to others.

c) He cannot be an official, chaplain, or approving member

of any government whose laws require slavery, exploitation, war as the price of its citizens' welfare or prosperity.

d) He cannot maim or kill in personal self-defense or for the sake of any he holds dear. Much less is he allowed to injure another in defense of property.

e) He cannot pay taxes for war or war preparation.

f) Under such a government as is mentioned in c) he may well be required in conscience to break laws that protect illicit war-making powers and properties.

7) Matthew, cc. 5–8, has been called the charter of the kingdom. It is a summation of human conduct based on the most exalted altruism, it demands virtue and constancy of a high, even a heroic order. The chapters, to be understood in context, should be placed against Matthew's account of Christ's passion and death. It will be seen how it all comes together in an act of love for the brethren.

This seems to be the crux of things, as Christ came to realize and to invite His friends in His direction, to love and die responsibly; to include others.

There is no guarantee of political or personal success; there is rather a sense of "rightness," of standing within history, in a way that confers health and creates spiritual continuity.

One is called to live non-violently, even if the social or political change one worked for is in fact unlikely or even impossible. It may or may not be possible to turn the United States around through non-violent revolution. But one thing is in favor of such an attempt: the total inability of violence, as a social or personal method, to change anything. On the other hand, one notes how a violent society justifies itself by forbidding its people to explore alternatives. So violence proliferates, captivates consciousness with the myth that it is the sole savior, and thus multiplies wars and victims, the boundless litany of human misery.

8) The best gift of such a tradition as the New Testament is what Gandhi called "soul force" and the New Testament calls grace. This often takes modest and humiliated form;

but its presence cannot but be felt. We might translate it today as the presence in individuals of their groupings, of inner
consistency, peaceableness, courage, good humor. In any
case, there is now and then the felt presence of the spirit.

Such a gift enables us not to give up. It keeps us at a distance from the tottering brinkmanship of spirit spoken of by
Camus—to whom the first question of modern life was that
of suicide. For us, the question must be quite different—how
to keep going, how to minimize human damage and destruction, how to love the enemy even while one's life stands in
opposition to him.

The presence of grace. We cannot know in any given age
whether we are going to "make it" or not; i.e., achieve even
on a modest local scale a viable and beloved community. The
question grows enormously more painful today, since of necessity such communities must culminate in a *world* order
of goods, services, communication, and governance. Moreover, the urgency of the question and the changes it entails
in our thinking and structures create a virus of fear and dread
and violence. All of which delays the real question and the
search for solutions.

In such an atmosphere, the individual feels trapped between upper and lower millstones, conflict and counter-
claim. Control of one's own life and destiny is ground to bits
by the machine.

One must at such times calmly evaluate events and his part
in them. Modesty; the times are so evil and winds so contrary
that survival itself is a kind of triumph; the survival of even
the smallest communities. It may be that one's hopes for the
world stop short; that they include only himself and a few
friends; that this will be one's total contribution toward
peaceableness. It may be that one will die stripped of all accomplishment, dignity and hopefulness his only contribution.
So Bonhoeffer, Gandhi, Jägerstatter. Yet their "soul force"
lives and lives on, in communities everywhere.

9) The contribution of prisoners is of import here. They

are among the exploited and powerless. Moreover, many middle-class inmates "pass over" through prison experience to share the common lot of blacks, browns, reds, those condemned to powerlessness from birth.

It remains important that prison be regarded as a boot camp for spiritual change, at least on the part of some. This would imply the following:

a) Rejection of defined crime and assigned punishment, as regulated by society. The dispensing of guilt and punishment is normally a slap on the wrist, designed to get one back to his gentleman's agreement with a criminal society. Upon release, one is supposed again to function as a good robotized consumer and taxpayer and wage earner and draftee. A unit of violence in a state of violence.

b) Discovery of a community—or its creation. I am convinced that until this happens, nothing happens. And this is precisely what is forbidden to happen. Look around: the dough-faced bureaucrats who day after day grind out their delaying tactics *against* education, dialogue, political awareness, worship, work with meaning, human relations . . . The cops, the front line of highly placed violence. Fellow prisoners, most of them living in the great yawn between unawakened past and unchanged future. Then the injunction: "do your own time"—a boot camp slogan for a society that is sodden with violence.

But what happens when we discover one another, share our poverty, our powerlessness—as also our insights, hopes, self-understanding, criticism; in effect pass from strangers (a permanent state of hell, in which one is "under orders") to brothers (the community of Jeremiah, Jesus, Buddha, etc.).

Nothing can possibly happen until that happens.

c) The odds against a) or b) are of course considerable in the case of prisoners. First, the violence of the system bears down heavily on them. They are supposed to be cheerful robotized field hands or factory hands or, in the case of a few, minor functionaries, their leash let slip an inch or two—

"lackey power." But in case something should (against all odds) happen to a prisoner ("something" being understood as a simple matter of coming alive) there are all sorts of ways of bringing the recalcitrant back in line. Let him dare act as some Panthers or Muslims have dared act in prison. Then the perfumed hand of John Lindsay and the calloused hand of, say, Jim Clark will press flesh; a moment of recognition, promises broken, dogs, clubs, Mace, imported violence. Official lawlessness must exact law; official disorder must have order.

Second, the violence of the prisoner's own past. Most prisoners are wounded and diminished, long before the prison grinder gets to eat their bones.

The affluent among them have played perhaps the saddest loser's game of all: checks, counterfeiting, stealing, defrauding, evasion. A paper game on a board; the pawns, cardboard men. Most of them are guilty of trying to "steal into" the society, as a ferret steals into another ferret's hole; more warmth, security, space for survival. Such men commonly have had no experience of poverty to awaken their passion, revulsion, dignity. So they have little sense of justice; they have not been injured by the society. There is in consequence little that could be called significant or exemplary in their plight. How to break such an impasse; how to pass from such criminality (breaking the rules of a criminal society, exploiters in an exploitative society) to the criminality of Jesus (hunger and thirst for justice; one dies of it). How to break such an impasse, so that they renounce their part in institutionalized violence for a place in the kingdom of the meek, the just, the powerless who seek new power?

d) The druggies are by and large part of the same scene; except that the wrongs done to them by outrageous punishment are far more overt. But it must be said that the energies and talents they have in such abundance are largely wasted or diverted from true purpose. Drugs may well increase awareness of the injustice, lies, and violence at the heart of society. At the same time, they dissipate the will and discipline required for human movement toward change.

10) The prison is the society up close; its laboratory, ghetto, colony, boot camp, isolation ward, asylum, hospital, morgue, church, incubator, school. With this difference—that all the images function in an atmosphere of palpable violence. That the mark of violence does not rub off on prisoners is as unlikely as the issuing of a white sheep from a red dip.

The solution of the vast majority of prisoners, as a condition of survival, is simply to go along with the game. "In order to survive," as they say. As a consequence, very few of them survive—if by survival one is to understand a sense of his brothers, renunciation of violence, rebirth.

11) For prisoners to get reborn (for anyone to get reborn) someone must pay. The payment for birth is blood; the cost of rebirth cannot be cheap. The question is not how to evade payment, but how to pay up like a human being. How to reckon coolly on one's resources, muster them, cherish and love and deepen them; in view of a life that (a) refuses to live off the misery of others, and (b) takes death seriously.

12) It is time to take death into account—seriously. Jesus did—so did Socrates, King, Gandhi, Malcolm X. Nonviolence demands that we do; the public facts of life make the issue real, bloodstained, up close, daily.

How does one take death seriously?

a) He disciplines himself, daily, hourly. This touches on every aspect of life here: use of time, reading, study, meditation, talk, food, and drink. It demands that we reject person-to-person violence, even when provocation is great. Many are devoted to *dolce vita*—even in the pitiful dole offered by prison—commissary living, sports at all hours, useless reading, endless small talk going nowhere.

b) One makes *love for the brethren* his chief concern. He is not perpetually caught in a net of personal turmoil, frustration, despair. He creates a space of sanity and cheerfulness, in which others can find relief. He does not exploit those

who are as powerless as himself. He knows the difference between daydreams, delusions, dread—and reality. He is more
interested in the fate of others than in his own—knowing that
the fate of others *is* his own. It goes without saying that one
who so lives is continually dying to his selfishness, ego, childish dreams and whims. He is taking death into account because he takes life seriously. He is doing that measure of
violence to his violent self that is the requisite for living non-
violently for others.

c) He connects, in every direction. Muslims and Panthers
have shown the potential of connecting with a religious or
cultural tradition that liberates and creates energies, allows
one to stand before his own soul—in a world that would
gladly exterminate him.

White prisoners have yet to connect.

So they sputter away in the dark, wasting energy, creating
no light for others. Those who come out of some religious
tradition throw it out—the baby with the baptism. But
what do they create, or substitute? And unless they do, how
will they live? I would be willing to venture that it is next to
impossible to live in a human way, except by connecting with
a primitive spiritual tradition, and testing its truth in the
daily struggle to be a man for others. If someone has come
on a better way, let him share it with us.

d) One is aware of the possibilities offered by the life of
prison. In a sense, we are all condemned here. In a deeper
sense, we condemn ourselves once we are condemned here.
We condemn ourselves to the merciless play of fantasy,
mood, conflict, waste of time, self-indulgence, lust, dread of
life.

There is, in reproof, an honorable tradition of dead men
who have come alive in prison. It is still happening; witness
Sostre, Jackson, the men of the Tombs (!), Auburn, Queens,
Brooklyn, West Street. But what seems to happen rather
constantly among blacks happens rarely to whites. Why? The
poor don't have to come to jail to discover the truth about

society; they are born its indentured slaves; whites, by and large the engineers, beneficiaries, or willing pawns of present arrangements, dream of little in prison except an auspicious return to the status quo—interest compounded.

P.S. This is a lousy place to die. Most do.

It is a good place to get born. Few do.

November 8

Came up in Quaker meeting today. The question of non-violence, as applied to those in charge of us. And especially in light of the suit we have filed, the crass neglect of human beings, the ironbound palatines, ignorant and arrogant at once, who hold our lives in fee. I thought Christ did not presume that the powerful would change or become human beings, but that He prepared his own soul to confront them, under risk of being destroyed by them, as He inevitably was. I thought also of the poor woman and her penny (Mark) and the praise she won from Him, whose eyes missed nothing of human beauty or truth. She gave her copper, not to be seen by men, not even in *quid pro quo* hope of reward from God. She gave out of love; because it was an act that corresponded to the heart's truth—her love of a holy place. It is of note that her praise is juxtaposed to the blame heaped on the scribes who "devour the savings of widows, and recite long prayers for appearance's sake . . ." But she "gave from her want, all that she had to live on." Life has a way of reducing us to our last copper; and then asking that also. But who is poorer than the dead? Or poorer than those who mourn the dead? I miss Merton as though he had died yesterday. I cannot understand.

In a true sense it can be said of Philip and me that we have nothing to do but stand firm in these months—to survive, to act as a silent prick to the consciousness of those outside—whether of friend or opponent, church or state. "Here we stand." On the other hand—there are the prisoners, the task of understanding, the discipline required to be men for the men, to grow in love, to use time as though time were indeed "tinged with the blood of Christ." To be here in a certain way—which is, to believe. We are writers and spokesmen for Catholics and must ponder deeply the state of the church, love her, keep far from us the corrosive hatred which is infecting the church everywhere. Not to be dupes or children, but neither to give up on the accumulated wisdom and prayer of the church which, in the earthen vessels of present life, are still available to us.

Above all (because it is the most insidious and pervasive form of destruction) to avoid hatred of the persecutors—the guards, warden, officers, many of whom literally ask for it. In their regard, to try for some form of human exchange, without paltering or timeserving; at the same time to seize on every human and legal means of throwing wrenches in the gears of their machinery. Example: our concern that legal aid be gotten to the men in the hole who are thrown into segregation without benefit of counsel, at the whim of authorities, without time limit, often for paltry occasional infractions.

Example: our suit against the warden, the justice department, and the bureau of prisons; a "class suit" on behalf of all federal prisoners, for violation of First Amendment rights.

November 11

We were told finally yesterday that we are to be allowed to teach—a perilous course. We will make it through the shoals, right and left. A "great books" take-off; we can treat of Christ, Socrates, Locke, Rousseau, Pascal—and then, if all goes well, some of the moderns. Every urge from authority is that we "take it easy"; the ideas are not to rock any boats.

If they do—? We shall have simply to survive from one session to another.

Meantime the smaller sessions in non-violence go on at the edges. Phil's paper received thoughtfully, so much so that another meeting is called for. I am reminded of those adult sessions we witnessed in the darkness of Hanoi in '68; men and women going forward with their basic training, under fire and bombs, the warden's rifles stacked in the corner.

The sparrows refuse to leave; they make jabberwocky at the barred windows, reminding us that a base ecological crime is being reversed; they outside, we within.

This combination of daring and patience! As though a high wire artist were in mid-act, knowing to the centimeter the distance to be traversed, the electric chance, the risk; and yet were determined, on a mad and beautiful impulse, to up the odds here and now, to turn a somersault in mid-passage—something "un-programmed," not in the act . . .

Consistency. We are told by the disenchanted: the prisoners only deceive you, they put on a "good conduct" badge before they approach you—they are in fact entirely different; selfish, vulgar, thieving, itching for violence, uncontained . . . And we say, of course!—but what other stuff is human hope made of than that men would want to be different, want at least a brief occasion to try out a better self than the one they were habitually condemned to?—and what if we are in fact the occasion of that attempt, that momentary change of soul?

At the same time, we must not be gulls. There is a point to be met here, scored by the "realists"—i.e., we must also point out the latent self-deception that supposes one can wear one face before the crowd, another before the priests.

I think our best gift is to make the same demand of ourselves, i.e., to show that Christianity supplies just that consistency and integrity to which the prisoners are instinctively drawn. That we be men on whatever occasion—and especially on those occasions when being human is most risky, unpopular, ignored.

Christ is our clue. To give his spirit space—in our meditation, speech; "Let your light shine before men . . ."

Everything is dumped in here; a city dump become a national dump; the federal dump system. The dumping of relationships. I am reminded of Alan Paton's touching tribute
to his dead wife; when one cannot keep a world, he can least
keep his own house. But how strange, almost old-fashioned
it seems—to defend marriage, to remind others that the
latest itch in the crotch is not the best index of a new love—
when there is a wife, and vows, and children at home . . .

I say to myself at times: O blessed Christianity, that gives
us so simple and ineradicable a sense of things—"not to deny
in the darkness what one affirmed in the light . . ." Some
prisoners dream of "leaping over" one life, a few lives; to get
at "the real issues." It is remarkably like the mind that uses
napalm "because it is merciful; it has saved so many men"
. . . A "genius" here, on work release, took off with a nurse
for an eight-day ecstasy and got her pregnant. He faces a new
dossier of charges, loses another two years—with children
and a wife who had counted on him as the chief help in her
struggle for health. What a bastard! I have no words for such
a shiftless screwball.

For Phil and me, who live in the hard, tearless grief of those
who know the good and see it violated, despised, and outraged, the task is also to live in the sodden swamp where
everything grows, everything struggles to kill, to assimilate,
to make it on the death of others. Hell is the place where
everything is allowed.

Alan Paton of himself and his wife (I thought of Philip
and myself): "And I write here that despite all our faults and
sins, our love of Christ and the good stayed with us all our
lives, and took us both into deep waters."

I wrote something on the fractioning of man, based on the
dividing of the cloak of St. Martin. Also knowing at a subtler
level a dividing and diminishing that takes place in me—I
live twenty-four hours a day in a cage with rutting jackdaws,

all of them pitifully drenched in every avenue, ingress, egress, and dead end of sex. I go about stupefied with exhaustion—one-half of me in function. Must one be half alive, half dead before he can be reborn?

The warden, the lieutenant, the captain, the guard, the social
        worker, the psychiatrist, the director of sanitation and
        safety, the director of education,
the chaplain, the director of budget, the director of food service,
        the overseer of industries
were all men born of woman; crossing the yard each night
with the looks of virtuous cats, the infesting rodents subdued,
homeward bound to the arms of chaste spouses, receiving upon
        and into their persons
hugs, kisses, food and drink, the rewards of virtuous hours
all presumably shipshape in the great holding tank (the hot phone
        long cool)—but that tank, that hole!
within which might arise, to pierce the ventricles of any heart like
        the blow of a knife blade, unwarning—
cries, imprecations, the very sweat, smut, smear of despair;
and which of you, sacred or secular gentlemen, treading
a straight path to appointed ends, generations of children,
wisdom seekers, friends, celebrations, about you
a phalanx of proprietary ordering presences—feels
in a midnight start of a bush or tree, an animal nosing the winds,
a start and slap of Old Glory against its pole—
the equinoctial fury, the storm, miles out at sea,
miles out, uncontrollable, unwithstood, unimagined
that shakes my bones, as I lie here.

November 14

I was certainly hustled and shoved about in the world a great deal—a great deal more than most priests—infinitely more than most Jesuits. Having from the start (let us say) of the '60s, or even earlier, made up my mind that I was going to sniff the winds of the world and indeed find out, if it could be found out, what caves the winds were born in . . . Wandering around Brooklyn in the '50s, boating alone for a week on Lake Cazenovia. In the early '60s climbing Trembleau Mountain to pick wild blueberries and read and write. Being the first to ask for a cabin alone on that lake, thirsting for solitude, for an opposite rhythm to the studies and crowds, even the liturgies . . .

It came to this: which might be considered, and is considered by so many, a dead end. A prisoner asked last night: don't you have any regrets? I searched as well as I could in mind and heart, and said simply: no, none. If I had any after three months of animal farm treatment, I should certainly consider it my duty to say so, to say that my purpose had flagged, or I had seen error or pride or the suicidal stretching of resources beyond their limit; or had come on a better heart. But none of these things lay within me, so I could say simply, as a result of a searching will and a purposeful honesty: no, none. If I have regrets, they are that I have beyond doubt placed obstacles in the way of a truer, firmer, quicker growth; and so impeded the ways of Love within me; as a few friends know, and still judge me with mercy. For such things are still to be worked out and atoned for in the months which lie ahead; to which occasions and their pain I say: *sit nomen Domini benedictum,* let it all be, let it come, whatever.

We begin teaching Monday, after much shifting of official gears and opinions, shiftings also in the unbalance of power, which has granted us, with the help of others, some leverage and measure of power for ourselves. To get the simplest things under way, what an enormous expenditure of energy and ingenuity; to get the conditions of life livable in a time of utmost chaos of will. What then? We shall see . . .

November 15

In this luxury housing, heated to a sweatbox, night and day
I have ample time to ponder the Sunday lesson:
In those days, the sun and the moon will be darkened;
He will gather his elect from the four winds . . .
John, whose grace and gentleness I learned here, light in a dark
          place.
Those fathers of families, husbands, counting the hours
          a stone in the belly—

Letter to J.C.

I said to myself the other night, sleepless as a night frog, bug-eyed between stars (real, unseen) and waters (real, unsee-able), why, I will write Him a letter. Possibly a long one, possibly a short. I do not know. I do not know how it will come off, whether He will favor it in this place where I am caught in a net and nailed down with some seven hundred others for an indefinite time. I do not know if it may come off, I am appalled and reduced all the day long, usually sleepless at night, guarded and kept like an animal, in a pit where Caesar calls the game. But I must try to think. I said so to another prisoner, whom I steal away to talk to in the hospital, usually with a cup of coffee in my hand for him and me. He is a young war resister, sensitive and intelligent. On occasion, with supreme rightness and good sense, he has flipped his lid in this place. Coming back, he is sane, calm, and of good judgment. And he said to me: OK. You must try.

It is, after all, fifty years since you fashioned me through my father and mother and brothers and school and the Jesuits and books and photos and university and cities around the world—tramping, flying, reading, arguing, and yes pray-

ing, everywhere on this globe. You have not been a stranger
to me, I have been no stranger to men and women. I have
been literally everywhere—usually, I hope, on your errands.
The things I have seen, the faces I have looked into! I have
skulked underground for months, before I was flushed by the
bird watchers, a most exotic survival, and brought here, and
caged—for the duration. And here, with Philip and the others I have not ceased to cry out to You—quite the contrary;
I have had daily to exorcise from my bones the constricting
horror of the lockup, the seamy underside of creation, the
little plot of earth hardly bigger than a mass grave, with its
tattered vegetation and dripping webs—a limbo of the heart
if ever there was one.

No stranger, Brother. Philip and I have held our scalded
hearts in our hands, for You to see. We have stood at the im-
provised table in the chaplain's office, summoned "up front"
over the loudspeakers—those faceless iron throats that call
men to meals, to lockup, to justice within justice. They might
as easily summon them to the furnaces. Eucharist!

The seven hundred are locked out, in principle. We stand
there in perpetual exhaustion, looking down at the bread
and wine, raising our eyes to the barred window and beyond,
the tatterdemalion November flowers, the shuffle of passing
men; the words stick in our mouth like a fistful of sand. Remember, Lord . . . Shall the Lord remember? Or has He not
forgotten us forever—the prisoners, the walking dead, the in-
habitants of some cold moon, the wraiths of All Saints' Eve?
Remember, Lord. Remember even us . . .

Fomenter of dread and fear, wielder of a sword wilder and
more bloodletting than Jehovah's, troublemaker, tenderest of
sons, brother of malefactors, of no-goods, junkies, beggars,
grifters, counterfeiters, liars, society's offal: remember we pray
to You—us, the scum, refuse of the world, those who play a
foul game badly and are caught at it; the itchy-fingered, the
lovers of dirty money, traders in drugs, the halfhearted, the

repeaters, those tattooed on the arm: "born to lose," and truthfully so.

Far world, far from the company of lovers and saints and hermits and virgins, and heroes and peacemakers, and guitarists and singers and children (far from the children our arms ache for . . .).

Remember us. Out of the depths; for we are brought very low . . .

They do not know what to say to us, they do not know what to expect of us. Their reactions generally are of two kinds: the young, who have no "connections," for whom the church is dead as a doornail (it is, almost; here, its last legs), and the oldsters, who expect fully that we in discarded army mufti and disposable missals will "show up" for the wretched Sunday service (which we do). The first sleep in; the second make do. Which group is right, or whether we are right in joining, for a half hour on Sunday A.M., the second, we do not know. I am not recording this in order to justify the option we take. We take it nonetheless, even when sitting or standing there or walking up to take the host, or consenting to read the Gospel (thereupon to hear it ground into hamburg) makes a stone grow in the pit of the stomach . . .

It is terrible to be powerless. It is doubly terrible to witness powerlessly the mutilation of the word, the death of a living, beautiful, and truthful word, by the slovenly retailers of religion whose vestment might in truth be a butcher's apron.

Out of the depths. Monday Tuesday Wednesday Thursday Friday depths. Saturday you are free to wander the yard, to talk or read, to roll the stone out of the depths. Sunday, out of the depths; a "religious" hell for a secular. You may sleep in, you may rise early for a bad sermon, a stale Eucharist. The choices are not large. Mauriac spoke of them; you do not come to this God as to a great one of this world holding court in a pentagon; the flag, the cross. No, you assemble, broken men, to break bread. At the edge of the world, where you scarcely are tolerated, where you barely can claim space, air; you gather, when all is said. To do what he did; with the same results, predictably.

I used to walk the filthy macadam yard at St. Peter's, Jersey City—how many years ago? Trying to put together enough reason, enough energy, to go on for another single day. In 1947: ten years later I was walking off my private devils on the Brooklyn pavement; bedeviled by insomnia, seeing no rhyme or reason in policing and drilling kids, the day only starting after school or on weekends when we would go, a few students and I, into Manhattan's East Side to work at some storefront, to gather some neighborhood youngsters, at Walt Janer's mission center . . . Or when I could read and study until 2 A.M. sleepless as a bat, toss until four and rise and steal out to say Mass alone.

I was back from Europe, I thought good days were ahead; I landed back where I most dreaded—high school drilling, cafeteria policing, the childish games that were supposed to prove one was with it. The headmaster, who played a poker-faced politics of loyalty and no opposition allowed, one day slipped and gave away his hand: "What did you do to land here?" he asked me. Alas, I had no crime to confess to, even for my own relief . . .

And tried nonetheless, with all the grace of an oil-slicked gull, to take You at Your word.

The old priest who guards the office where we say Mass here (he cannot bear looking in our faces) burst out one day: but why are they all leaving the priesthood, and you are not leaving . . . He would have been much more able to bear with the reversal of those happenings; if most were not leaving and we, manifest pot stirrers and poltergeists, were gracefully or otherwise bowing out . . .

We have tried to take You at Your word.

It has been for as long as I can remember, crisis upon crisis. How much of it was by Your will and intent for me? How much was my own wrong turns, my self-will and deception? I must, in such a place, at such a time, leave the answer to You, which is to say, to Mercy.

Beyond doubt the tongs of generation set a pinch of brimstone into my bones.

What a father we had! I was landlocked at Newark Airport (Dante's third circle of hell) sometime in February of 1970, thinking of him in that foul and dreary place, as I wandered outdoors among loading ramps, barrels, incessant noise and traffic, the greasy rain staining the earth to foulness. I thought of him, and of that night . . .

I had hurried home in response to an urgent call: he is sinking. Come. Jerry drove me over, we rehashed the last weeks; the intransigence of those old bones, the dour humors, the skill which never deserted him, even at ninety-one, to keep his family on edge, to deride, show contempt, order about, ignore. He was losing as he had lived, gracelessly. For some three weeks he had launched into a new tactic, since the last fall had broken his hip. He would neither eat nor take therapy nor in any way show a will to live. The doctors said his limb had healed without fault; there was nothing to impede his walking again, his old frame was sound and strong.

He willed to die: whether out of spite of us, or what else, none of us will ever know.

In a letter to You (as You see) he has taken over, as he always and invariably took over upon any scene that included his family. Pertinacious, self-centered, generally joyless, recounting the past interminably, quick-witted, acid, fierce to seize upon weakness, knowing his strength and determined never to lose out, an old-school tyrant—something to give the angels pause where they hovered!

We will never see his like again. No one will: least of all ourselves. There is but one father granted a man. The son will carry his father to his own grave; whatever else he can become, he is that man's son, born of his seed, parrying his shadow.

The struggle through that night! He took the oxygen like a desperate, spent runner nearing the tape, shaking the bed; the bed shook like a vessel in storm: What a man he was, the old nurse said in wonder, lifting his great hand to take his pulse, just see those bones!

We were alone, in that solitude death encloses in its wings—

I paced the room, I sat and read, I rose to look at you, to adjust the covers, the oxygen, to pray. I held your hand. I had never in all our lives held your hand. As you grew older, you used to embrace us when we returned home, but the embrace was always yours, not mine. I submitted to it, I could not give you my love, you had never known how to seek it—

I held your hand and repeated the prayers of your childhood and mine. Our Father, Hail Mary . . . O my God I am heartily sorry . . . and miraculously, your struggle quieted, the quivering of your frame; you were listening, you were praying with me.

In prison tonight, my father, I remember. Do you know, one year after your death, in another sodden November—do you know I am here? and why? And do you approve at last, and would you tell me so, with an altogether new gentleness?

Could there be a father who awaits us, his six sons; who is all you never were, generous, kind of heart and speech—a father you never were to us—and yet yourself, purified by fire, longing for that love we so longed to give and to receive?

He worshiped, bit in mouth; another task, an uphill climb on Sundays. We entered into that rhythm as children do, ignorant of any other conduct, the Sunday rhythm of Mass and communion, a better dinner than usual. Peaceful by mandate; Pa was in the house, at table, in the yard. I cannot remember your ever showing that Sunday would flow over upon us, that we had rights as God did, that we counted for something, as He counted so heavily . . .

We buried him in his shroud and a plain box. For a few dollars, with a notice in the paper that contributions could be sent to a peace group. Peace to your ashes, who had known so little peace! There was no "viewing," none of the expensive cosmetic daubing over the fact and primary presence of death. In the A.M., Mass; in the P.M., open house with a buffet for friends, who greeted us, ate and drank, spread through the house, came and went. Mom in midst, calm and dignity the crown of those mad hatter's fifty-three years, in which she had borne so much with such grace, attaining that inner light which is both sanity and healing.

We lowered his body ourselves, his sons, on the slope of a hill south of the city, within sight of the farmland where he had been born, ninety years before.

Requiescat. It is a wholesome thought to pray for the dead. From my prison I pray him deliverance from his; so that, father and sons, we may meet as free men in eternity—all debts paid, old rancors dissolved in that Love, that Light.

I have never found You an easy Master.

Undoubtedly, said a friend, you have a cave of dark pessimism at your heart. What I wonder at, is that you function so well, in spite of all . . .

So be it. And yet there are moments even in prison when the dark caul lifts from one's eyes, and in knowing You, Your presence, Your love, one may breathe more deeply the air of another land.

I wanted You to be Lord of the imagination; to help me imagine ways of living in the world which would be both true to the values I loved and an endlessly rich and spontaneous variation upon them . . .

November 18

I have never thanked You sufficiently for my father; for that dark and violent gift, whose mystery overshadows so much of my life; and lives on, like radium from the old bones we left on that country hillside, a year ago.

I am going to say thank you for him. An old-fashioned word, in a time when new fashion is so often a symbol of bankruptcy of spirit, amnesia, hatred of life.

When I think of why I should thank You for him, I look around this dark place, I look in the faces of my fellow prisoners, I taste to the dregs the bitter prison days. And I understand that gratitude is the only responsible act of a man. He and my mother brought us here, Philip and I.

Others were certainly involved—many in spite of themselves, and in bitter opposition to our lives. The Jesuits certainly qualify here. But before them, there was my father, who knew you, believed in you, in however twisted and quixotic a way. And taught us so to know, so to believe.

It is our own lives must straighten that twisted metal into an instrument of new virtue. Obviously. We cannot, we have no least desire to live the faith as he lived it (I almost said, as he imposed it). But even his anger, his despotism, became a kind of virtue in us—for he forced us to go beyond himself, not to settle our lives on his terms, to find in ourselves the virtue that would make love and truth and decency into active principles of conduct.

He walked with us to Sunday Mass, some two miles of open road, in the days when we were too poor to own a car or to take a streetcar or bus. At Mass, he prayed, as far as I can remember, with all his heart. He was capable of a sense of mystery. He was honest and generous and hard-working; for many years he slaved as a common workman for a Depression pittance; when he was laid off from work in the early thirties, he was not ashamed to apply for a public relief job, and to work for even less than before. Perhaps just his irascible, stubborn, angry will kept us afloat.

And though he denied us the first gift of a father—a father's heart—he did not deny us everything. He was proud when we entered the seminary, he followed our studies, our writing and teaching and lecturing, Phil's early civil rights struggle. Old, unquenchable, fierce, he took in stride the successive steps we determined on; to be publicly responsible in our ministries. We were always able to hash out at home the designs that lay nearest our hearts, even when they spelled trouble (they invariably did) for ourselves and for the family.

Perhaps something in his own hard existence led him further into our own; I cannot at any rate ever remember him arguing us down with that commonest parental argument, which is rooted in pride of place and ambition for clerical sons—because the parent wants at length the glory he was denied to shine fiercely in the sons. On this point alone, much will be forgiven.

When we wished to go on one of the early freedom rides into the South, his only urging was that he be allowed to come along. He was then in his late seventies.

I ask You peace on his old bones, restless, demonic, bent on his own will as they so often were. More, I ask that by Your gracious gift, he may be father to me, and I son to him, through all the years that remain to me—my father in prison, my father in the priesthood, my father in the heart and spirit I must show in order to live as I must.

May he, in seeing Your face, turn a new face to me, the face of a man twice born to truth, to reality, to vision; his sins expunged, Your covenant abiding in him.

May he, in the manner of a good father, be my guide and friend and steadfast counselor; now in the days of grace—as he was not in the days of nature.

Having lost everything (literally) in death—may he help his sons to the courage of those who have lost everything.

May he purify us of the bloodletting prison vices: self-pity, hoarding of spirit, complaints, acedia, laziness of mind—and above all the acid anger and hatred which unmans and weakens to the point of extinction.

November 26

Every strong thought turns me to water.
    I must forego, in the name of Bonhoeffer's "suffering fidelity"
all that cherished past   which in the level pans of justice
    weighs light as a breath: the "things of a child."
        It is the night, the night comes on, a beast
    scattering all before! I roll like ninepins, chaos is his game.
     O my dear friends, thought of you at any hour—
        the places we wandered, loving the earth, hands
an open space for gifts of time and place; how we held all
    things—
            must let them go. The desert monk
    measures his shroud, paces off his grave.
    Nunc coepi, the anchorite whispers. *Begin indeed*
        the exhausted motionless master, seated on a stone,
                counsels at twilight.

November 27

I work in the dental clinic with the following specimen: a
smartassed, tough, talented overweight head and gut. A
paisano with a perfect religion, perfectly pagan. He takes
Americanism one step further—i.e., into dollar criminality.
He reads everything, but everything, with the thoroughness
of a garbage machine. An authority on the Second World
War. Immunized against any alternative to his expertise.
Fights at the drop of a hat, makes mobiles and peace symbols and collages, sings like a steam-fitting bellows. Is in-
trigued by me, a new item in his folklore list; what a hit story
for the hometown folks, this fool priest and his brother . . .
I find him exasperating and exhilarating all at once. But what

hope is there for his redemption to something more human, the gift of his talents for others? He has pangs at times, unwilling even to try the Ry-Krisp Catholicism available here. But dreams and speaks, as winter comes on, of the *dolce vita*, yacht, Florida for the winter . . . the eating place he is going to open . . .

November 29

The indictments come down

J. Edgar has spoken. We are living through such times! Last night I hardly could bear the desolation, the thought of the loss of our friends, the confidence the past years have built up at such cost. Then the thought of being buried alive here for an indefinite sentence, when one is literally counting out his blood, drop by drop. Our worst fears are being realized, day by day . . . After such a night, one comes into the day like a drunk, only half in the world. I was lucky enough to be able to spend some time with Philip and so to be steadied by his unfailing good sense and faith. But the nightmare remains—for him, jeopardy so far greater than my own. With the hearing on reduction of sentence so near now . . . what more perfect way could they have found to spoil his chances, slim as they are in any case? But our friends rallied round, it is clear there is to be some sort of response in the Congress . . . What suffering for our family as well! I learned that I do not go very easily or naturally to our Lord, that I stew in my despair and in effect act as though there were no God. Or rather, conclude icily that He will simply have to come to understand. But all this goes forward in such a swamp of dereliction that I am quite lost, given over. The Psalms are some "carrion comfort" but they do not stay with me to any appreciable degree, as an *atmosphere* in which I can move and take life as it comes. The cruel past weeks, blow upon blow for us both: never easy.

December 1

I cannot "act as though" and still retain any semblance of sanity or selfhood. It is a fact too that I sweat blood and give up and call out, like the psalmist; it's not worth the candle. And You do not intervene. You are absent, like the dead. You have nothing to offer my fate—no palliative, no open door. As though You were not.

It is staggering and humiliating to be brought so low. So low one does not know if he will ever stand again, or see the other end of this night. One had thought it would end more gracefully, more honorably. It may not. Then the past, or others, will have to stand surrogate for what is in fact destroyed—without rhyme or reason. Except that one has been willing to go so far—and the journey was for the sake of others.

Coupled with the trip to Rochester, the developments of the past two or three days have induced a kind of stasis of heart. One would much rather dwell in a rich emptiness of silence than attempt a big explanation . . .

I was taken out in manacles, to testify at the trial of the Flower City draft board raiders. Was kept in solitary in West Street jail for one night. Not much of a penance, except that in such circumstances I tend to fold gradually into a dough, bereft of separate parts and incapable of autonomous acts—head included. A cage on the top floor, under the big ventilators, with two Puerto Rican kids—everything including shoes taken away . . . Up at six, breakfast, and out to the waiting cage to be picked up by the marshals once more . . .

There were evidently strict orders to keep me under wraps. We ended up, not in Rochester pokey, but in Erie County jail some forty miles out of town . . .

The trip was almost worth everything. Any lessening of inhumanity is so rare in such circumstances, one almost perishes for sheer relief. They took off the cuffs, took me into a lunch stand, and generally acted as though they were capable of respecting me and making a decent day of it. One of the marshals was pure Will Rogers—a dreamer and yet sharp as a bowie knife. He composed corny verses in free time, which he recited with delicate gusto.

The other was 99.99 per cent Catholic, macho, contemptuous of the young—very big on sexual play-fair, very big also on violence. Like his church, like his culture.

I had this unreal sense of being allowed an interval of beauty—a perfect late autumn day, all three of us carving our dreams out of whole forests, hills, streams, innocent life—between two stale ugly slices of reality—where I came from, where I was to go. There was no guarantee such a thing would happen again, indeed I had no claim on it.

As a matter of fact, it was withdrawn immediately, we being met at a throughway exit (security again) by another marshal's car; the waist and ankle shackles applied matter-of-factly (here comes normalcy again).

What a pokey! Stripped as usual by a big bumpkin of an officer ("Haw! Just made lieutenant"), led up and up three iron staircases, just under the roof. Solitary again. At least, I said, only one night.

Next A.M., after little or no sleep: "no court session until noon." Then at noon: "no court today." At 7 P.M. said fauna watcher came to lean and leer into my cell once more. I had not been out of the damn cage all night or day; he looking at his watch with the grand air of a Renaissance zoo keeper —"Well, let him out for fifteen minutes!" So he watched while I walked up and down, up and down, grateful for even that . . . At the same time a GREAT RESOLVE taking shape; having been refused access to chaplain, lawyer, family, razor, shower, books; the lights on night and day, the cell shrinking about me like a metal net. Resolve: I would cry out my cause in court on the morrow, so get to my friends and others; announcing I would neither eat nor drink until I was returned to Danbury . . . and if there were NO court on the morrow I would begin the same routine until I had access to someone.

O my poor old creaking soul which scarcely gets around in my poor old dray horse body—you still win a round or two!

Up betimes like Pepys; to be conveyed to the Flower City ward. Met midway by a damn fool dough-faced agent of something or other, armed with a walkie-talkie shoved into his thick hip and brain (not otherwise visible). Walkie wouldn't work. I applauded, like a manacled Zen man, one hand to the breeze, in the back seat. What a joy! Nothing works any more. I hope the bombers don't work today, nor the sheriffs nor the hangmen nor the evictors of the poor, nor the generals' carbines nor the makers of Mylai . . . They ferried me in by back streets, a security risk. Ha!

Coffee and a roll in the chief marshal's office. They always talk churchy to me and call me "Father" as though we were in the men's room of a mortuary chapel, hushed tones, averted gaze; we know, don't we, Father, the weakness of mortal flesh and how to split the take later . . . He came into the john and stood there while I shaved and peed; third floor up but you never know, I might take wing through the plate glass or something . . .

In came the Flower City Conspirators, I reeled as though pelted by flowers in late November, intempestive! What a beautiful barrage! We all embraced long and hard in front of the stony marshals (Let them all in today, no one stays in the cold . . .). It was a mini orgy in the cast-iron foundry. Down to work and tactics. Seven of the eight are defending themselves, the lawyer for Joe Gilchrist will question me at

length. Judge Burke, a great silver-maned St. Bernard of a
man, will allow any evidence as long as I stick to the substance of ". . . and so I told Joe . . ." I march into the courtroom, the FBI my shadow . . . a forest of hands goes up in
the V(ictory) salute. Two and a half hours later, I finish.

One of the women defendants, Joan Nicholson, kept getting shot down like a hundred clay pigeons in a trapshoot.
She wanted to ask me about prison, since presumably she
was to do time there. St. Bernard growled "irrelevant" and
receded further into his mane. I gave him time and leash.
Then, a quiet moment, I shouted: "I will neither eat nor
drink from this hour, until I am returned to Danbury prison."
"STRIKE IT OUT!" "The treatment of prisoners in transit
is utterly inhuman." "STRIKE IT OUT!" "This is the only
way (pointing to the scribes) I could get word to the press."
"STRIKE IT OUT!" I sat back. So did the judge. So did
everyone. "But you won't strike it out of our hearts!"—thus
our lovely defendant. Nor will they till hell freezes over.

December 11

Letter to Christ, continued.

I wanted to put down in some clumsy fashion what I con-
ceive to be my relationship to You. After all, we have been
on this troubled sojourn for some fifty years or so, and an attempt to get at "the thing" may be in order.

I wish to be short about this. It has to do with Phil. Simply put, no greater gift. I watch him with the men here; in
class, on the compound, at Mass, being himself. One of the
few who is free to be himself. And I come on a clue, both rational and embodied. There wells up in me at times such an
act of gratitude for being with such a man, for being, in a
sense, of one flesh and spirit with him, it seems that my life
can go on, fed by this single thought—that I have met a man,

and am in communion with all men. The gift is obscured and clarified, both, by the times. He would have been, like myself, something quite other, had not the deaths and lives of people summoned him into the cruel weather of the century, to speak and act there, in the fierce, pummeling, torrid, chilling winds that both create and destroy. Merton, A.J., Goldman, Jerry, Carol, Mom, others within that company, near and far, at rest or in our midst. But he stands at the center—his life still in combat, all the stigmata of the years on his face.

My clue to You. We are advised to go slowly with human images, to trust and welcome them to a point, to be courageous in going further, to interiorize them, to let them go finally, in favor of the death of all save Yourself. But one is involved here in a work of education. I thank You for him, who has led me so far—who has literally saved me, as You have literally saved me. A work of faith, a work of historical rightness. Because I can say brother, I can say from my heart, abba, father.

When I say all this I am not playing a game of put-down. He and I know how others are struggling through stages of doubt, despair, moodiness, sexual deprivation, fear, self-doubt, hatred, the burden of inhuman days. We find it viciously difficult to be patient. Other lives are both a call and a desert to us; our voices resound in the empty shells of lives which are either broken to bits, abandoned to their own misery and self-pity, or still unregenerate. We begin again and again and again. There is almost no one here who is capable of offering his life for others with any consistency or continuity. Indeed, prison is the playpen, the bear pit of the society at large, pressed close and small. The formation of even a few into a band of friends living for one another is a cruel, thankless, spotty job. We tend to forget the experience recounted of You and the Twelve in the Gospels—I even feel from time to time that we bludgeon them even with the Gospcls, instead of offering the tenderness, the wealth of feeling and response, the infinite adaptability You show.

This is only by way of reflecting on the course of a relationship that, held firmly by the years of discipline, concerted action, love, and family ties, tends by a law of natural movement to run off into other places and lives, wayward as water, no more to be dammed in or held to ourselves. All that we have, all that we are, a gift to the world. For the present, a gift to the prisoners; these cruelly beset and stricken and wounded and partial men, the detritus of a wasteful society, its pollutants, gathered to fester and befoul, in one limited place—a smoking natural dump yard . . . guarded night and day by the only ones who can be hired for such unsavory tasks —the mediocre, the quislings, the outriders and outsiders.

We are inserted here, to make whatever difference we may, to breathe the noisome self-destructing air, to be patient, to show forth the continuity of purpose which first led us to Catonsville, and beyond.

Someone wrote me: as long as the example of Jesus is of meaning to men, Your name will be blessed. The doctor here said to me yesterday: you can have no idea what impact your lives are having. To be worthy even to some partial degree of such words, one should be willing to bear a great deal . . .

The contradiction continues, one should be as relieved to be cursed with Christ, to be relegated to the limbo of church and state, as he is uncertain of mind at being the subject of cheap grace to others. "We are unprofitable servants . . ."

So we are come to our middle years, having been granted a longer time among men than were You . . . and being in prison, a strange lightening of the mind, a suspension of spirit—the perfect atmosphere, one would think, for the creation of men of the spirit, men of prayer, men in whom the life of faith is incandescent. Except, except—here too, one is subject to demons, the struggle is up close, bitter, humiliating, the issue most often in doubt, the right, the true, the integral are wounded and assailed. Cruelty, anger, self-

destruction, pusillanimity, doubt, active faithlessness, dread
of suffering, neglect of prayer, loss of ballast—prison is a
desert, and the desert is the dwelling place of demons. Amen.

Thank You for this place. Thank You for these brothers.
Thank You for these days.

Yesterday—one of the worst times. Such a horror of floating, unresolvable anxiety, no relief in sight. Prison. Locks on
a free spirit. Human wreckage. Sense of suffocation; the soul
imprisoned in the body, the body exiled among brute beasts.
At such a time in spite of all experience of the same, in spite
of all the skill one should be thought to have accumulated
—what? Almost yielding, almost a cop-out. One can only pick
up the debris and say, Lord have mercy.

I believe You are present to such days. I believe You are
there somewhat as Phil is there—powerless as I am. Yet supremely powerful to assuage in his uncorrupted immediacy
of understanding, his courage, his good humor, these gestures
which at every step bring smiles and glances and a better look
to things—a presence!

I creep off and play dead and try to get my breath again
for another assault on the cruel landscape—which to others
must seem fog-ridden and desolate and level, but to me invariably seems like another shark's tooth in the jaws of fate,
a peak with death for its revenge. Except that at such times,
death would be an exquisite relief, like freedom: never
granted.

Do not be free then, by any childish fiction. But for God
and man's sake, at least be a resolute and cheerful prisoner
—someone closer to the facts, to the truth of things. At least
this.

A young resister collapses under the regime—I visit him
for an hour each day, and note how well he bears his agony:
a grace, a courage like a naked bone under the whip of fear
and nauseous joyless loneliness. A young druggy goes through
the same thing. He, a flower child ("LSD, some three hundred trips"), wilts like a flower under the same cruelties. The

one man's whole life prepared him to deal with his emotions, even in the most fearful traumas, the experience of death afoot; the other had been a paladin of immaturity and self-indulgence, under the unassailable aegis of gurus, girls, life on the road, and drugs unlimited. I wonder, I ponder . . .

. . . We were stripped to the duff after our lawyers were here. The official philosophy seems to be: the Berrigans will undoubtedly try to pull some trick with these smartassed young Kunstlerites. It was a particularly odious session because the hack was so earnest, a body snatch on the prowl, and his disappointment mounted as he went picking through our shirts, socks, and crotches and found nothing to win him merits. Another item in the official scurrility—he was joined by another hack whom I knew to be a Catholic (daily communicant—thirty years, he had said once in my presence; something like the FBI genius who asked me five minutes after capture where my breviary was). Anyway, this second ghoul, who looks like a smooth-faced monsignor, kept up the most incredible sound track of chatter while the strip was proceeding. The evening sun was pouring over the hill through the windows: he was disquisitioning on the growth of real estate values on that hill and surrounding valleys. Like a medical student eating his lunch over the cadaver he was dissecting. I got a chilly whiff of death, or of Eichmann's ghost, in that moment. It was a demon's breath of extinction, indifferent hatred, and religion, all in one.

We were tossed our clothing. We said to one another: What a sunset! What a better day is coming! It was to keep up our courage—a spell also, against the demons of the place. They cannot stop what a history of good men can set in motion: but one must be unbreakable in spirit—not with the brittle hatred which is no more than a mirror-horror show to theirs. Another method entirely; as different from theirs as though it were imported from another planet—which indeed it is.

Now this little passage has the character and the truth of a prayer, as I firmly believe.

It is our attempt to be true to a fact of life here.

It is not wheeling You in, as the embalming comforter of the unsavory fact.

I rather think You were present to that tawdry scene somewhat in the majestic fashion of the winter sun; silent, all light, at center eye and edge of eye; enabling us to discern the meaning of the act and to respond to it, neither as dogs nor as men thrashing in a net of their devising.

The "religious" response, i.e., was simply the capacity to to deal with indignity; submitting to the inevitable, asserting our freedom by (1) despising and therefore blocking their blows, and (2) forgetting the incident, pushing it aside as childish, vindictive, desperate; thereby exorcising it of any power over us. A cleansing of consciousness.

If recalling it at all, merely and calmly placing it near the lives and deaths of others, in Vietnam, in Pakistan, in the black community; whose lives are so much more basely assailed, so much more onerous than ours.

I believe You stood so tall among men simply because You were so filled with the eminent capacities of man. A depth, a resonance, an unshakable though suffering fidelity, a suppleness of mind and eye before the condition and condign rhythms of life. A matter of quality, after all.

I would be like You, in this worldly, unadorned, unreligious response, before the foul inhuman fallout of all those who wield authority like a bloody flail.

To be patient, not in the way of a beaten, housebroken animal.

To retain a tenderness at heart—ultimately, I suppose, for one's poor self, who is beyond doubt brought low—unexpectedly, and for no valid reason under heaven.

To forgive these poor mercenaries of human flesh; to wish them, perhaps in some friendship or love we can know nothing of, much less engender, some form of salvation.

I wrote this two weeks ago, in solitary, in Erie County jail;
to You:

You; so near not existing
like a stillborn child
that rips the mothering world, her entrails, to a tatter
You; of whom many would state;
(especially that man, within hairsbreadth of fatherhood, now
        broken in hope
    his wife in a stupor, that bundle of guts and beginnings
        shoved in its grave)
it was all a nightmare, a chimera
though the earth, time, our lives sting like a nettle
    yet close upon this; a fistful of blood
                for a faith.

The following notes were scribbled on the floor of Erie
County jail. They are therefore part of this letter, which is
in essence a form of life itself; insofar as life in a shoe box can
be said to have a form. But in any case: *Sermon on the
Mount*: a blueprint of the human conduct of believers, ap-
plicable, rigorously, to all men in its insistent doctrine of
non-violence (man "is a link between anthropoid and human
being"). (1) It offers one image in response to the question:
how does one live in the world, especially in view of the inevitable conflicts that arise (a) among believers (b) between
believers and men in the world? (2) The code of conduct
offered by Christ is admittedly difficult in its demands on humans, especially if we admit clearheadedly our proneness to
violence of every kind, a tendency to which technology is
both an itch and a lackey; hypocrisy, selfishness, fear, dread
of moral change; the tendency to exploit and even to exterminate all who stand in the way. (3) All this admitted,
it must be said God does not command the impossible. Put
in this way, His commands express the outer reaches of human possibility; at the moment of intesusseption, these
"waters" create the new man; thus His will is *possible* (i.e.,

it has the attractiveness of a moral ideal), *probable* (some will be led to experiment with the ideal, at least from time to time), and *actual* (i.e., some will live and die in such wise). (4) The church, meant to be a sign of the community of the twice born, must in fact be censured as the chief obstacle, the denier, the one who first managed to cancel out these words. As Grand Inquisitor, she has given her own sermon; blessing herself or the world (the same thing finally) in terms contrary to Christ's (in fact she actively despises, fears Him and continually acts out His execution—to the point where her conduct, at first spectacularly sinful, merely becomes boring—a tawdry third-rate show. "Blessed are the rich, blessed are the cruel, blessed are the war makers, blessed the impure of heart. Blessed those who inflict persecution . . .). (5) We gain a sense here of the liaison which is possible, then probable, then so often actualized, between church and state. Many in consequence, once drawn to the divine logic and inner attractiveness of these sayings, can finally make peace with neither church nor state. What we have in consequence is all the frustration, false starts, world mimicry, explosiveness, and blindness of those who, in resistance to both official games, simply try to gather together and so live. These communes of conscience are probably the sole sign we shall have in our lifetime of the meaning of such words. Some marks of such gathered peoples at the edge: (a) political activism, "resist evil with good." The supposition of such words is verified once more in our day—personal and institutional violence are self-defeating, revolution is new, hopeful, or historically a breakthrough, only to the extent that it is non-violent in principle and method. (b) interiority; men so find ways to enlarge their humanity, their spiritual space, to give the life of mind and heart a chance; to meditate, to hearken to the inner voice. (c) public celebration. Christians find ways of replacing the old observances with celebrations of faith. Men who live have reason to celebrate their lives and deaths. Only the dead have nothing to celebrate; no good news. (6) Nothing genuine or truly human ever dies. Only institutions die. World religions speak of reincarnation, eternal life, etc., nirvana. Ways of saying *Vivat rex!* (7) It is the invariable dodge of the powerful to urge non-violence upon the powerless. This is a way of doubling their jeopardy, of "keeping them in their place," alive or dead. In such cases, Christ is involved, not as liberator, but as threat, sanction laid on the status quo. God of money, god of empire; or slave among slaves; "be obedient to your masters" —the early words were a mixed bag, as were the later ones . . . Whereas the Sermon on the Mount, applying equally to all, received equally by all, would bring a change of heart, a change of institutions on behalf of all. Liberation—from the slavery of power as well as the slavery of powerlessness. (8) Those who presume to speak the truth about the facts of power today are obliged to insist, in season and out, it is the men of power who are guilty of purveying, technologizing, and universalizing violence, as the ordinary and acceptable way of conducting human affairs. The violence of the powerless proceeds from a different ground of existence; it is as a result mitigated, respectful of life, and introduced as a last-ditch effort. Compare—by way of contrast—attitudes toward New York bombings versus bombing of a single village in Vietnam by B-52s . . .

(9) Purity of means alone guarantees purity of end.

(10) One remembers his future by embodying it here and now.

December 12

How much truth do we owe them?

Led to reflect this P.M. on the vagaries of life here, how it tends to multiply evidence of the uniformly sterile violent methods available to power . . . Two inmates escape; helicopters are overhead, hacks take off pell-mell in autos, armed with rifles. Manhunt. A local war is declared. Paul has just arrived and been admitted when they cleared the visiting room and ordered us all back to quarters. I thought of all those who had come such distances and must return with only a few minutes of normal affection or interchange. Everything is so quixotic and capricious that the "room count" may well continue for many hours before "normalcy" returns. (This after a press conference yesterday in which Nixon declared his will to resume bombing if while troop withdrawal continues there is harassment of our overflights. The Vietnamese are well advised to expect the worst. And so are we.)

The thin veneer of Christmas preparation is broken in a flash, as though an ogre or a kidnapper had invaded the nursery. The prisoners are to have their fun. But suppose one or another of them tries to break the rules? Then in truth the skies will fall in on him with a vengeance!

"My soul is calm within me, like a child in its mother."

Advent calm in such an atmosphere is not the loveless icy solitude, masking what degree of selfishness, of the professional guru. It is the peace with which one awaits the Savior of all; who, according to scripture, comes amid turmoil, passion, and the collapse of "normal" life. He comes to reassert the truth in a world built on deception and flourishing like a human jungle, on violence, fear, and division. It may well be a time of death as well as of renewed life—both in contention.

Images of bondage multiply in a world of interlocked slaveries. The prisoners must be reminded of their condition, the rebellious cities must be repeatedly pounded into submission, civil liberties circumscribed or snuffed out, crime punished more severely, cops praised, soldiery rewarded, generals charged with responsibility for a militarized future . . . Everywhere the world takes on the appearance of an armed camp. And all the while, a deceiving rhetoric poisons the springs of language; a lie is no longer a lie, it is a diplomatic bypass. Nothing is as bad as it might be, every assault on human integrity is a temporary expedient to meet a crisis induced by the enemy, domestic or foreign. One can only reflect, for cold comfort, that the atmosphere of the country is rapidly approaching that time described by the apocalyptic tongue of Jesus in Matthew's Gospel; the captivation of all but a very few by the beast of this world . . . The deadly God talk that buries you deeper than Pilate's spade could . . . That papier-mâché "construction" of theologizers; never to have tasted the world! Since the more one tastes it, the less inclined he is to pay tribute to a Platonic ghost, his moral armaments against man, his aping of the apes of God. We struggle and sweat here for some breakthrough in the net of despair that all but engulfs us—knowing that our sweet skins are on the block, that when chips are down, our deaths count for as much as a Vietnamese peasant's—which is to say, for nothing more than the price of a shotgun blast . . . So I think tonight of the two men who escaped, who were shot at, who made it for these few hours at least in the freezing weather, the snowfall. What are their thoughts tonight, the thoughts of their families? Where will they turn? Was theirs a desperation move or a coldly logical run for money, being unable to bear the bleak months ahead, the life that adds up to a vacuum, a mocking procession of empty days and nights? And where are You in the world, in their world? And who gets to write the story anyway—the story of the socialization of punishment; is it not most often those who have wielded the whips and passed sentence on the victims? And on what side of that (literal) fence have the theologians stood, who were the guardians and oracles of Your word among men?

In face of the ineluctable course of things, one's heart grows faint. Surely the theologians who were not narcoticized against events would be in courts, in prison, in the underground—in face of the destruction of peoples, the threatened destruction of the world . . . They would be pondering during such an advent the chapters of Matthew's Gospel read during Advent, the curse pronounced upon inhuman powers and dominations, the lying words of the beast who pretends to the place of God in the world . . . We have almost nothing of this. The Christian leaven is all but lost in the general corruption of life and conscience.

December 14

Brecht, Kafka, Pirandello! O Manes!
The marshal bent to putting the leg chains on us, making of Phil and myself the strangest Siamese twins of technological genetics. "Holy Cross man myself, Father. What year did you graduate?" We were off, "mad as the ice and snow," making our way across the glassy pavement to the car; belly chains, handcuffs, foot fetters, the pampered, protected, en-

dangered priests: "Might be some of those radicals trying to free you, Fathers."

At least it hones our edge clean and bright; anger, almost a euphoria of anger. We pass the hospital, dentistry quarters, prisoners leaning out the windows—"There they go!" The V sign.

O land of the free! Bullpen, chains, we're off to the wizard; three cars, ten marshals to keep two priests for a court appearance.

The U.S. attorney is young, a novice's first appearance. He is unsure in the first hour, more sure as he gets into "the credibility of the witness," explaining his line of reasoning to the judge. It is a matter of three letters apprehended in my shoes, months ago. I know now the government, stung by our suit on First Amendment rights of all federal prisoners, had done its homework—with the help of the kangaroo advocates, our "social workers." These (presumed) prisoners' advocates have laid it all out. Some "damaging phrases" are read out in the hushed courtroom. The question for me which I have wrestled over for months—how much of the truth do we owe them, to whom we owe Vietnam, the federal prisons, our lost years, the deaths of children, the fate of the Vietnamese? Can one on occasion be an ethical liar in service to a higher truth, when they have all the power, all the marshals, all the guns, all the prisons, all the Third World, all the soldiers, all the National Guard, all, all? When our whole court action is "about this," the necessity of hiding three letters in one's shoes?

We came back, in chains, the same route; strange when even Danbury prison is a great relief, a kind of homecoming; by reason of those who welcomed us as brothers, knowing our struggle is their own . . .

December 15

The question is whether we shall have a human life or will be progressively denied one—so gradually and skillfully we are never allowed to notice our metamorphosis into inventive chimps or housebroken dogs.

The question is whether we can bear the death and degradation of others more easily than our own.

The question is whether God is a brother and advocate to those in the breach, or whether He is the implacable, untouchable master of the machine.

The question is a choice between Nazis and men, and where we shall stand.

The question is so simply put, in fact, that a child could choose—rightly, from the evidence, the faces that summon him in this or that direction—life or damnation.

The question is whether we can bear to forget our brothers and call amnesia a normal condition of things.

Everything we grew up to believe was firmly in place and unchallenged is dying. Including the church. Including the Jesuits. At a deathbed where faith reigns, prayer and silence are the only worthy responses. We are called, therefore, to this sorrow. The man who gloats over such a scene is a monstrous reject—he has no healing power nor can he bring anything new to birth.

We go to court tomorrow once more in chains. Our friends are outraged, much more so than we, who consider the chains a badge of honor. In such a way, we bear the ignominy of our brothers, so long concealed from public view. Many are becoming conscious of the long-term domestic Vietnamization demanded by our "way of life"—which means that some must live and die in slavery.

December 18

The new indictments of friends for offering me hospitality on Block Island bring a freeze to the heart. At the same time one is trying to realize something. What does it mean in such days of hope that signs of hopelessness should abound, that the sufferings of friends should be so desperately multiplied? Is there any immunity from the virus of death? It makes sense to ask such a question only in a time of extraordinary life. We have first of all the impact upon two men of faith of a blow of such crushing force. A second birthday indeed: or perhaps the reason that the second was granted. Life is granted, first of all; only in time are reasons for the gift adduced—or its cost presented. Last August, the sequestered life of the island seemed impregnable—but it has been breached by the choices of last summer—and now there is to be no "outer solution" or other end to the act of faith that will be required. The books, the brave words, the brave struggle to continue the calm dissection of the powers of death in the society and the church—the books have wings—they come to roost, or rather their import comes due. I have the deepest confidence my friends will prove equal to the hour . . . Then there is the effect on the church, so rich, so inert, so filled with self-regard, with the safety of numbers and money and inheritances of the mind. So amnesiac; so willing to mediate the changes required and exacted of others— and then only to a point. Up to now, a point that has fallen far short of suffering and risk. It seems entirely appropriate that men of this quality, freed from priestcraft and properties, from the guardianship of God's tomb, would be the ones to lead the church from waxwork enterprises into the light of day . . . The impact of this indictment in calling the church, "befitting" the church to Christ's will in the world—what a

vocation of honor through the stigma of dishonor! I think of
Tony and Bill tonight and my prayer goes out to them; I
know they will be meditating the last days—the last days of
the empire, the last days of the world, whose signs always
imply a new presence of the Lord of the absurd, the Lord of
crisis and turmoil; "You will hear the noise of struggle near
at hand, the noise of turmoil far away; see that you are *not*
alarmed . . . Such things are bound to happen . . . Nation
will make war upon nation . . . with these things the birth
pangs of a new age begin . . . You will he handed over for
punishment and execution, men of all nations will hate you
for your allegiance to me. Many will lose faith, they will betray and hate one another. Many false prophets will arise,
and will mislead many; as the chaos spreads, men's love for
one another will grow cold. But the man who holds out to
the end will be saved . . . As things were in Noe's day, so
will they be when the Son of man comes. In the days before
the flood they ate and drank and married, until Noe went
into the ark and they knew nothing until the flood came and
swept them all away. That is how it will be when the Son
of man comes . . . Keep alert then, for you do not know on
what day the Son of man will come."

December 19

I do not believe we are going to get a perspective on things
by the enforced optimism that says, after such and such a
period—punishment, immobility, prison—things will again
reassert themselves and "normalize" "to a degree" and we
will take our "rightful, honored place" "where we stood before," "purified by our experience," "the prophets of the
'70s," etc., etc. The very clichés one has recourse to in this
speculation reveal the profound and depressing malaise that
lies at the heart of such thought. I think it is going to be nec-

essary to take death seriously. I think it is going to be necessary to take Matthew 24 seriously. I think it is a hard thing to be a sign for this generation, as Jonah was for his, and Jesus for His. I think the honeymoon is over—it has been over for some time, as most people in the world were forced to learn—(forced labor, forced poverty, forced migration, forced death). It has not been over for us, mainly for reasons that had nothing to do with faith. I mean we were prevented from reading the signs of the times because we had not ourselves become signs of the times—our lives were awry. Now they are not, in main outline. Now we must await the outcome. Which day after day is revealed as an act of man. What could be clearer as claimant, infringement, keeper of keys, denier of liberty, stifler of speech, preventer of birth, invitational of death—than imprisonment itself? But at the same time, all is revealed as well as act of God.

The question of faith in such circumstances has certainly altered . . . It has to do not with the temptation to give up, to alter our ground, to despair of God, to commit suicide. All that enters the case, of course, as it lives on in the world, and is the immanent, almost inevitable response of men under duress. At least momentarily, and from time to time. But for me, the whole question of Jesus is a "given," never to be taken away, never to be given away. The question then is how one deals with the given, how one takes it in hand and heart, what one makes of such a tradition, such a person . . . such a faith. Does one believe with the faith of God Himself, or is his faith "equable" in the sense of being reductive to the faith of any good man facing calamity?

Pop prison described

The pop prison; its hall of mirrors, its snack bars, comfort stops, newsstands, the functionaries who lock and unlock the future, the present, the past; the prestidigitators of release, opening again the can of culture for the dislocated—and then ourselves who are trying day after day to ride the mad current, to build something out of broken lives . . .

Jeremy's visit, his intensity and purity. The healing tensions built up by a man who to the deepest fiber of his soul is not "with it"—neither with the insensitivity groups, nor the beautiful people, nor the steaming religious flocks, nor middle, upper, or lower America. But is quite simply equipping himself in a time of the stripping of manhood to be a man; which is to say, to be the new man.

Phil spoke tonight of the enervating effects of living here, assaulted by the canned noise of the national culture mills day and night. Another place of dismemberment. Yet we remain determined to work through with the men we live with and are therefore responsible to.

What might it mean to be the last Jesuit, or very nearly the last? The times allow in principle for the enlarging of every carnivorous capacity and the emptying of every spiritual capacity. Everything is allowed. This is the touchstone of the new slavery which goes by the infamous name of the new freedom. Sexual license, military license, the freedom of slaves to reduce others to slavery.

Writing: the luxury of a mind which has not discovered its hands? . . .

Or, being here: the sinking in the guts, watching the stream of "ideas" go by, reviews, projects, spasms toward the light, and thinking; the evidence is all in. But will the thinking beast perish, like the unthinking one, his ideas going down with him, a sinking baggage?

We have only a few simple obligations here; among which must be counted cheerfulness, tolerance, the will to survive, the *conversio morum* of the monks, now at the beck and call of the secular masters—whose claim on us is total as God's. And utterly fraudulent.

They censor letters and send them back, marked variously "objectionable material," "unauthorized mention of inmate," "criticism of institution," etc. They strip search after visits, looking up assholes for drugs or demons or despairs. They are truculent, uncertain, overkilling us with complacency, sloppy in execution of the law, potbellied, lazy of mind, angry with those of us who will not grow cabbage leaves about the ears, who protest reduction of men to sticks and stones. In short, they want no interference with the death game. They count us avidly, several times a day, several times a night, because our bodies are their jobs. Literally, the politics is property.

I am in the mental condition day after day of one who is living with a dying relative or friend, one in terminal illness. The illness is my own, it is the atmosphere, infected with hopelessness, illusions, the last days of a dying mind. Strangely, a comfort exists in the thought. A kind of *quies*, an intersession between tasks. One puts aside the mind as a tool, to seize with his hands. Even in a dental clinic.

Philip and I are catching up on the years when our lives, so divergent one from another, merely intersected at this or that point. Living together at last for a sustained period—and in prison! Finding how searing that can be; determined as we are, not merely to circle one another in our work, reading, play, teaching, worship; but to suffer a kind of mutual eclipse, like two planets that cross, whose light is for a time denied its rightful scope. How much pain this implies—for both of us; each of us realizing, by way of unspoken consolation, how strong the other is in the bearing of pain.

January 5

Wanted to register an act of gratitude in the midst of the winter doldrums. To be alive even to the degree that one stands for the life of others; "in the midst of great darkness a light has shone." What sadness some of our friends show, almost in proportion as they have been generous and responsive to the times! Is one ever in his life ready for the outpouring of bad news, bad power, bad use of human and earthly resources that the days bring? I confess to a great loss of energy even as the months pass—that seems to be the most palpable form of death demanded of us here and now. When even courage does not seem to be enough—and every avenue of relief seems closed, as far as a future is concerned. Simply, we are reckoned dead men, and go walking on, in spite of death and all its minions, in the faith of Jesus, who loved us and was delivered for us. I am at the point where Christ can no longer be considered peripheral—at least less so than my many years as a Jesuit and a priest have allowed. The days are a terrible, even an overwhelming burden. I think I will have to share things more closely with Phil than I have heretofore.

Poetry quite dried up. Unable to escape from the piped

noise, all day, most of the night, the creation of a space of silence more difficult as one's reserves of energy and attention are lost. Prayer. Fidelity. Custody of the senses. An enforced cheerfulness toward others. Delicacy and sense of the plight of the brothers. One's existence truly found in them —and lost in them. Acceptance of those rhythms that render one physically weak and lightheaded with the absurdity of life, the inability to "grab" the whole round of life by the neck and claim mastery over it. Not at all.

January 6

Coming alive. Even the dentists are beginning to ask questions. Could it be that Baldwin's open letter to Angela Davis is helping? I gave it to Kaplan to read, we stayed two hours after work to rap on it, on the institution, on "coming in" to work versus choosing to be an inmate here . . . He is taken by my views, which is to say, he has no intention of changing his for mine. But we shall have to see.

Instance: J.J. is twenty-six years old, illiterate: "They couldn't find a teacher here low enough for me." He has been a state ward since age nine; in prison twelve years now. He is trying to get out of the trap, for the nth time. Very little understanding that he may be back again in short order. Where else, in the final instance, does he have to go?

A Viet vet Leroy, is proving to be an astonishingly bright and intense poet. The first job for me is always to read, to share and encourage. He is in trouble already for his correspondence, which reflects his anti-war, anti-racist views. Called in at high levels—what about this poetry? "Follow the rules!" Now, according to the rules, as per the warden's evidence on our suit in Hartford—no rules are in force! We are in fact operating in a vacuum, between the idiot's delight of the traditional rule sheet (shame on obscenity; we reserve the right to seize, destroy, etc.) and a promised set of rules to end all rules (however, D.C. is still working on these . . .). Of course, my name comes up . . . Is Berrigan connected to this? And of course, irremediably and irredeemably, I am. The twinge in the gut at knowing "my cause" is very much a live hot coal is very much like that earlier thrust in the guts which I remember from church authority when I would try the run for freedom in the early sixties. I am embarrassed even to set down the gut connection. Still, can one surmise that whenever authority is wrongheaded or -jointed, it always looks alike, no matter the sponsorship?

My relations to Phil undergo so painful and fruitful a revaluation. I feel in this as in so many areas that we must act as though our words, often stated, have face value . . . i.e., in such a case, we are asked to live out the truth that men do not grow in a community without growing in relation to one another and paying the price of such growth. Otherwise we merely ricochet off the truth, painful though that be, instead of granting it a home. We talk, we disagree, we give and take pain, and we trust that reflective grace will also have room and time in us—that we will grant it place, even first place. We are still, to one another, the first in the community. That does not mean that we ignore mistakes, clumsiness, wrong thinking in one another for the sake of appearances or peace (whatever that could mean). This is all a very stony path; it is, however, the only one that could conceivably lead us to the reality of other lives, or a rightful place in their struggle.

Our classes. All we can do is hope on: from so much errant and apparently formless talk, something genuine may emerge —possibly, before the whole enterprise is stomped out (for a while, it looked as though we ourselves might accomplish that very well). A general distrust and dislike of religion; based on the experience of the organized gigantic "thing" that has so adroitly leagued up with the state to bring us here.

January 10

Add to the ennui and glooms of January the particular sorrows and discontent of a few of us, who are enduring threats of increased legal jeopardy. Quite a mortician's liquid, to be shot into living veins and freeze them in death. A great effort even to set down these words . . . One has little to say; one adds, in any case, what difference could it make? People are glutted to the glottis with the evidence of national decay, bankruptcy, etc. So? If we cannot have a passionate life filled with bounty of the spirit, let us scratch about nonetheless with a bad one. After eagles are extinct, they reincarnate as lousy, tattered, filthy barnyard fowl.

We were asked to make a statement relative to the Catonsville play opening in New York City. I dragged through a few hundred words as though my fingers were my feet, my feet in irons. How is one to feel, when he is in prison, and his "crime" is about to be staged (the word is horrendous) for the world, while one's own life proceeds in a direction of plain two-cent death? What a stone in the guts! How do I feel? I feel at times as though I have lived too long, as though to live longer under such conditions were a supreme affront to the dignity of life itself; to the dignity my life has been able to muster so far. And then I think: but is your present life an affront to the dignity of the life of Jesus? Or does the truth of life only begin to be pressed out of the stones of such circumstances as ours? At least in these pages I can be candid about the truth of what we must endure, not knowing if my words will ever see the light—not knowing if *we* will ever see the light again. For the dreams of prisoners are denied us in principle; we have no family ties and are bound over to Jesus—captive to the world, in Him.

I hope and pray these notes do not give the impression of

dreariness of spirit. God knows, some days the tide rises high as the throat, one has the impression he is suffocating. But the feeling soon passes. I am reading Mandelshtam's *Hope Against Hope*; it proves both ominous and therapeutic. Ominous: so many scenes that parallel what we are enduring in thought control, prying, spying, snitching, and the rest. Therapeutic: to read how much may be endured, while the spirit still hopes on, even soars on. And that face in the frontispiece —a woman of genial mortified beauty, a mind scoured by death, exile, impoverishment. What has she not endured? As though indeed the century's terrors and reprisals and murders had all sought her out, a victim whose immortality must be tested by each succeeding horror . . .

. . . There is a character who visited me four or five times in the last two weeks: to deliver mail (no favor since he reads each envelope like a hack, assiduously, before tossing it down), to read out a carbon from the warden's office (describing Phil and me as his two chief problems and declaring "steps have been taken": one of those redolent euphemisms out of Stalin's brain pan). Then one day, this same prisoner asked for the "name of your organization" since "his sister and her friends have made a collection for you and want to go down [or up] in history as your benefactors" . . . Then last night he came in to denounce me in a kind of slavering rage, piteous to behold, mindless, violent . . . I had been saying things about him; that he was a CIA agent, that he was a snitch . . . He would break the hippies like chickens with his hands, they were lying . . . He implied also (amid slavish overtures of "respect for the cloth") that he would break my bones in like manner . . . In any case I put up with it and John and Shorty appeared successively at the door, wondering what the hell was up; it finally came to a halt. But I will not easily bear with a repetition of the same . . .

The difficulty here is to try to separate method from madness, malice from illness. The pathology would indeed include the truth about what is being so vociferously denied, i.e., the gent was, in the estimate of trustworthy men, indeed a "lame" of constant and proven value to the higher-ups. At the same time one must note a desperate will, operating now as a threat, now a promise, to befriend someone admired or trusted. What is to be done? One must be sensible and play innocent or ignorant on every occasion; at the same time one must take steps through friends, so that the violence, which I take to be a real threat, does not pass certain limits . . .

Also reading betimes, Stevenson's *The Still Point*, Bachelard's *Poetry of Space*, Stevie Smith's *The Best Beast*, Snyder's *Regarding Wave*, Guelleric Levertov poems. Finished Speer's *Inside the Third Reich* (a weasel-toothed book if ever was one). None of these seem to make me much better from day to day; what they rather do is make the days (and perhaps me also) bearable to others . . .

Hard time easy time; the worst thing is waiting, not knowing when new blows may fall, when we will simply be sewn into a shroud and slid overboard. This is a kind of death I don't easily get used to. Can one? Certainly '71 is going to bring more of what we have so far endured, rather than a lessening of things.

P.M. Ed the actor was admitted for a visit. He plays my part in the Catonsville trial play; very modest, direct listening type—a Minnesotan also! Stirred by the play, as are all the actors, uncertain as to how to proceed, what are the "handles" of understanding, "what are you all like?" A good two-hour session, but exhausting as well.

The enormous difficulty of getting off the ground friendships, which will be accessible and responsible to all of us . . . What does it mean not to be able to trust the majority of those one lives with? Mrs. Mandelshtam takes this up as a Stalinist-era question. For us, here, now the question is also a real one. Not to be able to proceed with a supposition of trust . . .

The play is important for the same reason any human

gesture expressing the "overflow of freedom" is important. I.e., we need something around which to gather in the night, some way of taking in our surroundings, of gaining perspective, to hope on . . .

The volcanic changes of mood one is subject to! At home there were the distractions, changes of scene, opportunity to run away from offenses, relief of all kinds . . . Here one is planted, like a vegetable. This makes me wonder at times how to survive, how not to prey on others or resort to violence at unexpected (it is always unexpected) provocation.

They have just locked me in for the one hundred and fiftieth night. I go into the sixth month.

We had to agree that one of the brothers could no longer meet with our discussion group. The paranoia, and its parasitic growth in winter, is unbelievable. This was a painful decision for us all—in the nature of things. But one learns from the past, or he condemns himself to the same old barren cycle and no relief. To being a fool, in sum.

January 12

To live from day to day, when any day can bring the sky falling in—and not on me alone, but on Phil and others. Can we live this way, even with joy; in a parallel way to the style we all tried outside? Things then were in a sense materially easier; but still we live with the sword overhead hanging by a hair . . . In a sense, one cannot even hope to prepare his soul for what may well happen. I think even the word "prepare" has something of bourgeois "householding" about it; but the soul is not a Dutch kitchen scrubbed up for a ritual sabbath. It is a cave of winds, source and sender of storms—whose walls have vanished; it is the world itself.

I wish to give my life for Phil and the others—to save them further pain and release them from bondage, as today's passage from Isaiah said. I hope he knows this. I fail him in many ways which I pray are small ways.

If one had it to do over again! I would have fought *not* to have him go with us to Catonsville; he having done enough when he shook us alive. I would have tried to persuade him to turn himself in on the appointed date, not to go underground. I am sick at heart for his desperate jeopardy endured for us all, so constantly, with such grace. Amen.

In such a way, the end of the '60s marked, if nothing else, the end of our innocence, or at least, a lessening of our illusions. We had not done our homework, we had not reckoned the cost of our undertaking, we had deceived ourselves about our strength, our spiritual resources, our self-understanding, our ability to form and maintain communities of conscience, our affinity with the oppressed peoples of the world. We had counted on a quick win, with minimal cost to ourselves. We were bugged by the noxious dreams of the culture —that anything was possible to us because anything was possible to our technology, our social engineering, our encounter groups, our rock music, our hip clothing. Didn't it all signify, beyond reasonable doubt, a revolution that would disarm the war makers, reapportion the fruits of labor, leisure, and love, would give birth to the New Man, bury the old man like a dusty Pharaoh?

It did not; *pace* Dr. Leary, Dr. Reich, the druggies, the hippies, the commune people, the Hell's Angels, the flora and fauna of Consciousness III.

It did not; *pace* ourselves.

It did not, Mr. Nixon declared. To prove it did not, he invaded Cambodia, issued a virtuous peace plan, bombed the north, welcomed Ky, ignored the Tiger Cages, sent paratroopers after war prisoners; did in fact whatever pleased him, on whatever occasion, to extend the war, to confound the movement, to discredit the peace talks.

He therefore merits our thanks, in whatever unlikely or ironic sense. For having joined his presidency to the former one, and declared himself the champion of that other "movement," not of middle or silent America (which is his creation and camouflage), but of the powerful, the moneyed, the great of the nation, whose place of pride is, literally, a matter of the fabric and substance of the republic, a matter of simple life and death, a matter of the way public and international affairs are to be conducted now and forever. In spite of all claims to the contrary, all constitutional or anarchic assaults on the republic (taken in its real sense, as a conglomerate of wealth and political control shored up with myths and mock-ups).

Thus the movement strove to become itself; unconscious, largely, that in comparison with the movements that had brought change elsewhere it was a movement of adolescents; and to that degree, captious, unreliable, selfish, moody, vulnerable, a pre-movement, in fact; easily deflected, easily discouraged

There is nothing quite like an opponent to reveal such a movement for what it is, in contrast to its own rhetoric and illusion. Events since the summer of '70 make this painfully clear. Mr. Nixon moved purposefully ahead with his own program, a blitzkrieg against a children's crusade; he invaded Cambodia, bombed the North Vietnamese, sent paratroopers to free his captive airmen, all with an air of virtuous and painful reluctance. His political career is intact, at present writing; the two irreducible demands of the Vietnamese negotiators at Paris (the removal of Ky and Thieu from office, the setting of a date for total troop withdrawal) are matters of hem and haw, of paper shufflings and bombings.

Why then a play about Catonsville, in the dreary winter of 1970? In the light of larger issues that harass us, does not the event appear as a kind of fiery tempest in a trash can? Can the play accomplish anything beyond a salute to nine men and women, who tried, and failed signally, to bring the moral issues of the war into the public forum of the courts?

One can only say: in a bad time, almost any move toward

sanity, moral clarity, community is a move of import. It is important to continue saying, whether from jail or underground or courtroom or theater, that the war is the first moral issue in America today. It is important to continue saying this, no matter how loudly public persuaders speak to the contrary, no matter how afflicted with amnesia or fear the "movement" is, no matter how massively the currents of despair or violence wrack the processes of political life, no matter that the indictments multiply against resisters to the war. Seen in this light, a serious effort to dramatize the Catonsville event must be accounted an important moment for all of us. In jail, it is a reminder that our action is not lost; that it makes moral sense to other Americans, and dramatic sense to a company of actors, many of whom declared, after the Los Angeles tryout last summer, that the play wrought a deep impact on their lives.

January 15

Trying to express, in light of recent indictments: (1) The irreversible character of events; such and such a course once embarked on, the momentum carries them—the war is the downhill sign of our civilization itself. The random character of things, the fits and starts of violence and repression at home mark this semi-consciousness of the "beast." (2) The task: to bring true consciousness to bear on this, so that all elements of distraction, dismay at the presence of death, inhibitions, fear and trembling, are removed or at least purified. (3) Being cheerful and calm under the most atrocious assaults. (4) "Suffering fidelity"—much more than a horse-drawn slogan out of a martyr's biography. We shall have to pay as dearly for peace as the peacemakers have had to pay in the midst of war everywhere. (5) Removal of distracting elements, which tend literally to rob one of his inmost command over his soul. Most people, myself included, are distracted by the illusion that a return to normalcy is still possible. It simply is not. This is at its deepest a biblical conclusion. The truth can be ours for the asking: at least in the sense that we can share the lives of the prophets and heroes, by a grace which we refuse to cheapen. I am asked to ask to be worthy of such a destiny—or to suffer it in Phil, for the present. But to live in that present without fretfulness or complaint, or (above all) without constructing a future which is a cop-out from reality . . . In this we can count on very few—even among Jesuits and churchmen—all of which is a measure of the suffering we must grow ready for, grow into.

Many will lose heart, lose trust, lose faith in us. Even now, many cannot even bear to meet our glance or our greeting (cf. Matthew 24). Our only defense will be (1) to despise the charges of Harrisburg in light of the murderous war, and (2) to be prepared that our sins and failings be made public. Not to cringe from the aspects of judgment involved in another trial . . . Our families too must suffer with us; Mom's last years are to be marked by tragedy—but so go the lives of good people everywhere; how can we hope for exemption? We cannot rightfully do so and will not. By such acceptance, our lives are freed from the constriction of mere tactic, to stand on the inward ground of conscious history, which does not give way as tragedy and chaos claim some for their own. This epiphany we ask to share, who are free and wish to share our freedom.

January 17

Letter to a congressman

Dear Congressman Anderson:

Tom Buck was here on Saturday; this is a note to say thank
you to him and yourself for support in very difficult times.
Sensitive men tend to find one another, by the Lord's good
fortune, in such days as we are enduring; you with your
heavy burden of public responsibility, we in prison; both you
and ourselves, as we pray, striving to be faithful stewards of
God's will and man's hope.

I will not dwell on the burden the past days have brought.
They have brought a share of anguish to our friends and
families as well. We are tasting, according to measure, the
suffering which the waging of war has always entailed: and
which the waging of peace must entail as well. This is the
thought which sustains us—a consolation which the support
of friends makes evident.

Such indictments as the one laid on the priests, nuns,
and their friends must be accepted as inevitable in such a
war as this one, continued and expanded beyond all reason
or goal. How else indeed wage modern war which is total in
principle and demands the total mobilization of citizens

into its designs? Their minds, their thoughts and speech
and actions must all be bent into instruments of war—else
the arsenal is incomplete. And as the rationale of the war is
more completely discredited each day, it becomes necessary
to concentrate on the punishment of those who refuse to
have the peaceable form of their lives, their vocations to the
gospel, their love of neighbor forged in the fires of nationalism into swords of vengeance and retaliation. By the grace
of God, we claim to be such. It follows, with the iron logic
of Mars, that we must be broken, discredited, punished—
so that the war itself may proceed on its bloody and tragic
course.

There are, however, several hopeful aspects to all this. In
the first place, it becomes clear that our actions have spoken
to the government, that those in power have heard us aright.
The churches can no longer be counted on to support the
search-and-destroy mission of the American military in the
world. We have served notice that belief in the Sermon on
the Mount forbids us to be a sacred cog in the great secular
war machine. This, especially for Catholics, is an event of the
highest historical import; for our church has never before
in its American experience repudiated an American war.
Never have its priests and nuns challenged the secular arm,
or undergone prison, or placed their bodies in the front line
of non-violent resistance. In cold war and hot, our church
has preserved an inert and questionable normalcy, based on
the all but irrefutable assumption that a war which was good
for America was good for Christian men and women—and
vice versa. Now that pattern is broken; in our hands, of deliberate purpose. Whatever our mistakes, our clumsiness,
our fear or tardiness, it will not be possible in the future to
assert that the American church added to the odious and
bloody adventure of Vietnam, the sanction of God's ap-
proval. We have stopped short; we have refused to raise
our hands in blessing on the war machine, and have instead

held them out for the manacles. Whatever the cost to us, this will someday be accounted to our honor.

Resistance to unjust power brings down the wrath of that power. Inevitably, the shabby justification offered for continuing the war demands a series of civil trials aimed at destroying the good name of those who oppose the war. So we face another crisis, another trial. It matters little to our accusers that they ignore the law under which, presumably, all citizens are to be held innocent until proven guilty. Prior to any legal action, doubts as to our innocence are sown in the minds of the public by the chief of the national lawkeeping agency. Moreover, when the indictments are finally handed down, a penumbra of guilt surrounds others than the accused; a group of co-conspirators is named. Legally, these latter have no recourse in the law to clear their good name; by implication, they too are part of the conspiracy, but the law is unable to uncover sufficient evidence of guilt. No matter; let them be named; the widespread net may not have drawn them in, but neither have they entirely escaped.

One cannot in good sense underestimate the harm done to the delicate fabric of society by such methods of justice, in support of such a war. One thinks of the trust and mutuality which govern human relations in decent times; one thinks that a government of the people, by the people, for the people has no need of spies, informers, or agents, wiretaps, a paramilitary and anonymous police force. Americans have normally considered such paraphernalia as odious and utterly foreign to the functions of a free society. They have deplored fascist or communist methods of maintaining law and order, considering them as inadmissible among free men, acting in private capacities. They have considered their Constitution as binding upon all in its limiting laws, and as protecting all in its guarantees of human and civil rights.

But a decade of war has placed all this in question. In a true sense, this may be considered the revenge exacted on our

people by the breakneck course of the war; we ourselves
are become the victims of the ruin we have wreaked upon
others; the war has indeed come home. To wage it abroad,
to shore up its bankrupt logic, to pay its outrageous wage,
we are bled white; the human needs of our people must be
indefinitely deferred, the poor must grow poorer, the very
freedom and justice which the war purportedly vindicates
abroad must languish and erode at home. After a decade of
such war, we scarcely know and can scarcely bear to trust
one another, are spiteful and alienated from the best of our
youth, are more divided among ourselves than ever in our
history. Natural flexibility of minds, openness to diverse cultures and styles, creativity in politics, compassion toward
the poor, that sense of sanity and welcome that once made
us a haven for foreign peoples—one senses that such qualities
are all but lost in our midst. The military metaphor rules;
we itch for the instantaneous, ruinous methodology of violence, in every quarter; agreeing, as we have come to do, that
a body count is a definitive solution to troublemakers, enemies, dissidents, first abroad, then at home.

What then shall we do with our lives? Once, our course
seemed clear. The law of the land was ample and humane;
we could work within its ambit for the common weal. We
had talents to offer our society; and the will to put them
to work. Moreover, a discipline and a tradition sustained us
—we were Catholic priests, vowed to service of our brothers.
We would labor, in concert with others, to bring to all Americans the possibility of a human life. Our gospel led us like
a lodestone to the heart of life; we were called to stand
at the side of the poor, the victimized, the excluded. We
were Christian optimists, American to the core. In the space
of our own lifetime, we thought, vision and constancy would
foreshorten the centuries of injustice, poverty, racism, and
unite once and for all the American deed to the American
promise. That hope sustained us through the '50s and '60s as

we taught, wrote, organized, planned, and prayed. And, of course, obeyed the law.

Then, the highest powers of the land violated the law of the land. So simple, so shattering an event occurred. We went to sleep one night, assured by our President that a few military advisers were helping beleaguered allies in South Vietnam: the discredited remnant of mandarins and collaborators abandoned by the French. We awoke to a nightmare of a full-scale war. As the war advanced, we were prepared to take seriously, as good Americans, any or all of the reasons adduced, usually after the fact, for more bombings, more soldiers, more money, more death. It was all worth it, whatever the cost; freedom was at stake, communism was advancing, our allies had called for help. In any case we had never lost a war, our national honor was in question, to withdraw would mean writing off the deaths of our sons and brothers. To continue the war, Congress was ignored or bypassed; world opinion was held of no account. At home, the question of juridical or congressional action was never seriously raised, except by a few courageous congressmen; the bulk of them, however, seemed content with their own decline as a body of lawmakers responsible to the people, mandated by the Constitution to bear responsibility for declaration of war.

What were we to do with our lives, in such circumstances?

In other circumstances, the answer had been relatively easy, in principle. As the war continued, the question became grievous and vexing almost beyond bearing. In a land that had nourished the fair hopes of so many, and had articulated its dream of justice and plenty, could we be forced to become lawbreakers, in defense of the right to life and liberty of other men? The ominous specter moved closer; we acted, we broke the law, we are paying the consequence, harsh as it is.

The Harrisburg charges need not lengthen this letter. They will be aired thoroughly in public, in what we hope will be a more equitable court than the one in which they were first revealed. Let me only say that we would bring bodily harm to no men; that determination must be placed beside the devastation of countless lives and immense territories, wrought by the war. We are peacemakers, the methods of the war are not our methods; its justification is worlds apart from our gospel.

Let me close by thanking you once more for your support and friendship in a dolorous time. It may be that out of what we endure, men will realize that Americans can still be compassionate men, that Christians take Christ seriously. The hope is alive, in us, for others to draw on, and take heart from.

The future will be different, someone said, if we make the present different. Exactly.

Daniel

January 18

After lockup, the guard yelled in at me: "Your friend J. is very sick. I spent an hour this evening with him in the hospital; he seems quieter now. Knew you would want to know!" Touch of humanity on a bleak landscape.

Literally everything including prisoners' rights must wait on the question of the war. That is becoming more evident each day. When everything is coming down, there is a hierarchy of even "crucial" questions.

It was reported that some friends said: "We were meeting together after the indictments, trying to decide what to do, and we decided to have a button made!" Bailing from the sinking ship with teaspoons!

We learn that Goodell will be here tomorrow. We are to be on the cover of *Time* magazine this week. Critic puts us in a gallery of Living Saints. What hogwash. Even under the assiduous eye of the watchdog, we are raked over for the pabulum of the masses. This notoriety—what a danger, not only to the trial of the accused, but to our very sense of who we are, why we are here, what we may contribute.

I flew off the handle today at Dr. B., thinking and reflecting aloud on the Jesuits. My continually crushed hopes in their regard. Tempted to contrast the provincial with Cardinal Sheehan of Baltimore and his immediate support of accused priests there. My sense, by contrast, is "to the devil and good riddance with Berrigan." The weakening of bonds, instead of their strengthening by one who is determined only on the solid phalanx of the average, and is utterly incapable of a charismatic gesture. So the ship slowly settled in the waters. But what grief from ourselves, who had hoped to offer something better—to be allowed to offer it in our own lifetime . . .

Points to be made in public, in defense from these charges of Harrisburg: we can repeat word for word the statement of convictions that governed our act at Catonsville in 1968; i.e.;

1) We would never, for any conceivable reason, do bodily or spiritual harm to any individual, for whatever end.

2) We continue to believe that certain property arrangements are immoral and anti-human. Destruction of such property may at times of social crisis be an overriding moral obligation.

3) The government shall not be allowed to shift the burden of guilt from itself to us. The war and war-making policy are the real issue of the trial. We maintain that the indictment is an attempt to distract from that issue by discrediting us and, by clear implication, resisters against the war. The Nixon administration has consistently used this tactic to continue and expand the war; it has countenanced atrocities, violated the Nuremberg statutes, neglected the step that would lead to the freeing of its prisoners, invaded a neutral country, resumed wanton bombing of the north. There must be a "scapegoat case" to conceal this international infamy. We are its Dreyfus case, its McCarthy victims.

4) The real conspiracy here exists between the FBI and

the justice department, in violating the law by declaring certain men and women guilty prior to a constitutional trial. Such a tactic, the initial statement of the case by Hoover, renders him indictable for violation of civil rights. We intend to pursue this matter.

A clearer statement of our innocence could hardly be asked than that offered under 1) and 2). Obviously, though, we are in a special and perilous time.

Goodell came, as fine and thoughtful and trustworthy as Anderson. Also his three assistants. We are always astonished at such goodness. Maybe part of the price of the times is precisely that one loses hope in the constancy of good men. We undervalue them, I say to Phil. He answers ruefully, "That's because most people deserve to be undervalued!" Which remark, it seems to me, quite closes the circle, unhelpfully. But it is true to a degree.

What to do when the sky falls in

There are three (or so) infallible, inevitable, invincible steps to facing down a fiasco such as last week's indictments (to speak of the soul of the powerless man threatened with such a whipping). Namely——

1) The sky falls in. Chicken Little glides onstage in Cassandra's robe piping ruination. She is well documented, an unliberated, ante-Freudian, ante-vote employee of FBI intimidation. But she has all the facts, and a gun at her waist. Look out; she is (says the male chauvinist) the deadly of the species.

2) You stew in your own special juices, for an unspecified period of time. John of the Cross is not much help, nor scripture, nor the notes of the Master of Novices on What to Do Until the M.D. Comes. Jesus is out of town. The Father is off on foreign assignment. The Holy Ghost sends a note from the inner office declaring his case load forbids seeing you: anyway, the union would object if he let you in. So you stew, indefinitely. Prayer is a dead yeast. You sit there or lie there or pace there, knowing everyone in D.C. and the Vatican and the Department of Injustice have signaled a post-

Superbowl victory cocktail party. Notre Dame won again. So what if you lost?

3) The boat, named the *Molly Brown*, slowly surfaces again, and rights itself. Friends appear, walking on the waters. Someone sends a dove around with a sprig of green in its mouth; it lands on a ruined masthead, smiling broadly. The good news is of course strictly qualified; we're still in this world, not by any means the best of all possibles. Indeed, the indictment, the death, the future still stand. But you've undergone a sea change. You can pray again, your guts have resumed something like their locale and function, you can take and eliminate food on schedule. Even a hack here and there looks at you as though he didn't wish you'd do Mother State the favor of dropping dead. The church shuffles some papers in the background and decides you can hang around awhile. (They know as you know there is nowhere for you to go anyway; and the embarrassment of your presence has to be weighed, at fingertips, with the, ahem, embarrassment of refusing you Christian burial . . .) Everything is about as lousy as it ever was, from one point of view; but from another, the world looks a bit different, almost bearable. Of course it's a drag being in the crappy spoiled fun house—still. It's like a vacation, three squares, guaranteed annual income, lots of crazy characters, nutty happenings—for a book, a scenario, or something . . .

4) You decide you won't give them the satisfaction of knowing they've opened your stitches, all up and down like a frayed zipper. You walk the yard and smile and smile and be a villain.

5) In your own head, you've metamorphosed—into a swan or a giraffe; here and there and nowhere you're migrating across the Alps or eating palm fronds in Zambia. They own nothing but a moulted feather or one of your hooves. Or a dropping. But these years, these precious years! Your own!

6) They don't own one idle tear, not one drop of sweat, not one footstep in their direction. They don't own a breath,

not a sigh, not a beat of anguish. They don't own father, mother, brethren. They don't own the children of Vietnam, not one scrofulous prisoner in Con Son. Nothing.

7) They don't own a greeting, not a glance of compliance, not a subway token, not the dust from the scam of your pocket, not a handout; not the slightest nod, not a pared fingernail, not a dirty snapped shoelace. Not poetry, not prose; not anger even, not regret, not the thump of a fist in a hand, not an obsessive dream of freedom. None of this to be wrung from me, in tribute; nothing to add in their ledgers, to be snooped out, to be reported to bosses, to be gloated over, to deduce victory from. Nothing. I am whole, entire, one, opposed, resisting, saying my *no* loud and clear, as into the winds and surf of Block Island. The same man in the same marmoreal gesture, life and death. *No*—for the sake of *yes*.

January 21

Lawyers here today; Kunstler unusually gentle and deferring to the other younger ones and so rightly, they having borne the heat of the last two tumultuous weeks.

Philip (a Dutch sailor with a wooden leg): "I went to the infirmary, they took my leg and locked it in a safe. Two months later when I asked for it, they opened the safe and my leg was gone . . ."

Today *everyone* but yrs. truly was fired at one fell swoop from the dental clinic, I felt gutted. We had spent almost six months trying to build something, a sense of one another . . . *all gone!* Or nearly all—and due to a vicious, vengeful act of one of the brethren too. Hardest of all to take. I ran around like a decapitated rabbit most of the A.M., from file cabinet to X ray to chair, not sure what would be next, not doing anything very well.

The atmosphere of *Hope Against Hope* is so terrifyingly symptomatic of the drift of things that one spends most of his waking hours in a cold sweat. We are possessed by noonday and midnight demons—and who will exorcise us?

I regret so little; how even answer the question—what is hardest about being here? I think survival itself is a very acute question and yet I survive in measure from day to day, with almost a monastic sternness about lingering over the past et ceteras that simply now have no existence for me.

The compound is seething with life—differentiated, agonized, unrealized, mobster, bleeding, inward, sullen; what fires, what ice! It is all underground, and does not know itself.

Often late at night one is granted a healing . . . "after day's fitful fever." The horror seems to diminish even in our little burial acre, the sky above is beautiful, serene, removed . . . One could almost believe the conduct of human affairs was a matter of compassion, not mere brute endurance. That this were not a prison, that the word were obsolete, that the tiger cages were empty! That we were granted a new chance in fact! . . .

Soledad Brother (George Jackson). Apart from the racist horror, it seems to me Philip faces a like future—indefinite custody at the hands of the war gods. And that there will be no more "normalcy" or "return" in our lifetime—that something similar may well be concocted in my regard as well, and so on, and so on.

January 23

Every time someone opens a door. Every time someone locks a door, unlocks a door. Every lineup for food, laundry, coffee at the company store. Every say-no behind every right (or left) turn. You may not do the opposite. The four limits of the compound; the guards' eyes, faces, jaws. The purpose renewed. The quiet battle. The will unassailed. Every bad news of every day—when was it we last had good news? Every sweating, wrung minute, toward dawn; the growing measure of an event which will have no heroic or noble outcome in this world. Every prayer, every effort to praise that God who is silent; to praise Him because He is silent, to praise Him although He is silent. To serve His honor in a darkening world, which honors only death.

Every search of the person, who is, according to our faith, sacred. Every ignoble transaction of the person, betrayal of the person, thieving, lying, betraying, putting one's own well-being first. Every sin, here also, against a community of persons, which must be born here, as in a lying-in hospital of the future.

Cheerfulness, Joy, Peace. Hardly won, hourly assailed, even here. The discouraged, the lost. Those who give up, by buying the pernicious public values. Those here for the wrong reasons, returning to the world for the wrong reasons, to do the wrong things with their lives.

The anguish of husbands and fathers. The hunger of faces, during visits; of hands and eyes, under the scrutiny of the guards. The artificial and artful and contrived scarcity of love, as a public resource, an energy available to all who would live, would live for others; who have begotten children and made love, and now are forbidden the presence of the fruits of their love.

Relationships awry. The necessity of silence, to preserve the little of integrity or health that exists in fact. The renunciation of wrong hope, wrong love, wrong words. The encompassing power of a silence in which God is free (He must be free) to bring the future into being. The forgiveness which is silent, which admits even the transgressor, the oppressing overlord, into the ambit of one's life, his concern.

Freedom from distraction—most of all from the distraction which is a vitiated form of life itself, in combat with the true life promised by the Savior. A whisper: embrace me, I will comfort and strengthen you and make the time pass; so you will "do good time."

Time as punishment: do your time! Time as reward, responsibility: redeem the time! Man as (official) slave of time, walking the treadmill: earning "good time."

"Any time is your time" (Jesus). No action, no passion, no heroism, no reward, no "other." Time as the envelope and atmosphere of selfishness. "My hour is not yet come"—His death will be the choice in which new life is contained and bestowed.

The wrecks, the hopeless, the diminished, the perennial children, the defeated, the bargainers, the betrayers . . . Over them all: the owners, the oppressors, the 9 to 5 keys with their legs, arms, eyes attached. The rattling of keys, the approach of power, the owners of bodies and spirits, the slave masters—and their slaves.

January 26

The situation at work (in the dental clinic) has been ludicrous in the extreme; something out of Gogol or Kafka. They first took on two extra clerks, thus putting others on the sidelines, there being little enough work for two, let alone four. Then last Friday, they summarily fired everyone but me. When I demanded an explanation, was told there was a minor scandal on the part of one, another has snitched, etc., etc. I was saved because I was not of their ilk, presumably. I "gave the clinic a tone!" Imagine that. Then today I learn in this breeding house of rumor that I was to be dumped also but was saved by the captain, who didn't want another *cause célèbre* on his lily hands. Prosit! By inference another bubble is burst—that my work there is of any real value to them . . . but is it? I read betimes, but try to take the technical side of things seriously, as much as I may, reflecting that the work is a real service to the inmates and I am responsible for a decent job. The enervating realization is that one is powerless —absolutely so, in such circumstances as we are in, that all decisions as to survival etc. come down from above, no inmate is worthy of being consulted about any decisions. One is an inmate in the same sense exactly as a mental patient or a terminally ill person would be. His life, work, etc. are in no serious sense in his own hands. The disintegrating effects of all this are evident in everything from the men's faces to their habitual conduct and demeanor. They are not allowed to give a damn—so they do not.

There is little to be gained by striving over all this. It is more fruitful simply to do one's best and leave the rest to God. Or at least so I have decided. We are walking on extremely thin ice. Our civil suit for rights of prisoners has been denied; six are indicted, the rest of us are co-conspirators, our friends generally are in disarray, stunned by the swift descent of ruin. We are just slowly picking up the pieces and evaluating the personal loss, recovering from the first shock with the help of a few who have appeared at our side.

This P.M. our class was "visited" for the first time by two officials—an ominous move, in view of the past weeks. We shall have simply to see what occurs and take our soundings accordingly. But the time ahead will not be easy. Philip will be taken off for arraignment, maybe an attempt will be made to transfer him permanently. There is so much anguish to taste, so much power and autonomy and time in the hands of the government officials, who have not even the threat of elections to deter them—at least a year, possibly two, in which they can cut their murderous swath at home and abroad, and no resistance to speak of. The war seems to be absorbed into the natural organism, like a foreign body or an illness—it festers there, but life drags on somehow. And meantime we are entirely in their power, except for the slight deterrence of public interest—much waned in fact since recent accusations against us. We go on, carrying a great weight of personal opprobrium, discouragement, etc. I can't remember when I felt life to be such a burden, so cheapened, so bereft of joy and hope. Yet one goes on—a compound attitude—partly out of habit, partly out of purpose. At least a few of us must survive, if not intact, at least recognizably *here*, and ourselves.

Most of the publicity has done great damage, reinforcing public suspicion of us as idealists turned to madness. Some would like to believe otherwise, and make gestures in our direction. But it is all disheartening in the extreme. I feel as though a blade were being held to our throats, we helpless as animals to turn it aside. Prayer in a spirit of faith is almost, it seems, no prayer at all. I felt this most acutely when the Quakers came to pray with us. They are good and sincere but so bright and cheery and caught up in their unassailed lives as to make one feel all the more acutely his alienation from the common middle life of America. They do not seem to sense what we are enduring—nor do they show in any real way a will to share our suffering. We pray and believe nonetheless—alone, or with a few, here and there, who are tasting the gall of life at their own lips.

Most days I am stupefied by the fact that locks are turned on me, by the noisy days and nights around me, by the atmosphere of distraction and abandonment to iron fate, by sleeplessness, by the uncertain future which casts so thick a shadow. Most of all by the sufferings of Philip which I share to the hilt—mostly because I do not yet share them. I am learning what it must mean to be his brother. I die of it.

We have Mass together and I cannot scrape together a single thought—whether of acceptance, aversion, hope, response. Stand there like a vertical corpse, take the bread and wine, empty as a plank, dry as a stone. My whole being, the open throat of a man who has died of thirst, who has no succor in this world—whose only justification for existing at all is that he believes, and so stands there. Let the Lord make of it what he will—nothing at all, or someday, a man. But after such days and nights one must surely count death his dearest friend. Except that I could not die without Philip, or apart from his fate. Will he ever know how I love him?

January 28

I am setting this down with my new pen, presented (with a matching pencil) to Philip and myself this P.M. in virtue of "our fine work with the education of the inmates." The atmosphere was a little chilling, the air of a posthumous award for "service to the party." Or at least so it seems to me. There are very few here from whom I would wish to receive anything, in truth.

The atmosphere, if one lets himself dwell on it, is terrifying for political prisoners. One becomes literally the sport of any fleeting rumor that happens to be in the air—like a poison. E.g., that one prisoner, whom indeed we have no reason to trust, has already agreed to testify against Philip in court. He confronted him, by my advice. It was for that fellow's salvation, as I saw it. Can he hope to live with himself if such a rumor be true? One reads every day of trials where informers supplied the heart of the evidence against the charged—much like the atmosphere of *Hope Against Hope*, which I am reading in horror. There is so little conscience anywhere and most are willing to trade their souls for a bit of time off their sentences. To keep a diary such as this one is an act which would be impugned as a crime. No wonder one's sleep is troubled, feeling to the heart the shadow that lies over us all. Practically all the prisoners drug themselves with the same diet they trade on outside—commissary and TV, and some meretricious reading. . . . One resolves in face of this to continue his diet of prayer, reflections, and reading and let the chips fall where they may. Someone sent me a poem by Neruda written while he was on the lam; he lived to be an old man, now is ambassador to France—but what will our future be like? The clouds are inexpressibly dark for us and our friends—and we know nothing of the other side of what we must simply suffer through, trusting in God that we are standing where men must stand—if there are to be any left in the world.

Letter to the Cambridge Jesuits

Dear Brothers,

I was surely happy for your invitations which served as a reminder to me that the fires of brotherhood are still alight, that our common life can endure—can in fact reassert itself more strongly in spite of separation, grief, ill fortune, the shadow of official disgrace.

You suggested I send you some words on peace, and I have been trying to absorb again the Lord's sensibility on this subject. Certainly this is not an easy task—but the conditions I live under tend, I think, to make it somewhat less difficult to grasp His mind and heart.

Prison is paradoxically a place where the peace He promises can take root in one's life, and grow. Freely entered upon, freely taken into account, life becomes a decision on behalf of peace. The world at war presses in, the nation at war, even, in a sense, the church at war—and these are a grievous burden indeed, for one has lost not only his own "normal" life by deliberately putting it on another track, he has made like assumptions about his brothers, in a sense risking for them what is most precious to himself. And in turn he hopes against hope that they will see the rationale of his course of action, its consonance with the gospel, will not separate him from the common life, will welcome and include his decision in their own choices on behalf of life.

I want to be very direct, and as simple as I know how in writing to you. The gospel gives us the right, indeed the command, to be prodigal in regard to our personal lives. There is a delicate rigor in the Lord's view of life—His own life, the lives of others. A Christian is asked to be serious about a serious issue; the lethal arrangements of power disposing of lives, the consignment of the living to death, for the sake of temporal gains, egoism, money, prestige, latest advantages— these are not the Christian game. Such methods cannot be our method in the world; in opposition to such methods, we are called upon to protest—first in words, then perhaps in act—the assumption being that our life is our own only when it is given for others.

In America, no one of us has yet been asked to give his life for the sake of peace. Some of us—a very few—have been summoned to spend a certain portion of our lives in prison; a contingency we would not have dreamed of a few years ago. Today, here we are, on ice. One is tempted to think at times that the prison thing will go on and on and on; as the war threshes on, its eerie, random swath a nightmare of ruin and death.

How then shall we wage peace together? I can perhaps contribute something by writing you to consider the course I have taken as a priest and a Jesuit.

I am struck first of all by the fact that Jesuit renewal seems largely stalemated. The reasons for this are undoubtedly complex; but I would like to risk one reading of the case. It seems to me that by and large, we have simply not realized the extent of the tragedy the Vietnam war has wrought on the Vietnamese people. We have proceeded with a domestic timetable of Jesuit good housekeeping, somewhat as though the shambles of the *alma domus*, the world at large, could be thrust aside—at least pro temp.

This strange inversion of values is simply another way of saying, I suggest, that obsession with the "good estate of the Order" is less a passionate desire for God's honor among men than a simple cultural illness. We believe in effect that all can still be well—with America, or the cities, with the uni verse, with the Jesuits—while the war proliferates, and the dragon's teeth we sowed on the prevailing winds of Vietnam spring up in Laos and Cambodia. Thus our minds come to resemble more and more a typical schizoid page one of the New York *Times*—on the right the President launches another scheme for domestic amelioration; on the left, we are prepared by indirection, fallacy, and deceit for more war. An Orwellian triumph; we destroy in order to save, we butter and bomb, we are compassionate and merciless; we cry peace peace and there is no peace. Truly we pluck to our own advantage the best from both worlds, heaven and hell.

I suggest that the Jesuit view of gospel and culture is not notably at odds with all this. Most of us are, in fact, good Germans in a time of death. Our immunity from the razor edge of the American sword dulls the truth as it strikes against our minds. We neither pay taxes on our institutions nor are drafted into the war, nor are our links with the military, through chaplaincies, grants, research, investments, seriously questioned. We are, as a body of men, caught in the culture; bound like every institution today to the corporate web of death known as the war effort. Can we, in face of such facts, expect the peace of the Lord to descend in our midst, in our hearts, in our lives—together with that flowering of peace which results in new directions, new and imaginative ways of living for others?

Admittedly I speak of difficult matters, a future hard to come by, a present life which is marked by renunciation of lawful hopes, of normalcy, of an untroubled existence in the world. But all these things are vanishing from our midst in any case—not (as one might hope) by way of deliberate choices freely undertaken, but by the cruel revenge taken on us by the times themselves, which demand that we dismantle our earthly kingdom, or see it snatched from our hands while we recoil in fear and dread.

Daniel

February 1

The month opens in an atmosphere of foreboding and dread. It really seems as though in such circumstances things have only one way of proceeding—breakneck, downhill. Philip is feeling the pressures, he has taken a heavy cold and looks quite haggard. I feel like a stone set in ice. I pray, and it is a non-prayer—all one has, like winter itself, is the courage somehow to endure one day, and that alone. I count death as a very small undertaking (!) in comparison with these weeks. The reality of Phil being hauled off for another court proceeding—how is it to be endured? It is to be endured because in this case as in any other, necessity must become a virtue . . . one endures like an animal; there is nothing gracious or "chosen" about life—or precious little . . . A bad time for all concerned; for human rights, for the dream of free men aspiring to public freedom.

Yet, as a matter of fact, stories from the other prisons reveal something far more barbaric than obtains here. When one approaches day-to-day life searching for personal freedom, there is a large field indeed in which to be a man among others. And what is more desirable at such a time than that one should, by using his head and heart, create something for others—especially for the majority who are feeling the burden of the days so much more harshly than ourselves? If Philip is taken off, so are many others, in worse conditions,

with fewer resources, convictions . . . Today, a young black
wanted to speak of God and we went around the compound
together, talking of the man Jesus, our brother and friend . . .

Hounding us to death; we can only oppose the calm will
which is based on faith, on a burning sense of the wrong
wreaked by war and war makers, on our willingness to suffer
everything they are pleased to heap on us. In effect, by showing the superiority of isolated moral courage to the vast
papier-mâché strength of the armed pack. This necessarily
brings one face to face with death and its analogates—not in
some intangible or mystical or painless way, but by the literal
loss of everything one had presumed as his own. It is necessary to create the future by paying tribute to its coming, to
its presence. As though it indeed exerted the pressure on our
choices of its nearness, its voice, its call to a new style and
way.

February 8

Two events: had arranged tickets to Catonsville play for
three clinic employees. But it transpired that they were unwilling to step to the box office to pick them up, since the
tickets awaited them in the name Berrigan. "Too much FBI
surveillance!" Ha!

Those who accept jobs that bring big privilege pay for it
with their manhood—such as it is. Everything here has a price
tag—the only free man is the one who has nothing to lose. I
am still far from this. It may be it will come on the day when
I too have lost everything. Philip seems closer to it, an event
of life, in favor of life, than I am. I remember trying to convey
such a sense of freedom in the case of the Carmelite nun,
Edith Stein, who was finally killed under Hitler. I believe
with all my crooked heart that we are guilty as a nation of
unutterable crimes against humanity. I believe the majority

of prisoners are positively unaware and blinded to the nature of these crimes. With varying degrees of despair they are trying to sew up the rotten fabric of some "normalcy" for themselves and for their children. This makes for a series of desperation moves which becomes the pattern of life itself. They live in such a way as to make manhood impossible . . .

Now on the day when I see the possibility of freedom receding, I will have to embrace a new stage that includes the most horrendous form of death (continued imprisonment) that I know of—for myself and for my family and friends. When I come to say my "so be it" in those depths, I will either perish or emerge reborn. There will be no other choice.

Today was the day of arraignment for the Harrisburg Six. It was also, by report, the day when Phil's reduction of sentence was refused. Another door has closed. Naturally. We still do not know if all the doors are locked, or if this is a set-off induced by the official madness. But in all the nation there are very few whom God could discover tonight standing for life in any visible way. The six will be esteemed someday for having so stood. This will be their honor.

I tried to fast today for the others and to be in communion with them. I also refused to celebrate Mass without Philip. It seemed to me to reduce the act to a charade merely to stand alone at the altar in the midst of such inhumanity (I never before met a "Mass priest" in the flesh) and say the words of life and liberation.

God give them all strength for the months ahead. One thing is certain. There will be great surprises as six persons of such burning desire and quality speak up.

Dealing with fear is a continuing struggle. I said to myself in the hours before dawn some days ago, as though the word came from without: "It is the end of the time of grief and dread. It is to be the time of strength from now on." And so it has been. No great perception of how, no dramatic change of heart. But there is a curious imperceptible lifting of a nearly intolerable burden, and I walk more easily.

The little trees are glossy and creak in the wind like Tiffany jewelry. There is a daily change rung on the few living things; it brings one's breath up short. *Multum in parvo*; in tune with the midwinter life in lifeless places.

February 11

How easy it is to fall into a tragicomic sense of one's self. Something of destiny's noble dolt, caught under the lash, fore and after, keeping the upper lip stiff for some reason more or less crudely related to pride, or the indolence that refuses self-scrutiny. I am led to all this in midwinter, when we are more or less cut off from friends and the healthy externals that make for health. We are all tossed like doughnuts or serpents into the same bag; and in close quarters, under rigorous shakings, doughnuts get broken and serpents turn on one another. It takes great resources to keep cheerful in spirit, to count the blessings of life and love, wherever they show themselves, for what they are, to thank God and man that one is where he is, even in jail. That one is *what* he is—a man striving to be a better man, and to pay the cost with a certain grace of spirit. Many around us are paying a harder cost in their separation from children and family, in their consciousness of guilt. Our cause, moreover, is publicly available, people are praising our play, reading our books, etc. The church is becoming more thoughtful about the questions we have tried to raise and the way we have lived our lives—in public and in private. It is going to be difficult for the government to move against us on the latest charges; a bit of daylight is beginning to show through the cruel night to which the indictments consigned us. The discrediting, indeed, is on the other foot, as events are showing more clearly.

All this lightens the grievous burden of the past weeks,

which I confess has been very nearly unendurable. What an act of faith was required of us—an act which found me, for one, unprepared to the point of near extinction. But all that seems to be lifting. It was lifted by the sight of our friends who came among us with their lives, their faces, their hopes, so nearly intact as to grant us a stay of death. Need it be added that they came to us seeking like gifts also?

Our mother is seriously ill once more. The word that strikes hardest is the word of her pain, deadening, continuous physical pain, which gives a vivid coloration to our days and nights. She is also bearing the cross, she knows what it is to be where we are, in a way churchmen might envy were they also saints. She knows because she loves us, and therefore trusts us and has no need of declarations of loyalty, pure intent, etc.

The cost of the days; to have poetry plucked from one's life. To be so nearly and continually exhausted that the "overflow" of spontaneous joy can no longer be counted on. One lives in a kind of continuous twilight of the spirit, trying to "make it" through the next hour or two, the present day, with so little to offer the needs of others. Vivacity, play of spirit quenched, or nearly so. One drags on with about 50 or 60 per cent of his resources. It would be easy, and at the same time quite lethal, to lose trust in oneself, to begin even to hate oneself for not being totally "with it." This is, I think, where a Zen sense of things comes into play—to flow with life not "muscled up" but simply granted (and therefore in measure, and on the scale of one's hopes, withheld as well). The diminishing implied by the passion of Christ reenacted here and now. I have been meditating on St. John, as a constant, haunting parable of the continuity of youth and age: "I tell you this: when you were younger, you tightened your belt and walked where you would; but when you are old you will stretch out your arms, and a stranger will bind you fast, and carry you where you have no wish to go. He said this to indicate the death by which Peter would glorify God. Then he added: follow me."

Catonsville on stage: the weight of an endless and powerless folly

The question has arisen of how we feel as the *Catonsville Nine* play is about to open in New York City, with all the panoply attendant on such an event—distinguished cast, top-drawer director and producer . . .

Something that transpired in May of '68, with the fear and trembling attendant on such an event, has been claimed by and delivered over to history. Surely in May of 1968 no such possibility entered our minds: we were steeled only to act, the times and our own experience counseled modesty. Hanging heavily on our minds were the suffering and death inflicted on a distant people by the mad charade of the war. What might be exacted of ourselves, as we strove to resist, had first nudged us, then gnawed at us, then attached itself to our mind and flesh, like the fox in the Greek story. At the end, there was no escaping. We concocted our napalm, like medieval necromancers, around a coffee table in a friend's home, conscious of the weird nightmares of that liturgy, the spreading of wild fires that had muttered in our minds for months. We went down to our cars, and drove to Cantonsville. The rest, as they say on stage, is history.

Two and a half years later, February 1971, the Catonsville

people could forgather only by an act of fiction—or an act of God. One of us, David Darst, died in a flaming auto crash over a year ago. Another, Mary Moylan, is at this writing at large, but underground. The rest of us are scattered about the federal penal system, chaff to the winds.

Phil and I are thus out of touch with the others, dead and living, except by acts of affection and intercession. So we can pretend to speak only for ourselves in the reflections that follow.

Our first reaction to the opening of the play is one of profound grief, on many grounds. We mourn for the war; that useless, grotesque, debilitating, downhill rampage; in spite of everything, the war goes on. Neither we of Catonsville nor the Four of the Customhouse, nor the Eight of New York nor the Beavers of Miland—nor senators, nor self-immolators, nor preachers, nor the Weathermen, nor three Presidents and all their promising, pledging, or hedging—none of these in all their sum of moral passion or inflected punishment, or duplicity or purpose, have availed to halt the war. We mourn that our lives have made so little difference in the brute scales of power. We are in prison, our friends are in prison or stand under actual indictment or the threat thereof. And the war goes on. We are locked up for the duration, paying tribute with years of our lives to a system of crime and punishment that punishes the crime of peaceableness and refuses to indict the crime of war. And the war goes on.

Our lives, let it be noted, are difficult only because they must bear the weight of an endless and powerless folly. Other than that, we are treated with decency; physically we are not consigned to Tiger Cages or interrogated under torture. Indeed, Danbury appears to the inner eye as a kind of pop prison, a superficial art form where comic money changers, publicans, con artists, spies, rich Mafiosi, the poor who dig too deep into the pie mingle and do their thing (do their time) together with a sprinkling of draft resisters and ourselves. Nothing very bad happens, nothing very human is allowed to happen. Ninety per cent of the prison budget goes to locks, stocks, hacks; we rejoice in a plethora of guards, a paucity of books, indifferently good food, indifferently bad religion. Inmates work for twenty cents an hour making missile parts for obscure projects related to "national security," or they pick up butts on the compound, or swab tables in the dining hall, or clerk or type or sweep, or in my case, help in the clinic.

Philip and I, moreover, teach a course, have access to periodicals, meet with lawyers and friends. Our brief against the regime has little to do, except on occasion, with indignities of personal treatment. The system, after a few feints and starts, makes room for "special cases" like us—not a great deal of room, but room nonetheless. It is thus difficult to formulate or convey the sources of that grief I spoke of—a constant friction of the spirit, just above or below normalcy, neither serious fever nor chill, a heavy drag of soul.

Probably the feeling is shared by men and women everywhere as the war goes on. The first fine frenzy of the late '60s has passed. Then we had thought to make a revolution of love, reason, and hope; to make it moreover in our own lifetime, even in a few years, by the simple victory of good sense over violent means, of love over militarism, of hope over the rot of despair. We shared the optimism of those who had yet to achieve hope—quite unconscious that optimism is an American illness (it breathes like a quartan fever from the military dispatches, the war always won and never over). We concocted a theory of social change, radical and rapid, populist and innocent—a theory persuasive only to those who have never engaged history, and its powers and dominations, in a fight to the finish.

We had thought to enjoy the fruits of such change, without knowing what the change would cost, or indeed what the alternatives to our own social system might be. We had gone after foreign gods—whether of Marxism or Maoism or Christianity—all imported, all impotent. In the process, we had dusted off the domestic god of violence, invoking him with a rhetoric we fancied was new and would win him to our side and make him, Moloch as he was, a god of good intentions—our god, and therefore good, beneficent, working through obscure and bloody means to our beneficent ends. Only to learn to our chagrin and dismay that he was in fact a double agent, and cared not a whit for our innocence. Since he was in fact the numen of public, sanctioned power, and betrayed his promises even while he multiplied them.

February 13

How much of the truth do we owe them? I have a clue to the question today in the example of Christ . . . the question, I think, becomes largely irrelevant when one thinks how the Savior rephrased it, not by submitting before the powers, but by submitting to the will of the Father. Into thy hands.

Thus the question becomes: how much of the truth do I owe to the community, to history, to the future, to God? Phrased in such a way, the question can have only one answer: the truth of life itself, the man who walks clothed in his words, to the direction and destiny the truth reveals to him as his own; neither stolen nor imposed, but his own, because the Father's.

All the lying pretensions of the state are vaporized in the face of such a gesture.

I am drawn more and more away from the Bonhoeffer ethic, "to be a liar in the image of the king of liars." Is it because I am not pure enough or strong enough to make such an ethic stick? Or because (as Ramsey Clark said to us yesterday) "all of us have everything to gain from the truth, from the purity of the truth"?

I think with a trembling heart of everything the truth may

exact of us in the months ahead. We are again at the beginning. The other end may be either vindication or catastrophe
—God knows. A wrong throw of the dice—thus our fate
would appear to the cynics; and the loading of dice has become the favorite occupation of those in power.

Can the church be enlisted around the issues of our trial?
We had best keep our thoughts and expectations modest—
the cold war has not only chilled the abstract state—it has
frozen the bones of believers as well, who are as exposed to
arctic weathers as the best (or worst) of men . . .

We can do for the church what we can do for the state:
present the truth of our lives, entrusting ourselves to that
truth, as a most powerful inner energy that is available to
all who seek.

It seems to me that Jesus so conducted Himself, before
Pilate as before Caiaphas; My kingdom is not of this world
. . . Are you then the son of God? Your own lips have said
so . . .

In such a light, the enlisting of the church on the side of
the truth is just about as absurd a project as the military
draft. From both areas the truth is by necessity exiled.

What we would best do is to allow the truth a place in our
own hearts, knowing that the heart hungers, by the law of its
existence, to know the truth and embrace it; and that to offer
the truth is the noblest task open to our lives. It is a task
worth dying for.

I write this with many a queasy glance at myself, many a
qualm. There were times this year when I felt as much a
stranger to the truth as were my captors. I am not proud of
the episode of the three letters last August: the issue returned
to haunt me in the courtroom at Hartford. I can only say: I
was still dwelling in the shadow of Berrigan at that time;
moreover I was enduring the onslaughts of much anger, required as I was to learn the game here.

February 14

A sense of pervasive gloom. The bad news concocted by
the betrayers of man . . . A sense of sorrow numbs the pen in
my hand as I try to set this down. Where indeed is it all to
end? The war crosses over the bodies of another people; we
have shelved human life as an issue, in the universal morgue.
The movement seems stricken with despair and inertia, the
same forces that remove its nerve, its will, descend upon my
friends and declare our freedom forfeit for the duration.
And where is the church, where is truth and understanding?
We huddle in the dark around a candle which must nurture
us, but which at the same time is slowly consumed. Who
will survive these days? Faith grows weak, even those who
trusted us are touched with palsy and fear and lose all direction . . . I am putting the case in all its present darkness, an
effort of understanding. I am seeking salvation in the way
of a blind man, the future being so insecure . . .

Yesterday a friend put it so: would that you too were to
be indicted . . . what a dimension that would add to the
case! I grieve most of all for Philip, who must bear the larg-
est weight of the cross, who does it gracefully and strongly
—but what a life opens (or closes) before him! Our lives
touch with agony all those whom we love and dare call friends.
And the war, the war like a terminal disease goes its way, by
its own laws, irrevocably, a Greek tragedy where the last
page is the first—known, reckoned up, ineluctable, beyond
escape.

The reality of Christ! I seek *salvation*, Gandhi says on
the first page of his autobiography, that marriage of inmost
word and public act. And he goes on to reprove himself bit-
terly for his inward division, a reproof we can scarcely share
in light of his heroic life and death.

But to seek salvation—within and without, where Christ is and speaks to us; or is silent, leaving us and our world to its own cruelty, its own "devices"—diabolic and anti-human, to the deliberate souring of nature and the universe in the service of death . . . Who shall draw us forth from the body of this death? Our Lord Jesus Christ; to whom all honor and glory; the task being to live and die simply as men and women in a most inhuman and forbidding time . . .

Reflections on reading Gandhi's autobiography for the nth time:

Truth as *experiment* (title). The search for the truth of existence is as rigorous as a scientific experiment. I.e., it requires that the soul of the seeker be an analogous laboratory —freedom, rigor, purity of soul, readiness for suffering, respect for others. One prepares his life for experiment as he prepares a specimen, a complex of equipment, an organism of tissues. One is as rigorous in undergoing, in evaluating, in welcoming the new and unexpected. One is, in sum, imaginative. He realizes that the original hypothesis, i.e., "man is a creature capable of the truth," remains a pious sentiment to be mouthed by the worst charlatans, killers, manipulators of power—until it is embodied in a personal and social style.

One calls on the powers of the universe, embedded in a religion or culture, in deference to this quest. The *numina patrum* of Virgil; he takes his gods with him. On this score, Western man is at odds. He wants to go it alone; like the waiters for Godot. Or he wants not to win the gods to his side, but literally to steal their fire, like Prometheus. The result is technological catastrophe as a fact or a threat.

One wishes also that the quest be a social one. The truth is not the possession of the seeker, after a loner's journey. Relations to others are the field on which one determines both means and end, judges their impurity or validity. The seeker is also the liberator—he releases (vacates) fields of force in others, unsuspected, latent resources of heroism, new directions for the enslaved.

Circumstances may make the English, in possession of the land into the "enemy." But the seeker knows the enemy lies much nearer; the will to enslavement, the dismembered consciousness of the enslaved; the willingness to give life over to impersonal fate; to die as one was born. Laziness of soul.

We are free to sneer at cultural childishness in a great or holy man. The question remains, what made him great? or: how did he see himself emerging from childhood, family, into the world, a gigantic leaven of an immovable mass?

(1) Sexual taboos; (2) dietary taboos; (3) betrayal of father in his death. Interesting that these three also trouble the process of breakaway from old culture (Slater) to new consciousness in young America.

The unacknowledged, boiling connection between sexual codes (monogamy, puritan marriages) and public violence (cf. L. B. Johnson's metaphors about Vietnam war, as told in "Tuesday Cabinet"). Also my conversation with federal marshals on way to Rochester . . . "degenerates, against war, yelling, 'give us your daughters.'" Also: geography of allowable sex—violence; whites long looked on blacks as an open reserve for sex and violence. Daniel Lang's account of rape slaying in Vietnam war declares open season *perpetually*; contrast with the *qualified* open season at home on nonwhites. Mylai declares the unlimited time and place allowed to such incursions.

In light of this, Gandhi's quest for sexual control emerges as a healthy sign. He declares himself as unbearably lustful toward his child bride. We would easily pooh-pooh such scruples. Our culture, the new one, allows for an open season on others. But considered as violence toward others, sexual urges that take no account or little account of the other person often become another symptom of the permeating violence of the culture. Hyperdelicacy, on the other hand, can be a sign that a general conquest of oneself, including one's will to violence, is under way. One has identified a concrete obstacle to humanity, and is in process of facing it. Gandhi said later: only the violent are capable of non-violence. It is in light of so profound a truth that one can understand the right reason under his rather jejune narrative.

Attitude toward women, specifically his wife. Like many strong men, he paid a mere lip service to the full humanity of others. He wanted her to learn to read and write, and mourns righteously that she showed little interest or progress in letters . . . Her life was a footnote to his own ego. He awakened her, to make love to her, the night his father died: and he mourns the failure of his love (but only of his love for his father . . .).

February 17

Not finding it easy to keep at this diary. Not because "nothing happens in jail" but for quite the opposite reason, as it seems to me; too much happens to be able to absorb.

Mother is coming back so miraculously, so unexpectedly from her illness. I had prayed someone would come by, so we could send her flowers for her eighty-fifth birthday Friday and lo! Francine Grey here, flowers sent!

Ramsey Clark wants to join our legal staff and will be here also early next week.

People send books; no letters are allowed. There is a picayune vengeful spirit in American authority; where you cannot get away with wounding people in large ways, do it in small. But they cannot, for the sake of whatever devil, leave them alone or encourage their living zestfulness. Stomp! Even on a fly . . . I am struck by the random charac-ter of this policy, in large matters as in small. The dropping of charges against Tony Towne and Bill Stringfellow is a case in point. One asks: is not the case against the Harrisburg Eight at least equally flimsy? It is. Yet, apparently for higher stakes, the charade will go forward.

The authorities preserve tender ways, up close, in their families, while they fling their full boned fury abroad in a swath of death. Can the same organism be life- and death-dealing?

The weather is cruelly cold again, sudden onslaught of snow this P.M., as though the sky had suddenly exploded with fury. I slog it along from day to day, only about 50 per cent functioning, smiling on all comers like a Bread Puppet. Determined in a pre-mental, instinctive way, like a dying dog's clutch on a bone, to see this thing through.

"Every man has secrets." (Nero Wolfe)

The hack who is wheeling, dealing with one inmate, while supervising the strip search of another.

Our silence in the books class, dealing with Gandhi. One has a sense with all Americans these days of a birth perpetually postponed. Through accident, outrage, freak in nature, natural calamity, we are unable to bring ourselves to the moment when the face of the truth appears. We live in the world by veering away from all those occasions when "something may happen"; thereby hoping it may never come to pass . . .

February 18

I wonder if anyone has been called to a tougher life than I —with so few resources to go on. Maybe this discrepancy between faith and task is at the heart of the suffocation I feel day to day. How will one finish a day? How will one begin another day? One prays badly, and forgets afterward—so soon afterward—why and how he prayed. The crowning impression is one of a rather desperate, even hilarious, always touching effort of the former bug in the rug to conquer Everest . . . I don't want to be theatrical here about a serious matter. It is not a light matter at my age to take off on this latest episode (if it were put in Gandhi's terms of a "testing of man" I would have to declare with empty, discomforted hands—a loss!). Still, one can say—there seemed to have been no one else around, and the thing had, in all conscience, to be done . . . So what else could I do?

(I am incarcerated in "quarters" for a day or so—heavy cold leads to heavy reflection . . .)

In any case, if faith is not knowing the other end of this adventure, and still giving myself to it, I guess I have some slight measure of faith.

And yet while I could live so much more nobly, fearlessly, cheerfully—I could also live much more selfishly, fearfully . . . so it goes. A life with and for friends whom one does not even see . . .

February 20

Letter to a hellion

Dear friend and brother:

(now it is my turn to write) I can see from my window, at dawn and dusk, a single struggling maple, taking on its changed form of spring. The sparrows cling to it noisily. Today being Saturday (no work) I was able to stand beneath it; on each bough a tiny hand and fingers were sprouting; the buds had opened, their inhumanly delicate colors, from green to pink and white, were drinking the light. From a distance, the tree seemed to stand in an anchored cloud, somewhere between a gossamer and a sigh of acceptance. The yard is alive with the catcalls and yells of the ballplayers.

And I think of you; something of the precious endangered order symbolized by one tree. As though I were to stand at the window one morning and see with a start of horror how the tree had been hacked down in the night and lay there breathing its last.

In a sea of disorder which is the world, a tree stands as a sign of an order that is never quite defeated. This is what I had hoped to see in you, what perhaps you had hoped to see in me; some vindication. A sense that even in prison, which stabilizes disorder in the name of public and inner order, some order was possible. That men might speak the truth and express in their lives a measure of truth and moral beauty, in spite of all.

I could not help you do this. I was too old, or too white, or too selfish, or too sterile, or too preoccupied with my own troubles and defeats, which began with the January indictments and continue with the obscenities out of Harrisburg, to this day.

Your face is heartbreaking to me. It will not leave me. I met you, our lives collided without ever touching: a field of force struck us apart. The prison system has two solutions for men like you: either you make it peaceably in a stagnant corral with other animals in process of domestication, or you are shipped out to become somebody else's problem: the marshals', the Midwest's. You are a misfit even in a tank where the piranhas behave and bide their time.

If only, if only—it is the bitterest cry the Platonist can utter. If only your gifts were really together, if only you had an inkling of who you are, if only bad theology and worse sociology had not soured your guts, rising to your head with a befouled vision of short cuts, ways around the Man, ownership, mastery, messiahship, thumbs down on patience, ignorance, tentative judgments, nix on the honesty that alone confounds the keepers and draws the captives into one. If only you had not turned your blackness into a bludgeon that prodded and wounded others—and inevitably yourself.

That hanging "if" is like a hanging limb: it is our statement of loss, as well as yours. We needed you; you refused to be the house nigger of our suburban mausoleum minds. For that, we could only honor you with our hope: that you would be, not some slack-headed disciple of priests, but a fiery and tenacious opposite number, to release through you and ourselves that vital charge that would turn on the lights in the house of the dead.

Daniel

February 24

I wonder if ever again (presuming this phase of things will end one day) I shall experience the free-floating desolation of these days. I had not thought it was possible to die of grief, but must confess the passion of Christ has taken on a new and ominous meaning. Can Lent bring anything January and the indictments did not already bring? "They got to me" —one reaches the literal end of his rope; i.e., there is no more space left in which to negotiate survival . . . Yet as I tried to share with Philip, I had to face that too with a certain calm; what remains obscure is the extent to which one yielded passively (too passively?) to the conviction that the end of something was in sight . . .

There is sin perhaps in dropping back to the delicious sense of death by freezing. I could only have recourse to the larger pattern of things, in which one tries to be faithful to prayer, faithful to faith itself; then, on an immediate rearing up of crisis, nothing of what went before seems enough. What one has recourse to is literally an act of God; He must act—or He must not—which is to say, Providence remains free to summon me or not. But I at least know that very little can be "mandated" as a task of grace—the energy is simply not there. Or if it is there, it does not move in the direction one would have hoped for.

Am trying to give some thought to Lent in prison. I must say I see little light on the subject, except for the need of (1) more discipline in prayer, (2) better custody of senses, mastery of sense of suffocation, of despair.

But a great deal of this can become a kind of weight lifting. If only I had the deep-breathing sense, even at times, of such vitality as would grant command of the life here! Will I ever again experience the vital joy that says life is sub-

ject to one's control, one's own direction, one can dispense
life as a gift, freely? I do not have that sense—perhaps have
not had it for some time—but at least I have felt there was
enough cushion, variety, acceptance, enough of the rough
and gentle rhythms of the world to grant access to others,
a contribution, a gift. One drags out the days here, as though
he were trailing his own entrails behind him, wounded from
the outset . . .

February 26

A terrifying dream tonight which seemed, after the event,
to say nearly everything about the past year. An airplane
ride, a storm, a crash on the mountaintop. A long scenario of
ruin and rubble, everything systematically pulverized down
the ridges of the mountain. Bits and pieces rolling downhill, a heap of detritus brought up silently against the side of
a silent, unoccupied house, standing there half revealed in
the storm. A horror, literally. I took it for an image of my life
since January when the indictments came down. If there was
any salvation, it was simply that I survived, a kind of tourist
at the event, to record it in memory, impersonally. I have
had to accept impersonally all that has happened to me; as
though to another person, where self-interest or panicky will
are concerned. A certain classic detachment which "lets go"
what is normally most precious for the sake of what might
possibly get born, given the chance that the former good,
deciduous, apprehensive, and "nervy," might yield the scene.

Everything, everyone went. No survivors. The death of one
is the death of all, in principle. So might the birth of one be?
When Jesus died, what light was left in the world? But we
are told, and invited to believe, that He rose again in immortal flesh, in the world which had claimed life-and-death power
over Him.

March 1

I was reading over an essay by Griffin on Merton, something so beautiful, redolent of the life and atmosphere in the cabin where I had passed such joyous hours with him and our friends in those "lost '60s" before he was to be lost to us. What will the '70s not take from us? They have begun like the seven plagues of Egypt. There seems little left, from planting to harvest, but death.

Yet I think at times (the logic has yet to reach my heart) truly Phil and I are being asked to take off from where Merton started. The kind of life he rejoiced in is less and less possible—solitude, immediate healing nature. We are all being thrust into the polluted caldron—of the cities, of jail, of censorship, bugging, lawyers' jargon. The courts of law which are by no means courts of justice, the muskets going off all around, expectations of life lowering imperceptibly, like the supply of pure water, air, land; inferior, mean minds literally turning locks on our freedom, the church less and less at the center of our passion, loneliness, and alienation. One could go on and on. There is a kind of ascetical freedom required in "leaving thy low vaulted past!"—the very opposite, one remarks, of the evolutionary miracle sung by the poet.

We are literally in for it, in a way Merton could not have known. That knocking of the knees, the fear that clutches and freezes the heart, is an altogether accurate premonition of what is really coming for Americans, which they are first of all inflicting on the world. And there is no getting ready for such an event—one simply does what he can to survive from day to day, with the suffering fidelity of Bonhoeffer, and leaves the larger tragedy to descend when and as it will; God find you faithful on His day!

Fr. Mitchell and lawyers visiting today. Oppressive sense

(from the first) of the attrition of small talk. I simply had no energy to introduce large issues, to outline my grievings about the silence and abandonment of the Jesuits. This is by now such an old story I cannot quite confront it. All the promises of some six months ago have been swept aside or forgotten—nothing done, nothing struggled for. We went on and on, small talk, gossip. The superiors seem consumed with keeping the peace, ensuring some sort of tawdry consensus with communities which live well, eat well, keep the factory going. Evidently the best they can offer someone like me is to pray for me—which, given everything else, seems a sorry enough boon. I was forced to reflect in the middle of it all—what do I have in common with such men? What sort of fiction am I keeping alive by claiming fraternity with them? When they do come to visit here, they seem constricted, hesitating to ask questions about my life or work, convinced that life here is a huge yawn, a hiatus or rupture of my former style . . . There is, of course, a great deal that never gets said or appreciated on such occasions—the deep goodness of a number of the men, the struggle of the younger priests to live authentically, the secret communion with a minority who, through us, are experiencing the travail of the days—the war, the breakup of the church, the struggle to get born.

Class tonight took a good turn. We got from Gandhi to a discussion by two of the young resisters of their feeling about being in prison—torment, meaning, community. One of them, a particularly perceptive Jew, spoke of his sense of abandonment by the "movement"—in such wise as would remind one of dereliction of Jesus Himself. I am so moved by these hidden analogies. They are true also of Philip and myself. In such times, old friends have vanished, or been silenced or forbidden access by the regime here. And new friends come very slowly.

March 2

My face white as a powdered clown's
looks long at me; white lips, faded eyes,
a Lenten ghost, fifty years haunting the earth
(as Levine saw me, a grin, a putty knife's mark
a strut, ball and chain, a silly candle
the dark snuffs like a shark). Absence of feeling.
This cardboard show of existence
Murder, a knife at the back
leaves us standing, dead, dead, dead
on our feet.

The place where nothing happens; but where we are called to make something happen; *descendit in infernos, captivam duxit captivitatem* . . .

I sense the temptation, which is precisely to give up, to live with half one's batteries turned off, to respond to the kind of life "suggested" by the atmosphere, with non-life according to that atmosphere. As though indeed by the banks of the Styx one were allowed only to be a wraith . . .

Then comes the call of Lent; to enter the scene of the crucified as a man who accepts death as the preliminary to a new creation. Philip and I have so often, so often been called to begin again! Our whole lives, if they are a testimony to anything, are a call to this innate power of grace in us, which makes of most unpromising events—prison, underground, the very atmosphere and sentence of death—something new, some beginning of a new creation which must be verified in us, if it is to have validity anywhere, for anyone at all.

The Quaker stubbornness of the intentions at Mass. No one there, everyone there. We cling to the names and presences of our friends like two drowning men to spars and lifelines.

Powerlessness before the new trials. No mobility to think things through. Lassitude of mind, that "sleep of sadness" of the disciples in the garden. Quandary: a Zen conviction, letting things go until I have something to offer, and on the other hand, a laziness of spirit which would be unworthy of the heat and torment of the moment.

Poetry would be such a relief—inability to organize a poem, scattered, wearying round of the days which allow so little light and warmth to the mind.

Mom's illness, her intense physical suffering, weighing on us also. The burden of Philip's anguish, his lucid, massive anger at the course of things, the social madness which we, alone among the prisoners, seem to sense or bear or think about. The sense of having reached a dead end in the society of which we are a part, a society on whose fevers, violence, anger, misused resources so large a part of the world's future depends, willy-nilly.

A full Lenten program presented by the times, for us to shoulder. The Christ of history who mysteriously and actually shoulders the cross of the world with us . . .

Fun and games in the molar factory

Woke to the sense, washing over like a tide, of being in jail; how many days! And thought of all 750 men here, all awakening from the neutrality of sleep, its free-floating geography—one might be literally anywhere. To be in jail—stirring and moving into that depression of spirit which seizes on one before he is fully in command, lowers its harness on him, restricts, enfeebles the movement of his mind, puts him at rigorous distance from family and friends, orders him about, decrees that this day will be like every other day—the worse for being a day added to the crushing burden of the days . . . So that awakening is another hiatus in the vast toothless, tasteless yawn of existence-without-choosing-one's-existence. Purgatorial. The hard task of making virtue out of a necessity that grinds one down . . . Some of this I feel for myself, all of it I feel for the others, especially for those with families and wives; the loosening of ties, the enforced distance from love.

I wonder if in purgatory one would be able to make necessity a virtuous choice. Sometimes I am able to walk—head high, breathing the prayer for all of us that we would keep

alive in our hearts the flame that first brought us to Catonsville . . .

The difficulty of writing anything down at the end of the
day. Turning to reading almost as a narcotic, a way out,
through the experiences and lives of others—out of the fact
that one is living and experiencing so little for himself.

Caught, as I feel, between Zen as a vice of laziness, letting
literally anything happen to myself; and on the other hand,
forcing the hand of life, wrenching it to one's own "uses," as
though to endure all this had no value in itself, because one
was quite literally bankrupt and had nothing to offer others,
the future, the brethren outside . . .

I was demeaned by a crude hospital official who made a
cruel pseudo-humorous crack, and then went his way, after
other prey no doubt. Stood the humiliation for some five
minutes, realizing I would be unable to live with myself if I
let it pass. Sought him out in his office, told him face to face
what I thought of such a crack. He relented, apologized, followed me back to the clinic to apologize before the others
as well. End of the matter except I believe I set up a legitimate line between the humiliation of being an inmate and
the gratuitous humiliation dumped on one by an inferior
spirit playing hobs with the feelings of a powerless man . . .

In course of a conversation with another assistant, spoke
heatedly of "g.d. idiots" making war policy. He registered
dismay at my language. "Though you're a convict I respect
you as a priest etc." I was unable to concur with the basis of
his "respect" and advised reading of the imprecatory Psalms
and Old Testament prophets, whose language is scarcely of
the boudoir or sacristy. Religion is politesse. I say, a plague
on it. So it goes.

The men are out late tonight breaking up the ice after a
hailstorm that tore apart, at one blow, the false promise of
an untimely spring. Across the compound in A and O, men
are showering, reading, playing ping-pong. There is a semblance of order and discipline.

With inquiring eyes, priests, lawyers, friends, editors come to seek out our life. We are as exotic as birds or beasts in a big city zoo—or terminal patients in a hospital. How do we live? What is the day like? What do we eat? What is our work? Do we brothers get to see one another, to talk, to share? Indeed, what seems killingly ordinary from the inside (peacocks lead the life of rather mangy barnyard cocks after all) has about it the subtle glow of the caged and captured gorgeous bird, brought gingerly from afar . . .

We rise about 7:30. Sometimes I manage a cup of cocoa and coffee, missing breakfast habitually, manage also to say a quick prayer, a Psalm perhaps, straighten the bed, dress, wash, get to work by 8 or 8:05.

The clinic! The morning can bring any bit of comico-tragedy, and usually does. Every Tuesday we give a quick, thorough checkup to the new arrivals, as part of their medical induction. Then the day: cleaning sinks, sweeping, X rays to be taken, developed, mounted; helping at the chair, mixing filling material, sterilizing instruments—there is no end to it. But there is an end; the periods of quiet over cups of coffee at mid-morning—to me the most typical moments of the day—a prisoner's day. The eyes of a convict go dim with memory, men lean out a window (barred) offering a rare expansive view of the countryside, memory or expectation turn one to the past or future—or a cloud of despair descends, the present, the accursed present . . . We cross the wintry yard and line up for the midday chow—some 750 are served a nourishing, varied, generally tasteless meal, from 10:45 to 12. (The food is like the religion is like the discipline is like the tenor and atmosphere of time—everything tastes like everything else; i.e., things that should have distinctive odor, gusto, moral, sharp outline, should spur or start reactions, chains of thought, sensibility, spurts of love or aversion —nothing tastes like nothing. We are in prison.)

Back to work by 1, roughly to 4 P.M. Eat by 5. First count of day at 5:30—the hour when the zoo keepers render account of the bodies whose lockup is the rationale for the employment of some hundreds of key-bearing, goose-stepping custodians of private and public weal, the retention behind bars of menaces like myself. So on and on. Two nights a week to classes in Great Books. One night, if not prevented by putrefied offerings, to movie. Several nights to reading indoors or walking the geological squirrel cage outside. So, dear reader, to a turn of exercises, to Psalms, to bed.

At least for the duration of this present long haul; as innocent, though not nearly as dispirited, as a molting captive dove. Indeed, Picasso would have to draw me in mid-flight even here, striking fire from feather and beak.

March 5

We are back, hog-wild, into winter. Nixon is gazing earnestly and paterfamilially from the tube, assuring the nation of firm leadership over the next frontier. Which one will it be? Only God and the generals can be thought to know. My terror is mitigated by knowledge of the first leader, unutterably increased by the second. Lent goes on, the world's passion goes on, men learn so little and change so hardly. Yet it remains true that one Gandhi, one Merton, one King, one Philip (let me say it) binds up the suppurating wounds of the century, makes one feel in the midst of loss and collapse that "man holds a winning ticket in the cosmic sweepstakes." Yet it is all up for grabs, over the night skies of Hanoi, awaiting—with what foreboding and anguish we can only surmise —the next remote-control brainless move of the generals who hold the lives and deaths of children in their manicured hands. A bad time for man, a good time for man. We live on in the fleeting, questionable hope that Christ binds up the wounds and blesses the vocation of life itself.

I have been thinking: what an opportunity for the Catholics to seize anew on the truth of their tradition, and following the example of even a few of us, to plunge into that tradition, simply make man their vocation in this century. What if even a few of them were able to read the signs, to substitute world passion for self-interest, compassion for selfishness, the Sermon on the Mount for militarism, and so invite the kingdom to earth? We Americans have never before had such a chance for vindicating the honor of Christ, betrayed by silence, inertia, and the "good life" (which has so often resulted in the enforced misery and death of so many). It was possible in ordinary times to be ordinary, i.e., peaceable, by rote; with such peaceable moral mediocrity there could be no quarrel. Since the bad news had not reached such unquenchable proportions, nor penetrated consciousness so deeply.

The innocent are condemned to death by the conditions of life; that is the bad news. By and large, the news is a big power arrangement in the world—an American arrangement. To realize this requires of necessity a change in consciousness, a rearrangement of the moral consequences of being human and Christian. One can no longer live as though the good news that surrounds his own life were partaken of by the majority; as though most men had even a remote opportunity to live in the dignity that befits them: peace, plenty, political freedom. Most men lie under the guns that decree their reduction to slavery, so that the haves and have-nots may be a continuing criminal arrangement of the tribes of the earth.

The next genetic stage for Americans is to get reborn into the community of man. This will be a bloody business. The preliminary stage to this birth is upon us. It is called resistance. There can be no viable plan for the political birth of a new community until a sufficient number are speaking, loud and clear, their resistance to the claim of death on the community. I do believe this. It is the only stage of things not veiled in obscurity. It is a clear and present duty of those called to be Christians.

We were discussing "right and wrong ways of being in the world."

One wrong way was the profitlessness of gaining the world and suffering the loss of one's selfhood.

The opposite of that seemed to be the profitableness of suffering the loss of the world and gaining possession of one's own soul, spirit, selfhood.

This is beyond doubt a crisis situation, to be verified according to the plain news of the day. One is called to such loss; I am called to such loss. The opposite, the "gainful employment," is such idolatry as transforms the world, an instrumental network of institutions, into a potter's field presided over by idols.

"Presided over" is said deliberately. The idols are infused with malign power beyond that of the dislocated and inflated ego. Institutions, militarism, racism now have the malignant presumptive power of gods. They order men to die in their "name," to kill in their name.

The youths in the fiery furnace, Daniel in the lions' pit know one word—resistance. One saves his soul by resisting the idols.

Prison is a constant geography and dramatization of the idols in action. Their command: refuse community, reject one another, reject the God of compassion, hope, joy, freedom. Serve Caesar in chains; do your time.

It is absolutely necessary to be cast into the furnace, the pit, the jail, in order to vindicate the truth of God. It is there the pretension "Caesar saves" is broken, once and for all. Daniel is unharmed, the youths sing their chant of liberation. More, they become figures of hope and truth; they break the chains of others who follow and gain grace to believe, to trust, to hope.

The idols are not to be seen as rude clay figures; they are institutions exerting a force, a claim on us. They are historical movements. They summon men under their banners; they have formulas, goals, methods. Men give years of their lives to service of such, and commonly consider themselves decent, religious men in so doing. The *yes* of Jesus (Paul) must be seen as having another side, another word: *no*. It is the old word of the biblical resister—a *no* spoken in the face of the powers that claim the power and name of God. It is a *no* spoken in face of the power to commit one to death; it implies actual criminality before the laws of the omnipotent state.

March 5

Letter to a congressman:

Last night I heard the mechanical doors of my cell close shut for the 200th time. This A.M. I lined up for my 600th meal, along with the other 750 inmates; last Sunday I attended my 28th Sunday Mass, reading the Gospel, receiving communion; this week I had my 30th strip shake, a down to the skin search for almost anything (contraband) after a visit of lawyers. So life goes on. I have walked around the level squirrel cage of the compound perhaps some 4,000 times; were I a classic Greek fatalist I would salute the goddess named Necessity, whose buried and broken image must lie somewhere in the depths of the frozen mud and grass. I have watched the green leaves on the dozen trees turn dark and sanguine and fall; the trees creak today in their sheath of March ice, there are pre-buds swelling under the harsh weather. Men have gone, men have come in; my number of 23742 is now expanded by some 300 more, arrivals, departures.

I am a prisoner; much of the implicit horror is exorcised in prayer by now. Marvelous what the human organism can adjust to. I am counted, supervised, fed, clothed, housed by the state, another item in its gargantuan stockpile, a trouble-some priest, stripped, with no equivocation, of his normal ministry, dumped with some 22,000 other delinquents into "centers of rehabilitation." Thus the ironic crown is placed on my thirty or so adult years of writing, teaching, traveling, speaking in public. The text of John has come home to roost: "when you were young, you went where you would, but when you grow old, another will bind you, and lead you where you would not go."

March 6

The deep suffering evident in the three young priests who arrived here. The sea changes in their faces, as though from a long drowning. Into new life? We struggle and hope and like the broken father of the dead girl in *The Virgin Spring*, acknowledge that we do not understand God. Who might have arranged things otherwise for us all—for all the world and for His own Son . . . As I write this I feel like crossing it out, like a coward's renunciation of cowardice. The fact being that given "the world, the way it goes" we could not but be here, in continuing trouble with Caesar and with one another. The chalice cannot pass by—it is held to our lips, having passed through the tortured hands, the blood-ied mouths of all those who lie under the same Providence as ourselves, and bleed there. Including Jesus Himself, who prayed that the cup might pass Him by, if only . . . The "if" could not be sustained, the cup must be drained. It was the first offering of the new law. Beyond all argument at such a conception of things stands the unkillable example of One who "in fear and trembling" gave His life for the brethren, preferring to suffer violence rather than to inflict it on others. *Non in multiloquio.* The final gesture is one of kenosis, the offering, the drawing of blood. (I fear these notes; they become too wordy, and I fail in a hundred ways of an average day here to measure up to what is possible. Yet I hope for self-understanding, and go on—and hope day by day to exorcise hatred, pusillanimity, backward glances, indulgence, all the waste and welter of time's debris, of being another piece of that debris.)

A good discussion continued tonight on the "being in Himself" and the "being in the world" of Jesus. We inch forward, trying one another for size, conscious of our deep sorrow at not measuring up.

March 7

Reading Solzhenitzyn's *First Circle,* wondering at the rounded, large arc of the man's genius, able so skillfully to encompass so many lives, so many aspects of prison experience. Especially the sharp cut of prison moods, the way in which all this changeful, almost uncontrollable inner weather is exploited for the purposes of the prison and the state. What a deft and moral hand he places at the very core of motivation, exploit, wit, heroism, corruption! I was struck especially by the way he understands and treats prison visits. What after all is more taken for granted outside than the presence of others, being able to sit and converse with a wide variety of people, with the worthy and true and dear, as well as the falsehearted, the boring, the bureaucratic sellouts—to bear with some, to delight in others, in every case to have one's life strike off fire from other lives, to grow and rebound and *live* . . .

Here all that precious opportunity is cut to the bone. One is alternately bored, outraged, indifferently cast into chancy, haphazard, outrageous occurrences that have no power to restore the mind and heart. So a visit becomes a truly great, sometimes unexpected event. The lifeless prisoners have no visits and make do—creating their whole lives according to the gray, shapeless pattern of the day's round. But a visit! One goes back to the yard literally lightheaded, as though he had drunk the wine of the real world, other faces, beautiful clothing, smiles, those hints and evocations of a forbidden life which for a while one is free to conjure again, to imagine, for a little space.

I know after the past two months and the new indictments, I know that grief does not kill a man. Otherwise I would be dead. Grief is to be taken in degrees, and so taken, like a just-under-lethal dose of poison, it just fails in its lethal errand. I am somewhere between the middle march in this regard—not dead, certainly, but not living either. It remains to be seen whether I can really come to life again—living with what the months ahead are certain to bring (the trial), what they will probably bring—the conviction of six, or at least of some.

What is one to do in the meantime? If I have learned anything in fifty years, it is that I cannot pull myself by bootstraps into some higher world of the mind or heart. I have gained great respect for economy of expenditure, for passivity, for operating at 50 per cent or 60 per cent of my capacity —this at the price of surviving at all. Faking it in the noble Zen tradition has kept me on the road so far, when the chances of psycho-survival were not favorable, even from my earliest years in the Society. Yet here am I, a prisoner of fairly long term, learning day by day the feints, rounding the corners of the barbed-wire enclosure of mind and body. I may even survive to write another poem, which seems at such a time the best way to put the miracle of rebirth.

Strange what one gets to live with, when he must. I feel at times like one who has undergone radical surgery for cancer, and been turned loose—a half man stumping about his half world, where everyone else is whole and wholly in possession. Except that one lives here among the basket cases, a near terminal hospital inhabited by those who barely made it from under the bucket and saw of the mad surgeons.

The blessings attendant on such a life, in such a time, are very great nonetheless. Strange that when one set of "connections" has been cut away, another grows in its place. I suppose our public presence has never been so great as when the locks closed behind us. This is all part of the great unexpected workings of a providence that remains untouched by human frenzy and effort. When all our plans came to a halt, their sum a cold zero, other things, better things began to happen. When we chose to lose everything, people began to notice and ponder our lives. The Catonsville play continues to draw sell-out audiences, the former writings and tapes appear publicly, friends make sure publications appear, the remote prisoners are the talk of the movement.

Themselves? They are required to do precisely nothing, to live their half-baked, small-talk round of prison existence, to be themselves, i.e., to be powerless and inept and humiliated in the thousand ways prison is skilled in exacting. Astonishing. A weird logic flowering in the ground of supreme illogic. It was something of this respect for the inherent force of a life of truth and solitude which makes sense in regard to Merton; now he is gone. He realized, I think, how little all the gigantic sum of talk, logic, effort, sweat, striving, machination, reasonableness, prudence make—all said and done. He put his ear to the ground and heard as from a gigantic shell the humming inwardness of the universe. He sensed the long stretch of history. So he learned to be patient and ironic, to parcel out his anger in small doses, to refuse to play God—the last temptation of the great, to become an idol unto himself. Maybe this is why I miss him so grievously. He was a very emperor of illogic, a Zen man who waited on God, who in the manner of a godlike man refused to interfere with the patient workings of the great Absent One. The fortitude of that stance, the courage it required to refuse to play a debased Westernized Prometheus, spoke to the best in me. It gave me perspective and solidity where I stood, it kept me sane and cheerful.

If we could hold converse with the gods, and they were not icy deceivers or sedulous apes, they would counsel us in just such ways. And we might be transformed into religious men.

The prisoner is a monk without portfolio; he is required to be patient, chaste, poor, obedient, industrious; all in service to H. M. State, who receives his vows with bloody hands; and will, if at all provoked, freshen the stains with new blood . . .

The things not allowed are the very things commanded: to be a brother, to be a passionate witness to the truth of a compassionate God who abominates violence and resists death. Hence the tension.

Philip and I give up here in essence what we already renounced, years ago, by choice. This should in the nature of things liberate us to be true brothers. Why have thought of tomorrow? Neither script nor staff. The Son of Man has nowhere to lay His head . . . My heart fails in me when I set down such lines; their demand on my soul is rigorous and cruel, and I am, as always, unready to submit to them.

The real issue here is a struggle between church and state. And then, a second thought. Would that the struggle took such form! No, we are in conflict with both parties; warmaking state, silent church. With such allies as issue from both camps to witness to peace; if necessary, to die "outside the walls" of both enclosures.

March 8

The enemy in such a place as this may well be routine or segregation or the gnaw of hatred or acedia or waste or fear of the unknown or the faces of certain guards or the pabulum

of bad religion or the stink of the days or some witches' brew
of all these—probably the whole shmear. I don't know of
any way to inoculate against it all except by letting go, with
whatever deep breaths one can summon. For me the place
and authorities and all they stand flat-footed for around the
world are slowly vanishing. I take it a little better with the
days; maybe body and mind are really getting to another
world and the logic of it makes better sense.

March 16

Sometimes the requirements of non-violent love seem so
picayune and suffocating (e.g., here, now) as to allow very
little through as to greatness of resolve or horizon. How to
believe that our being here is making a difference for others?
We are truly in Lent, truly in a desert. The truth applied
not only to the daily grind, which seems trivial and enervating, but to the vast horizons offered by our former life, and
if the plain truth is told, by our talents. Yet Philip and the
others must drink still deeper of the gall held out to us . . .
In light of the insufficiency of almost every human means
—genius, eloquence, passionate speech—in breaking through
the icy wall of wrong power, do not such perspectives
seem a sort of satanic temptation (as in the vistas opened
to Jesus by the devil—"all these I will give you")? Can one
be destroyed in the role of suffering servant? Here we are; we
are to believe, as I do most firmly, that being here is the natural crown of everything that went before; not merely in a hu-
manistic sense that good men inevitably come to ill, but in the
sense of the crowning of a journey of faith by the opening
of a wider vista of faith. The reward of faith, that is to say,
is not vision, it is a life which both requires and bestows a
greater measure of faith; the ability to see the journey through,
stage by stage, so that the promise, still withheld, remains it-

self, pristine, never canceled. "Come, into a land which I will show you." Showing, Epiphany; it is the journey, its continuance, the adhesion of mind and heart to what was first offered and is never rescinded. Thus our discipline continues.

If for Gandhi this was fairly clear, the reason must lie (1) in his unmatched purity of spirit, which kept him moving headlong into the heart of social chaos, clear of heart and mind and lucid in word, and (2) in the comparative clarity of his social struggle. He could count on a measure of humanity from the oppressor; they were willing to weigh the nonviolent forces he was vitalizing and to yield before them in measure, with a certain respect both for Gandhi and for human life. We can count on very little of this latter; and our distance from the grandeur of the Mahatma is, let me assure friends, foes, and my own soul, a source of constant humiliation. As well as of emulation—as witness our passionate reading of the autobiography in our weekly classes.

Thomas Merton on Peace has finally arrived, in proof sheets. It contains enough memories of Tom and ourselves to keep one awake for many a moon. As well as G. Zahn's introduction, generally fair and perceptive. What sorrow attends all our memories of this great and good friend— and what vistas his death invites us to, even by way of shattered hope! Beyond all speculation as to the way his life might have gone, one feels simply that he should say thank you to the God of all for the gift of such a life.

Putting down this dog of exhaustion day by day; never quite downed, never quite at one's best. At least a bit of perspective after fifty years allows a certain aesthetic distance from outright despair at the unaccountable failure of energies. One has made it before, in all probability, too, will make it again.

Bro. Skunk, reduced by two thirds by winter's rigors, noses about the yard, a scrawny muff on the move. A lenten skunk, by all odds. He is indifferent to us as the skinny moon; skin and bones himself, he slides under the big gate and seeks to share for an hour or two each night the circularity of the prisoner's journey, going (for a time at least, doing time) nowhere precisely. Brother Butter is now Brother Bones.

The silence of Jesus during Lent, that ultimate and unassailable dignity. Which, being required to die, sets around its countenance, a free zone of contemplation, an uninterrupted depth which it both plumbs and possesses—the Father's will.

What cannot be counted can be counted on

They count us at 5:30 P.M., 9, 11, 12, 2, and 5. So many heads; then phone the number to headquarters, a quick general computation is made, and the "all clear" is given; in our case, the cell doors are opened, except from 11 to 6. Presumably then we are of some account, a kind of vanishing species, which might, were not the accounts strictly kept, melt or vanish before their eyes. Some would say: jobs depend on our being present, all sorts of economics are involved, the "security" of the system, egos, future involvements, advances on the ladder. Not so long a time ago, the same number game, connected with the same implicit rewards and punishments, was also a rule of thumb in the churches. In the Jesuits we had a yearly *compte* to be submitted to Rome; so many sermons, baptisms, conversions, entering a huge hopper at headquarters, presumably justifying one's steward- ship in the world. I wonder in consequence what happens to humans when this numerology succeeds (1) Christianity, a religion of "spirit and truth" as announced by the Master, and (2) a state where politics are governed by social concern, passion for human welfare, and the quality of life of its citizens. The numbers game thrives when both realities are scuttled. Then we get from the state war as a way of life, with its body counts; and a church hankering more and more after Caesar's booty of captives, slaves, faithful sheep for the fleecing.

Once men are numbered they lose their names; in fact and *de jure* they become instruments, either in death or captivity, of the lustful egoism of others. Reduced to objects that prove something like the totalizing character of war or "justice."

Numbers erase individuality which is always troublesome, itchy, questioning, fighting against tyranny, death, stereotypology. Under the count, one acts as he must against every attempt to put him to death—he lives on by acts of imagination, rage, courage, ingenuity. Under the guillotine, new ways of life; under edict of death, new ways of being a man. In all prison literature (*First Circle*) men react most strongly by (1) cultivating their resistance, weeping, thieving, living, defending and sustaining one another, mimicking the oppressor with ridicule, asserting in every way possible their recognition of the presence of death's power; (2) dramatizing the alternatives left to them in moments of life, love, satire, scatology, community.

The "count" is to time as life is to time consciousness. On the one hand, stale time, dead time, dead souls. Being condemned to death one is supposed to "live" like the dead —never to smile, to act out his slavery in submissiveness, silence, dread. Every refusal so to live creates life in the empery of death and cheats the emperor of his prey. I used to wonder: why do none or so very few of the prisoners ever smile? I decided to smile deliberately, as an act of defiance, to anyone I would meet or pass a greeting to. I was to learn the cost of this and understand better the deep groove of sadness eaten into men's faces by the acid of time itself. But to continue in my defiance.

One counts: money, cattle, possessions in general, real estate, hunting catch, conquests (sexual or material), litters of offspring, baked goods, gross national product, dead enemies, votes, offenses real or fancied.

One cannot count: living conscious people (in principle), sacraments, occasions of love, acts of non-violence and reconciliation, attitudes, starts and flushes of love, moments of insight, ruling fears, truthful words and deeds, children, musical motifs, epiphanies, masterpieces of art, excellent wine, bread, cheese. (With some of these, numeration is simply irrelevant; with others it is manifest blasphemy.)

March 19—St. Joseph's Day—Mass at noon

It strikes me as an example of the day-to-day style (!) here that I have yet to give space or reflection on the indictments or their mental, spiritual, political effect on me.

First reaction—pure, profound grief verging on despair. I remember vividly Shorty coming to my cell to say, "The eight o'clock news says six were indicted, Phil among them." We went to seek him out. He was in dining hall rapping. Took it calmly. We walked the compound in a dense silence, like exhausted explorers in a North Pole trek, their supplies all but gone. One round, and Phil excused himself and went inside. Thus began the latest chapter in the dark night. I was to know more of it, but that night set the pattern of insomnia and hopelessness, nightmares of abandonment of friends, despair of relief. What would those think of us now who had trusted us implicitly? Were we to be buried out of mind? Who would be able to respond and come to our side? I do not recommend such nights to others. They happen, inevitably. One is not properly "religious" by spontaneous response —more like a stricken animal, beyond recourse or aid. It has to be gone through, the Eumenides are in control.

Then a slow comeback, as from a wasting illness. Bill K.

around, full of fun, ginger, and love. He met the press afterward with a good statement. Next day, prompt as the good Samaritan, Bill Anderson, perfectly, exquisitely unflappable. Presence and strategy. But most of all, presence.

No crisis like this is apt to bring out the religious legions of relief. The Jesuits kept their distance; the provincial came only weeks later when the radioactive dust had settled. I suppose it is simply because the spiritual equipment boggles. Men of the cloth cannot imagine what it is to be buried here, then twice buried under such a cruel avalanche. I do not blame them; one might as well blame a paraplegic for knitting cashmere sweaters.

We began the slow work of habilitation of community. Lawyers signed up one by one, a stellar cast that in the beginning showed us a good deal more rhetoric than substance. We found ourselves hassling over their tactics, listening wanly to their speeches, forced to put off the essentials of getting to know one another, the accused, in the new red landscape of death. That work is, at present writing, just getting under way. Another way of saying: hope is again afoot, shod, girt, ready for the next stage of exodus.

Astonishing forms, methods, voices, insistences, self-givings; support everywhere in face of the insupportable. The feeling now being one of qualified confidence: we will, hook and crook, make it.

March 20

One of our tasks must be (in regard to something we touched on yesterday) not to become further sources of alienation to others who are only too willing to latch onto us as their salvation. "The salvation of man lies within himself." (Gandhi) Just as we have taken steps in our lives which seem appropriate to the times, so must others. There is a delicate balance here between keeping adult connections, as required for any movement worthy of the name, and ourselves being sources of "umbilicalization," keeping others dependent on the great symbols who in this case are transformed into idols. I think one of the moments for this was the hours of class, when we came to realize mainly through John that we could not be the magicians, but must simply enter a fraternal group which would find itself in the act of reading and reflecting. People are starved on their diet of mass media and Cencral Foods, General Motors, General Electric slop—junk; religion plays its obvious role as well. Christ becomes the great "universal solvent" instead of a summons to humanity on the part of those who have learned not to be cowed by the world . . . We must, on our part, refuse such a role. We can only offer our lives, if necessary our deaths. In between are all the interstices they must fill with their own deduction, modes of service, all the rest.

March 21

Fun is where you find it. One genius was busted for having twenty-six hard-boiled eggs in his cell. I had this surreal image about him, a big dun green-brown bird hopping around flapping his arms laying these golden nuggets here, there, and everywhere, backing into his locker, perching up on the window sill. Twenty-six, hard-boiled!

Another had twenty-eight pillowcases, all of them sheathing his pillow. He was busted to the hole. Said in explanation: It was easier to take them off, one at a time. But to have to put on a clean one every week! He languished in solitary; but not really, bounced right back, as most of the young demons do.

March 21

Portrait of a prince of hell

I remember him as one of very few, perhaps the only one of
the inmates who could strike me with the fear that I associate
with evil. Just as I ordinarily, invariably associate an instinctive confidence, a search for the good face and an expectation
of finding it, with the assumption of my guts and experience that human beings are decent. I first met him on the
stands of the athletic field in a summer twilight, shortly after
being dumped into the general population. I was feeling like
a shored sea animal after the B.I. episode and used to look
for empty stands to contemplate the ball game of existence
and commune with my team, The Losers. And he came up
and began a long monologue, gratuitous, and slippery, an
old hand with a dumb priest. The pitch was to grow familiar. He knew the game—that could hardly be doubted. But
he knew my species about as well as he knew the thoughts of
a threatened school of seals. Nothing daunted.

Thus the message. I was to trust no one—repeat no
one—present company always excepted. I would be taken
advantage of, I would lose everything, I would give too much,
talk to the wrong persons, etc., etc. Now supposing all this

was the literal truth and the threat of my being a country mole in a zoo of weasels and marmosets was true, the talk was wrong, the occasion and timing were off, the vibes were rotten. I put up with it. Years of putting up with it made me at least qualified not to take him seriously—the message, the medium, the whole bag . . . We parted, pointedly, when I moved off after a half hour or so to better air . . . Some weeks later, he accosted me again. I was walking with Phil, who had recently arrived from Lewisburg. This time, the exchange was truer to his real form. I had been seen sympathetically exchanging words and advice with a young homosexual prisoner, had presumably encouraged his friendship with another homo (a married man). This time I was subjected to an irrational rant, relative to my obligations, which were, as I then learned in some astonishment, to despise and turn my back on such outcasts. I took the advice badly, as being outside the scope of his expertise, but the moment was a delicate one. To rebut him, I would have to break a confidential matter, so I said nothing. Following this assault, he ignored me pointedly for several weeks, turning a stony stare on any effort at reconciliation . . .

Then, mainly due to Phil, he began talking again; this time it was a rush of confidence, advice, requests for book loans, reports on his recent readings, etc. He came on, now, as the reformist whose conversion was due to a hard-won insight into the duplicity and maltreatment of the prison system. He was ready to stand with us, at any cost, in whatever project, within or outside prison, which might be thought to bring the system down, a tower of tongues assailed by a hero armed with the sword of truth. He began attending our classes on St. Matthew's Gospel, which were just getting under way. There he favored the gallery with long diatribes on the failure of the church to communicate the human substance of Christ's life and example—all true to a point no doubt, but tiresome and reeking with the righteousness of the Christian *manqué*.

He had a special driving skill for wearying his hearers without notably enlightening them. Struggling as we were, under circumstances of personal oppression, loneliness, and despair, to draw together, to warm our chilled lives with some flame of renewal, his words evoked a long susurration of weary forbearance. We were so tired of every effort to force upon us another buck's weight of the wrongness of the world. Beasts of burden as we were condemned to be by the decree of our punishers, we had turned to the New Testament, for some relief, some hint of joy or fervor of spirit, some way in or out . . .

Luckily for all of us, he gave up after three or four sessions and appeared no more: by a deliberate decision, as he virtuously assured me later; so that he might be able to confess real ignorance of what went on in the class, when he was questioned by the authorities . . .

The indictments came down, our hearts were split open once more, our spirits tried to the marrow. He met us walking, one night; the moon was full. "Who will teach us to bay like animals for our pain?" he cried aloud. I have no doubt he had his moments of honesty—as far as that virtue could penetrate him; which is to say, at times he thought he was sincere, he acted it out, in public or private, he rose to occasions. Under the moon, something of our own passion was reflected in his tortured eyes, whose suffering had far different sources than our own. Was there hope for him?

His friends told us in the paranoiac weather of that late winter that he had made a deal with authorities to win his parole. That deal included an informer's role against the H. accused. We were stunned. To believe the news without substantiation seemed monstrous. There was nothing to do but confront him, give him a chance to respond . . . The scene can scarcely be imagined. He denied the accusation with untoward vehemence; there was a particular agony, as he told me later, because he knew he once could have been tempted in such a direction; and the knowledge that his past made him vulnerable to such suspicion was beyond enduring. His migraine headaches, a recurrent malaise, attacked him with savagery. A day later, meeting him, haggard and whey-faced, I was shocked beyond belief. It was as though a healthy man had been dipped by torturers in a vat of boiling acid. This was his dark night, his molten existence, the hell he carried within him.

I could only say to him, with what calm I could muster, "If the tale is untrue, you know it and so are vindicated before your own conscience; if it is true, know that we are at your mercy; for what can we do, either to prevent your course or persuade you otherwise?" He was not comforted . . . I see him then, in retrospect, that shadowy, chunky con man, his words, spurious, vehement, declamatory, whee-dling, debased, and betrayed by mother love and money love, violent, spasmodic, unpredictable, murderous in mood —a bonebreaker, a churchgoer, a liar, a Jesuit "old boy," a master croupier, strong of arm and sick of mind; wanting to become, in plenary denial of his past, a student, social worker, reformer, revolutionary, God knows what.

Of the truth or falsity of the charges against him we know up to the present—nothing. Will he be unwrapped from "protective custody" like a Judas from hell, to walk into the courtroom at Harrisburg in the autumn, ready to condemn his friends? Will he turn over a new leaf with that spatulate, well-manicured hand, from the last page of the *Inferno* to the first of the *Purgatorio*, an autobiography of hope, an ascent?

He had been grifter, extortioner, homosexual, *bon vivant*, mama's boy, snitch thief; out of prison and in, he had kept friends and been kept; lost friends and been set adrift—it was a biography that would bring horror to the face of a studi-ous griffin . . . Finally, the evil I smelled in him was the evil of money, the suppuration of a human body that has sweated through its deeds of violence and betrayal, whose acts and words of renunciation only multiplied his betrayals. The odor stuck to him, he emanated a kind of death. It was

he who brought home to me that in this place, a prison where
men languish, despair, curse, endure; where some men slip
into that death which is recidivism; and where a few men,
only a very few, get reborn, come on the truth of their tor-
mentors and themselves, see the umbilical which joins them
to the torturers, the crime to the punishment—in such a place
some few so nearly die as to refuse all efforts at resuscitation.
Some few die, or so nearly die, as to show forth to all the extreme condition into which we are thrust, the miracle that
sustains us.

He is at the edge; whether he will disappear entirely,
whether the claim of death on him is irrevocable, is still unknown. But in the meantime, far from human recourse,
twisted and self-damned, he becomes a strange figure of hope,
lodged in my mind. His kind is so rare, even in prison. Even
he could not entirely, once and for all, have done with
us, with Phil and myself. He kept coming back, for more
punishment and suffering no doubt; at the same time for a
drop of cooling water held in our palm, to assuage the fevers
of one who burned in hell.

*   *March 22*

The following exchange in the compound, after our class
on Gandhi:

P: How can I get my wife out of her fundamentalist bag?

I: What do you mean?

P: Oh, she's always talking lately about Jesus or hell-fire;
take Him or get it in the neck . . .

I: Well, I don't know your wife well enough to offer an
answer; but speaking of Gandhi . . .

P: Yeah, go ahead.

I: I'd say maybe a little more love on your part, a little more
truth, would help.

L - O - N - G silence.

P: Well—I'll have to think that one over. Why don't you say something more of what you mean?

I: I've said what I mean.

P: Dan, that's what gets me about you. You make these cracks and then go off and refuse to talk any further, to say what you mean.

I: I've said what I meant. You asked a question and got an answer.

P: Maybe I've got some guilt involved . . .

I: Then deal with that one too.

P: (Huffily) I'm going indoors.

Comment: You start here with the idea that my interlocutor P. (from all prior available knowledge) is pretty nearly impermeable to common or singular good sense, that he is moreover of at least ten minds about P. himself, that he talks into space balloons continually and launches them into the ether, with no return envisaged, that everyone has trouble connecting with him—etc., etc., etc. Then you say: he's the kind Ma spoke of years ago: some people you just carry. Someone carries them a mile, someone a further mile; but they carry no one, not even themselves.

Right on.

March 24

One of the characters here exhibits all, all the colorations, claw to tooth, of "ye compleat Capitalist." He is to be released to a breathless world next week, in virtue of a $2,000 offering before the altar of law . . . His wife, on instruction (the wives of all compleat capitalists are limps), is driving up, as per instructions, in a candy-apple-red Caddy, just purchased; as you or I would favor ourselves with, say, a new pair of pants for the occasion. They will leave with car and baby three days later for East Europe and Russia, where he in red (honor of Marxism) Caddy (honor of capitalism) hopes to make a movie on uplifting themes. He is cold as gun metal, an exponent of positive thinking who runs like a metallic dog in the evenings, round and round the compound. Definition of a capitalist; a gun metal man running, round and round, the world.

An hour today in the hospital with a twenty-two-year-old who cut his wrists last Saturday evening. What a bloody cry for help—after two and a half years here for heroin. A slice, so to speak, of life for me also. He has a classic oval face and skin and chinaberry eyes of an angel by Donatello, and moves just as slowly, eyes, expression. Very intelligent, beat, broken, up for repairs—in Hawaii, he says, where he hopes to connect with his brother. But it is all as vague as a heroin dream. What he has going for him could fit under one of his long fingernails and come loose as easily. I brought him art books and he promises to work and talk for his remaining sixty days.

It would be so easy to slide into despair at such human wreckage, so young—and completely useless to do so. The chaplains and medical doctor, who by consideration or profession are supposed to offer some counter to inhuman power here, offer zero. So the medics come to me, at the wrong end of near tragedy, to talk with the victims—which is ironically of course one reason why we are here at all, and perhaps one way of starting over. But what pain! And what a sense of helplessness—a lenten feeling deep in the heart, as Lent moves toward the passion and death of the man who was equally powerless to do anything except give his life; and see what that would do.

Strange stirrings on the indictments, new moves by the government, evidence of their thrashing about witlessly in the sack of their self-enclosed violence. One has a strange sense that the tide is turning in our direction—but that great perils lie ahead, through which only devotion to truth will carry us . . .

It comes to me at times to question: what is it I most long for in the world of good former times? Certainly only a fool would fail to recall with utmost gratitude and affection the people of Cornell, the energizing and varied landscape, the intoxicating variety of human friendships—and "free access to the world"—the constant persuasion and gentle proof that one is *human*, offered by the challenge of facing others to face, going before large audiences, preaching, lecturing, all the rest . . .

But when I search my spirit for a pang of loss, I am at a loss; there is none, or scarcely none. Sometimes, to be sure, in the first weeks, detention was like an iron hand on my throat, inexorably closing. The sense of death nearing, passing. We are visited, cosseted even by admiring friends, in the manner of explorers from the Far North, hospitalized for a time, their burns and chilblains like honorable stigmata on their bodies. Every day is a stretching on the rack—better still on the loom. New colorations, new textures of existence, a new man slowly taking shape. The worst thus slowly approaches the best. What better indeed, than that one be placed so near the springs of life (suffering, hope, isolation) in order to be required to create his own soul? To be responsible, to some degree at least, for the soul of his brethren? I know I am able to set down such words only many days and weeks after the lethal shock of the indictments. I looked death fairly in the face, and was for a time literally turned to stone. But since then, something has happened, a better mind has set in . . .

Sometimes in regard to the past I accuse myself of a want of feeling—how can one have had so much of the pip of the world on his lips, and not regret its withdrawal? Yet I hope I can be grateful, and energetic enough to set my mind solidly toward the present and future, with all due love for what has been, and no longer is.

March 25

An outspaced brain, slow speech, angular head, black hair, a tomahawk profile. Yes, I'm part Cherokee. Picked up at the Canadian border; couldn't swim the river, carrying something that had to be kept dry (!) Now he's bound for the West in cuffs—Texas this time. Thinks anything west of the Mississippi *must* be good: got to get on the other side of that river! He showed me his possessions as he prepared to hack out. A headband Indian style, a few grubby letters, and a single pearl. A gift from a girl friend: it glowed there in my hand, a pearl, and in this place!

Same kid; pretty well gone, in the same or other shapes, forms, ominous presences of schizoid condition. He hailed me out into the yard this A.M. to share his nightmare; twelve years on drugs, five intense LSD years. Now voices and presences and evil little men squirt through his veins, head, bones, like flies or locusts. I was of two minds (!) as to whether to get him some hospital attention—roughly like asking them to drug up the druggy. But got him into the chow line instead. A few other fairly normal good-humored people pummeled and joked with him a bit. He did a sudden switch, smiled tentatively, got off his hell trip for a while. And while he didn't seem to connect with much of anything around, at least he switched tracks and seemed more peaceable within. But what to be done over the long days ahead? Will simply have to see.

We celebrate Mass usually two times a week (no one but ourselves allowed to be present) in the chaplain's office, which is so like the chaplain as to be uninhabitable by any spirit but his. The desk littered with pointless odds and ends, a stale sacristy of the mind, bookcases filled with dusty old tomes unread for years, the American and papal flags moldering in far corners, emblems of lost battles, the walls a sickly green, last year's calendar. A place where literally no one comes or goes, the dead heart of a dead place . . . He is supposed, according to some handbook or other, to interview every Catholic admitted to the prison, but confesses under direct questioning he has lost the files or they are not in order; he is visibly upset at the prospect of having to see any new face, face any new life . . . When we came here, he used to admit clerics to see us, for an hour or so, always in his presence. The authorities ordered the practice stopped. He, being a man subject to Caesar, promptly complied, as he invariably does, it being beyond imagining to him that he should lie under another sort of authority . . .

So we go in and read scripture and eat the wafer and drink the wine; and are against all expectation strengthened to bear our lives one day more.

From time to time a few wide-eyed new arrivals approach this worthy cleric, more or less in hopes that something can be done, that he will try something new, will show some semblance of heart or compassion. And are, as all before them, promptly put down, put off, put out; and in this as in everything, learn that joining the population is so simple a thing as having one's hopes deflated, growing used to having nothing happen, knowing that religion is another cut of the tasteless, odorless, colorless life here—and so learn to keep their mouths shut, to keep the peace, to become part of the vast "peace-keeping machinery" that beats men flat, empty as newsprint or rolled metal.

Prosit. Personally, the trouble with me is not that nothing happens here, but that, if I have the instinct merely to follow the scent of life, so much is happening as to be almost beyond bearing. The suffering we witness! The men, especially the young, locked in here and there, sent to the hole, sent to the strip cell, in immediate need of some help, counsel, intervention! The sicknesses, the aberration, the despair.

All the detritus left behind by the rake's progress of justice, medicine, religion, family, crime, court, city jails, night transport, illness, and trouble in families . . .

March 27

The lieutenant yaps at us like a cocker spaniel for "taking food from outside, when you have the machines here." We laugh in his face, not contemptuously, but simply and joyfully, like men who encounter a minor inconvenience—at the end of a perfect day by the sea. He turns away laughing, unable to go on with his law-and-order rap. Of such moments are the bearing of long days and nights made.

Tomorrow A.M. I put on white pants and shirt and proceed to the clinic on time, clean the floor, wipe out the sinks, set up instruments, mount the X rays, get ready for patients and doctors. An uneasy week begins its cycle, like every week. With the dentists things usually go well. Tomorrow our clerk, the irrepressible voluntarist and compleat capitalist, leaves; the new clerk, a lawyer with the face of an El Greco cardinal, takes over.

April 2

Finished *First Circle*, since then both exalted and oppressed. I suppose "work of art" is a pretentious term when applied to the unimaginable suffering and death of good men, even of indifferent men, in prisons. I mean, I could read the novel with less pain than I can read the New York *Times*. Does that say something about the difference between art and bad news? I think so. So, as our own lockup clicks its jaws shut, I pray tonight for our dear friends who were here today, for all in danger of the law, for all whose future looks bleak and despairing because they too feel in their deepest heart the stirring of a sense of others. Dangerous men— those for whom the death of another is real, and therefore can be imagined.

If man does not promise much these days, neither does God. At such a point I can only begin what the experts call "imprecation"—a form of worship in which God is so real that He can be cursed. Cursed i.e. for doing what He is very old and skilled at—refusing to play god. That Love which is silent.

Though the days go forward and are unrepeatable, it seems as though weeks and months reverse themselves. It is like a computerized nightmare of time, literally nothing but cycles; a circular track, like the compound itself.

Our friends come like spring and leave like autumn; all in the space of a few hours. Talk about time!

I would no longer bother even to hide these pages. Let them have them if they want. I can always start again like Genet and others, if the ax falls. Why do they so fear a literate man? There must still be some hope for the written word . . .

We have to thank the concocters of indictments for one thing—they leave us very little time for heroics or tears over our "fate." There is simply one day after another to be gotten through—never gracefully, never quite graciously—but gotten through nonetheless, always with the suffering around one to keep him canny and alert for opportunities to help. Someone shipped out, someone sick or discouraged or demented —someone simply worse off than oneself, whose condition calls one to his side. I want, if our own situation betters, to get some legal aid to those who are being tried and broken around here . . .

There is one supreme motive for not allowing one's own spirit to be broken—it would not be useful for others.

The doctors and medicos wander in and out of the clinic. I try to be courteous, at the same time I am conscious that I am not one of them, even though I am drawn into their conversation on this or that occasion. To be faithful to being an inmate, to be distrustful of the quality of such men, who never will be prisoners—for any cause.

Here lie the good Germicans

We had come from a particularly exalting visit with Jerry, Carol; there was the usual strip search to be undergone. What a deflation of spirit! After the wild free variety of the world, one is cornered and raked over like an animal . . . I think of the years that may lie ahead for Philip when all this is to continue. They go through our clothes with impassive faces, we are suspected of carrying something from the land of the living, land of the loving, land of nature, land of laughter, land of promise; into no man's land, into the cancer ward, into the first circle of the damned. Where we are supposedly living according to their maps, their architecture, their plans for the living who are forbidden to live. One cannot summon religious props on such an occasion; at least I cannot. To think of the stripping of Jesus is no great help, though it might be to a saint. I am outraged, brought low, my worst feelings are briefly in command. I think of conserving my energy for the real trials which one encounters at every turn here, and which lie ahead, and try not to waste feeling on the unfeeling. Dress again as quickly as possible and go out.

One of the younger men, thrown in with us, had the gumption to question the guard: "Don't you feel how wrong it is to treat priests this way?" His answer: "I don't feel very good treating *any* inmate this way." Which wasn't, all considered, so bad.

But like almost everyone these days, from Laos to here, he went ahead with his job, palming and feeling the scraps of clothing, while he revealed his second thoughts. Almost everyone capable of any thought has second thoughts. Almost no one is capable of acting on them. Which is why men order others to cross another border, or man another bomber, and are sure of being obeyed. Which is our epitaph: here lie the good Germans; and over there, the victims. Almost no one will die without his hands around the throat of the victim. The mass grave is à la mode; only the hero dies in solitude.

I am driven back to these pages, almost like an addict. A good page of reading, a chance meeting, a face, a word of complaint—even a greeting—set me off. A passion like a disease of the bone—deep, deep, a pain felt only in movement, in the constriction like a drop of acid on a limb joint—one is ill, but all the more determined to move, to exercise, to punish the limb into normalcy. Alas; maybe everything one tries saves every other thing from becoming a narcotic.

Even here the world of action and the locale of work, exercise, eating, sleeping is vivacious, various enough so that no deadly sclerosis sets in at any point. To keep everything going of which one is capable—not to let life go cheaply into death, not to give up! I think sometimes the Zen testimony is the truest of all.

And even when one chose jail and anonymity (the hand of Mars placed brutally to his mouth), quite the opposite happened, an act which surpassed all human expectation. When we were muzzled and chained, we were heard most powerfully. Men were not longing to hear from "usual" lives which could in some fashion assure them those lives they were forced to lead were rewarding or virtuous or in no need of relief from outside. They needed to be told the truth, something so simple and beyond expression as the fact of their own slavery. And some hint of a way out.

The guards go home to their families, as the Secretary of War, the President, the chief rabbi, the cardinal all go home to their families. They wrap themselves, after long weariness, vexing decisions, the sweat and pomp and fevers of power, in joy, recognition, faces that love and respond, lives that ask only to live and be lived with. Whatever the nightmares of their days, men know the intoxication of evenings and nights, when they can be restored once more to face the nearly unbearable, nearly insane demands of "the world, the way it goes." It is only ourselves who must live "in the factory" day and night, under the smokestack and the towers and extinguished lights.

To keep us, to count us, to have a complete tally four times a day! Some of the inmates undoubtedly have never before been so valued. Some of their wives, some of their children beyond doubt devoutly give thanks that they went on the lam, disappeared, were locked up. Only here are they a precious species, pelt and feathers guarded like the slumbering gold in the vaults of Fort Knox.

There is an inspector from the Department of Prisons in D.C. stalking around the premises in a raw silk suit; he talks only to the bosses, and will report everything is shipshape here. Which of course it is; a slave ship running on schedule takes no note of the demurring of certain noisome, sweating characters in the hold.

The chaplain is porcine and stern of face—a savior gone to seed. It is as though the voice box of Jesus got stuck in some wrong reincarnation, in the blubber of a Nero. He is literally beyond belief. He conducts witless seminars in outmoded ridiculosities like "Communications" for which a suffering inmate, applying for admission, can be credited $5 a term. Thanks to the transmogrification of religion into prison cunning and cruelty, he draws a fat paycheck, plays superhack, and quite constantly and coolly defames the honor of Jesus Christ. A small matter, for which there is no calling him to account, he being a useful senior member of the slave ship bureaucracy. I expect Dante could have dealt with him quite adequately; so, presumably, will God the Father and Judge. The rest of us are helpless.

April 12

". . . how many years do the Americans want to fight us? Five years? Ten years? Twenty-five years? They will find us ready." (Pham Van Dong) And how many years must be spent in jail? . . . It is just this kind of patience brings our rebirth to pass, day by day.

An extremely exhausting week ends; trying to push one foot ahead of the other, meet visitors with reasonable cheerfulness, work and study and pray—a sense at the end, quite humiliating, of doing it all clumsily, with two left hands and feet. Strangely impatient and short of breath, which is to say, short on spirit. Without a Lenten program to grab and be grabbed by. Dead time, like stale rooms to be passed through interminably before the open air is reached. Unclear about Zen flow and inner laziness, the burdens of others largely unmet, the universal bad news from above.

Yet in the midst of it all the great good news, so hidden from beneath. Paris, the meetings with the Vietnamese, the greetings that get through. Jerry and Carol, their cheerful staying power, good humor, vivacity, the ability to laugh in the teeth of the guards and locks and frowns. I thought today: we are the only ones who break into great bursts of laughter in the visiting rooms—certainly a minor victory. Amen.

April 13

I am learning so slowly! The swing of a rhythm that will
allow for personal survival here—and something more. Not
too much of anything! So go easy on the clogging periodicals
that bring the ills of the world entirely too close for non-
contamination. Does that sound supercilious? I am speaking
as simply as I know, of survival. "Thy waters have en-
compassed me . . ." To the point where one loses a sense
of what is truly available and possible on behalf of others, in
such a place. I mean a serenity of prayer, intercession that
does not lose heart. In comparison with this calling, its
nobility and depth, one can become a merely troubled
scavenger in the off-city dump, brow furrowed at the callous,
meretricious shark's existence that lives, dies, in such a way
. . . No, one is here not to rub his nerves raw, but to give
room to the spirit, to grow in awareness, to offer another way,
deliberately at odds with the lemming's beaten track. I am
choking to death on bad news because I am neglecting to be
good news. Is this not so? . . .

One friend was tripping on acid. He seemed as usual, except that on one subject his needle stuck in a groove. It was
as though we were doomed to go round and round and round
the compound (as indeed we are) and at the same time
helplessly, inevitably to be struck in the face by some diaboli-
cal hidden stretched rope. How come? . . .

For the first time, I would venture, the question arises as
a serious question—should not one refuse parole in order to
stay on here, if he has come on a good thing—community,
work, books, friends? I am astonished at the lucidity of one
friend, a redheaded granny-glassed young monk who lives
day in and out with great skill and intrepidity. I listen to his
pros and cons, and refuse to give a decision which must in any

case be his own. But pro and con, his mind functions well—
it has been honed to an edge by meditation and service—and
not least of all by the classes at which a dozen or so of
us hammer at Gandhi's door twice a week. Does it all get anywhere? It got to him!

Suddenly embraced in the yard by an inmate this P.M. It
was his way of offering and accepting forgiveness for some
recent teacup tempests. Not a bad moment, for two felons?

The hardest thing (at times) is the noise. One seems
awash in it, as though in a filthy mid sea into which all the
craft afloat had dumped their *stercora*. I am practically helpless, much more so than 99.9 per cent of the others, for whom
air is not air, atmosphere not itself, talk not talk, work not
work, unless it is all awash in racket. God help my silences,
my deep breaths, my inner whispers, my hints from afar.
They are all dying of strangulation.

April 15

Quakers here. Great heated exchange about a demonstra-
tion in April at the gates or inside. A bummer. No consulta-
tion with prisoners; a day at the zoo. Vociferous outcries of
indignation etc. It seems as though by now a few things
ought to be clarified for the "movement": (1) Prisoners are
not "another group" to be consulted in a project like this;
they are the heart of the matter. (2) Prisoners, in any case,
are not the main question of the day, as though we were maltreated etc. here. We are not. The main issue and pressure
remains the war. (3) Decisions which send us here and keep
us here are not made here. This is the small end of the horn
of ills. Let the people assemble where decisions of power
are actually made—which is to say at local federal buildings
and in D.C. (4) The net result of civil disobedience outside

this prison would be revenge taken on the prisoners—not an ideal outcome, to any humane view of things.

The word at present is: the project has gone too far, raised too much momentum; it cannot be stopped. Too, are we talking here of the peace, or of the war?

April 16

Snowing rapaciously outside, peaceful as December inside.

Phil and I lose enormously in not having any critical opposition that might be called real. On the one hand, the slack-jawed liberal establishment on its stony arse, jawing such nostrums as make the heart shudder with a sense of the presence of death. The New York *Times* takes the whole mordant mess as a deific "given"—anyone from Allende to the Weathermen to D. Dellinger to anyone who would dare to probe into the roots or nerve centers of things is to be abominated.

On the Catholic (or let us say the wide religious) scene there is simply no one to be heard from. The paperback from Holy Cross is a good indication; they could find no one but Fr. Greeley to stand up and say *no* to us and Catonsville, and his *no* is so intemperate and mean-spirited as to put off anyone but himself, presumably. No one of the quality of Chesterton, or Merton, to approach the questions we try to raise, to modify them with a better historic sense, to let whatever is of value in our writings filter through the personality cult and come out the other side.

There is almost no one left to love the church enough to help it to flourish, walk, learn, know ecstasy, grow up, experience the act of love, be celibate, go to jail, sing, contemplate, remain sane, shed blood, break bread, taste wine, laugh, play the fool, be wise as a phoenix, stiffen like Scylla before the buccaneers, grow flowers, take decisions, swallow hard, stand by . . .

Most are ludicrously attached to their own instrumentalities, mental constructs, or skeletons in closets, bones in cupboards, bread on waters—too attached to be able to enter in, as subject, to the prodigious act of creation that would bring the new world to pass. It is a matter of illuminating style, a lightning strike, the professed despisal of non-life and omnivorous death, the professed willingness to live as though the life of a brother or his death were indeed a weight on the scales . . .

The latest in a long line of well-wishers arrived yesterday, asking for the inevitable "statement" to speed the departure of King Tut. Practically no one in the media has any conception that man is saved by anything but newsprint. If our being here means anything, it must be simply a new and interesting place from which to issue the ultimate words that raise man from the pit. Alas! Along with this, a complete innocence reigns with regard to the extreme delicacy, not to say jeopardy, of the times. We are not about to aggravate the beast who has us, already, by one limb. Very few seem to care about that aspect of things; we are supposed to be grateful that Moloch finds us tasty and wants us for dinner.

April 17

One might consider (in deference to Swift) a traveler to a place where every citizen has, at one time or another, been a prisoner. Everyone. And in the following manner. The guilty are chained by the right foot to a certain spot. The chain is lengthened as they fulfill prescribed rules of conduct, to the point where their freedom allows them increasing opportunity to see, converse with, meet with others of their kind. On a certain day, usually coinciding with the commemoration

of the freedom fight of the nation, all but the most flagrant
prisoners are released from their iron tether, to a more attractive compound. It lies in fact at the center of the nation's
capital. Those "freed" are persuaded that they are now indeed free men and women in a free world. They have "free"
access to all sorts of media: they lounge about, wander the
supermarkets or movie houses, choose the factories or em-
poria or churches or education centers where they wish to
employ or divert themselves. The elements of their freedom
are pointed out to them in careful rehabilitation sessions:
they are reminded that choices abound of the most diverse
forms of the good life.

Still, more or less obscurely understood, the metaphor and
fact of prison are lodged deep in the minds of the people.
Citizens wear on their persons either of two ineradicable realities: chains, or the mark of chains once worn. Those who
are in chains keep up their courage, even their pride in the
reflection that today's chain is longer, even by an inch, than
yesterday's was. Those who are closely held, either because
they have proved mettlesome or because they have recently
been sentenced, dream of tomorrow. So the saying arose: "not
as short as it was, not as long as it will be."

Those released to the "ultimate compound" often display
to one another the marks of their former misery, skin-deep
or cloven to the bone, with all the pride of martyrs uncover-
ing their stigmata. The point of such unveilings is in fact a
gentle, ironic, and prideful sense of competition, together
with a post-Christian sense of accomplishment. Behold: Holy
Mother State, to whom all things are possible, has rehabilitated even me. Which is to say: even I, the most intransigent
and unpromising hulk this side of the Himalayas, have been
so softened and reduced, so pierced with shafts of remorse,
so blessed with secular asperges, so dunged and pruned and
planted as to become a fruitful flower, a domesticated ex-
emplar of whatever is good, whatever noble, whatever worthy
of note in humankind. Behold the state, how she loved me;

with unconscious and touching parody, the citizen holds up his wrists and bares his ankles. The cruel purple cicatrices glow like medals of honor.

Most citizens manage, after a certain number of years at large, to "think free," as it is commonly put. This device, an improved form of an old "Jesus prayer," consists in a pause of normal activity, whether in public or in one's home, several times each day. At the given signal, every citizen repeats a saying attributed to one of the founders of the state; in translation it goes crudely:

"1 2 3 4 5 — I am by gift of Mother State alive."

(a deep breath)

"1 2 3 — Mother State has set me free."

(several deep breaths followed by a leap in the air)

Finally each one turns in the direction of the national obelisk and observes, like a deep-sea diver, a moment of held breath.

A recent national convocation of social planners, engineers, psychiatrists, clergymen, and hardhats has issued a joint statement on the benefits to the nation of such a modest program of renewal, religiously observed. The vice-president for war, peace, health, education, and welfare observed on this occasion: "To think oneself free is beyond doubt to be free. To foster such feelings has long been the aim of this administration."

Still, such efforts are not always availing. Prisoners on short chains have been known so to gnaw away at their bonds, so to madden themselves with mirages of freedom lost, freedom beckoning, as to die of malice and distemper. Like beasts condemned to the water wheel, they dig a circular rut in the earth and lie down in it, never to rise.

Nor has restoration to freedom always healed the wounds

of the past. Some, locked in the stern ring of their early imprisonment, their minds tight as a wound spring, turn and turn about themselves in the streets like animals in pursuit of their tails. Others, more benignly afflicted, chase after the moon in her nightly course, baying like timber wolves; others strive to climb aboard the vaporous rainbows. Still others follow a large but nonetheless locked and circular path in their day-long meanderings. They can be deflected neither by the stern fences of the propertied, nor by watchdogs or guards. They invade alleys, break into homes, front to back, climb over barriers, furniture, leap out of windows, all to preserve the arc which encircles their wandering minds, a band of tightened steel.

For the milder cases, a circular village of healing has been devised. There the victims of genetic damage or undesirable childhoods are gradually cured of their spastic circularity and slowly, ever so slowly, returned to the square world.

April 22

'The chain: not as short as it has been,
     not as long as it will be

A peculiarly empty, nowhere class on Swift left me feeling
as though we were all a company of Yahoos acting out their
pointless cruelties on one another. A long patience indeed is
all that avails to keep one going in such times.

April 29

Life around here is dead as a dog's jawbone, long buried.
Officially speaking, that is. That bone may have bayed at the
moon, turned up its burning eyes in a seasonal love howl,
ground member to member in ecstasy of a small kill, a fight.
No matter; you turn it up with a spade in the spring—dead,
calcified, grimaoing, jeweled like a Neanderthal necklace with
its row of rotting studs . . .
Official death. Everyone is supposed, not to like it precisely (crime like virtue does not reside in the head), but to
put up with it, as a condition of life. You are supposed to be
"resigned" to being here; like someone bearing a terminal

cancer, or (lighter cases) an old woman with an arthritic joint. There is no relief for it except the relief of death itself, or the less drastic medicine of hope—future release to friends, family, life outside.

Sometimes the death pattern gets broken for a while: in spite of all the surveillance of official frowns. You can't put some 750 men into a space designed ungenerously for 550 and not expect some trouble, effervescence, some chemical blowup of inordinate pressure. Sometimes again it is the spectacle of arrivals and departures—comical, tragic-comic, tragic—that makes for the relief. So many types, ages, backgrounds, looks, colors, languages, styles; so many "head changes," so many creepers clinging to the human upright, so many umbilicals, antennae, radiants that go out from him, under the gates, over the walls, joining him to you know not whom, wife and family and partners, neighborhood, pubs, parishes, cronies, bank account. He is like a severed limb still on the move, still twitching with the unbearable catatonic memory of what main body of man he was bloodily torn from.

It all makes for the scent and color of life, a "high" on the death scene. Who will go home tomorrow? He will undoubtedly be leaving a large hole in the fabric of someone's existence. Who will arrive? What new constellations will join? What adjustments, what moving over of friends, to include him, to enrich their circle as it grows larger? What new dreams, illusions, absurdities will be set in motion?

May 3

I want to speak of one man who crossed our lives here for a period of perhaps one month. Why of him? I am not entirely certain beyond the peculiar circumstances of his coming (and going) and the altogether peculiar scent he leaves behind him, an uneasiness, a qualm in the blood, a shadow as of something not wholly exorcised, nor wholly welcomed. I have grieved before about failing to come to grips with another human, have paced the floor in despair for my clumsiness or uncharity or intemperateness. God knows fifty years gives one ample time, if not to resolve his ineptitudes, at least to savor them to the bitter full, even perhaps to learn from them.

He came into the dental clinic one day, put a note into my hands, and left, after announcing his name. The procedure was not as weird as it sounds in the telling; the clinic is busy and inmate visitors are not encouraged. The note announced him in somewhat official prose for the circumstance as Rev. So-and-So, friend of —— and —— and ——. The ticket of entrance was, in short, impeccable. He knew several movement people, he was telling me his credentials were in good order. In days following, we went through the usual ritual of getting acquainted; a bit heated up, for he was no ordinary prisoner, but a minister of some obscure church, ordained (as he explained to someone) at the beginning of his studies instead of at the end . . . It was a good indication of the ass-backward method of his life. He had been in a number of federal joints; most of his sentence passed on the road in the interminable circle the system sets in motion for troublemakers, malcontents, seekers, mental cases, those who for one reason or another make waves in the stagnant pond.

The first serious meeting came in the course of one of our biweekly classes. I had had a sense, obscurely dogging me for a week or two, that all was not as rosy as his smile, his ready tongue, his omnivorous reading habits would indicate. He was somewhat frantic in all his dealings; not with the endemic speed of youth precisely, but more with the spin of a human off balance, someone bent on keeping score, making points, proving himself. Then one night the discussion hit hard; he started a speech on some point or other vaguely connected, vaguely disconnected, with the point at issue in the text In a freewheeling course such as ours, where the participants come and go and the struggle to maintain a core of consistency is hard and close, one puts up with a great deal. But he pushed so hard and careened so erratically, I felt bound to move up the breastworks; there are limits now and then to what one can put up with in the name of free expression. His method was pernicious, his logic was off; and I said so, as strongly as I knew how. I had a sense that I was saving something precious, for myself and for others. In prison, where the structures of reason are under constant assault from authority, it seemed to me a kind of crime for prisoners to ape their keepers' self-indulgent witlessness.

My remarks were badly received. A day or so later I received another letter, this time one of dismissal. I was, so I was told, a typical Jesuit intellectual, venting his mental arrogance on prisoners as he had undoubtedly honed it on students. Bad, bad. Moreover, my theology was faulty; I did not appreciate or convey a sense of the Savior who listened and learned and was patient . . . Another note followed, a few days after, in the same tenor. He stopped attending classes. It became clear in fact that he was struggling to come to grips with some deep-working wound, which I had opened or worsened. I stopped by one day when I observed him alone in the typing room, assured him of my serious reception of his thoughts, and proposed an early meeting. Which never occurred.

He shifted from our class to the leadership of the black history class. One night with some ten or twelve students, he walked into our group, doubling our number. He and his friends sat silent as the grave, while we continued our rap, uneasy with the meaning of this silent invasion. There seemed, in fact, little rhyme or reason for it. Things had grown dull in his class; he had proposed that those who wished come in and "see how the man was doing it." Another raveled strand in a general tangle.

He took to attending Sunday Mass, playing the piano gustily, singing with more will than skill a hymn or two; a bit off key, a bit too fast, an edge of the frantic. Used or inured to the spiritless hebdomadal gruel, equal parts cliché and inert moralizing, the middle-aged Celtic aficionados would snicker in their prayer books. South Boston had never seen the like. On Palm Sunday Phil and I joined him in a reading of the Passion at Mass. He took the part of Christ; read badly, stumbled over unfamiliar words, his timing off.

He was trying hard, it could not be doubted. Too hard? One had a sense he was playing both sides of the street, buying here, selling there, pushing to win a bargain in either place. Black power to the blacks, a generous measure of hate for whitey; and with us, a more complaisant role, a search for a place in the "common struggle."

None of it quite came off. But within a week or two, his own head came off. One night he fought morosely with a white over a seeming trifle. It was a matter of a television program. (To convicts, television and food are serious matters indeed, matters of substance, of machismo, of access to rights —narrow gates to the world.) He and his opponent were placed in solitary a few days later. I saw the other depart in chains for Lewisburg. The same day, he himself was led out, to take the road for Marion. The vicious cycle was under way once more. He had failed to make it in one more compound.

Would he ever make it, in any compound, including the larger one stretching coast to coast to which birth (or death) has assigned us, to which all of us will one day, ironically, be "released"?

May 8—Eve of my fiftieth birthday

What more fitting place to celebrate fittingly this fitting day. Ha! I feel in my bones and cranium thirty-five at the least. I want to start all over. I want to write one immortal line. I want to perform one good non-violent act. I want to re-activate all the dead cells that cling to my skull like last year's honeycomb, sweet and musty. I want to undergo a (faint) trauma (I do) when I pause in that last breath before sleep and the stone in my gut speaks like a Magian: *what have you done with the years?* My God, do not remember the waste since ordination, since entering the Jesuits, since entering jail. I want to get out of here; I want to get Philip out of here. I want the end of all indicting of uncommon virtue for being uncommon. I want America to get reborn into gentleness. I want to survive, if I survive, as A. J. Muste did, or to go out tomorrow with grace. I want to die if I have to die (O my God) like Merton—in an unexpected way, with my saddlebags on. I want Mother to walk again, to see her. I want Jerry's eye to be healed. I want all jails to go up in smoke, like a kicked dry toadstool. I want to walk in the woods and kneel down in a sodden place and stretch out on pine needles and never get up. I want to metamorphose into a pine tree growing out of a rock wall on Champlain shore. I want everyone to have the above-mentioned gifts. All swordfish to be liberated from the mercury in their guts . . . To hang around sane and sound for a few years in which the above may be seen occurring . . .

A rainy, dense, dreary, befogged day on the compound. I slept for an hour and dreamed (unusual happening) thusly: Was summoned by the big blare to "control." Told by the lieutenant to "follow me." Led *outside*; nothing seemed unusual. At the foot of a hillside I had never seen was a graveyard, an open grave, fresh mound. He said: "Step in there!" I did; he drew a gun. (All day in the fog, the sound of gunfire outside the dream; prison personnel are required by law to spend one day every six months practicing for the apocalypse). It dawned on me: this bird is going to shoot me. I shouted out NO! "Who said I was to be shot?" He hesitated, perplexed. "Who said so? Wait, I'll check." He came back: "You were right, it's all a mistake." I climbed out of the grave, out of the dream.

(This being continued at the window after lights out) Strange sense of recognition here, as of taking notes under bombs in Hanoi, or in the grave (at the window by meager light from the compound's unblinking federal eye).

To say thank you for being in the right place, with the thanks a flower might want to utter for being in the right soil, a bird in the right sky. The concomitant responsibility (what a weird word for conscious flower or man) to wear the true colors of one's existence, to trace the right geometry in the heavens, the pure form following on the purity of existence . . . Knowing that to die in such circumstance is to lodge that in the earth which shall enrich the earth, that the risen Christ is the in-vigorating which allows these lives to occur, and the hand and smile behind them, in the lurid, meager light granted by the times and powers . . .

(A project for the autumn unfolds, the opening of the Kennedy Center for the Performing Arts in D.C.; New York Philharmonic director Bernstein wants to come and talk turkey about my prose and poetry for a Mass on opening night. I am of two minds on the subject; is one to play that game of the '60s again, fiddling while the underground is afire, artifacting while the rats gnaw and shit in the rotten wainscoting? Resistance can be a work of art, as Catonsville showed, and what extraordinary results on and off Broadway attended on that event! We'll have to see . . .)

I want to get lost on B. Island again. I want to walk the fog and stones and sands with Phil, if not in this despensation, in another to come . . .

Hoped to hang all this on a star, but none was out tonight. So make the best; wishing for wishing's sake.

The radio still rackets away at midnight, obstacle to contemplation, sanity, joy—they turn it up when the lights go out so that in accord with the Brimstone Manual the men can neither (1) read nor (2) sleep. Then the thing seems to seep off rather than turn off, as though it had carbolic acid in leaky veins. It just dribbled out.

It is midnight. Fifty years ago my mother bore me. She could not have more exactly shot me to this place if she had loosed an arrow from a bow with the eye of an Iroquois. I thank her, and my father, who rests in Christ, and Philip, in whose heart I rest. I thank the living Christ. I adjust my bib and take prison for my choice birthday portion. And like Oliver Twist, ask for seconds.

I can almost sense the prayer and thought of others straining in my direction tonight. I turn prayer gently around, for the children, the wounded, the dying, the bombed. A judge said today, sentencing four in New York for conspiracy to bomb (maximum sentence), "We cannot countenance this irrationality." Jesus Judge, echo that one in a voice of thunder in the ears of our uniformed and civilian killers.

The silence comes down like a gift, a benediction. Happy half century, Daniel. Would that all priests were as fortunate tonight as you. I grin like a sleepless monkey at the full moon, thanking the birth Man.

May 14 (scribbled at the window, in darkness)

sense of the heavy burden of people, millions of people.
the nation becalmed and rotting like a Liberty scow
lashed to the Hudson pier; rats, rotting, the captain mad
or drunk.
sense of the heavy burden of those who resist; the meeting of this afternoon, the lawyers, their suffering with us.
Philip, as though my own soul were enduring in another
body; Liz, her goodness and calm and strength. The
priests, Mary, everyone at one on essentials, a sense of
the common bond, our faith.
sense of the strangeness of spring in this place, nature
going about her work, the leaves, the cherry blossoms,
forsythia, tulips in the compound.
the many worlds revolving, careening, conflicting in this
place. The suffering of families, the rupture of affections,
the clinging to a few comforts, coffee, commissary, drugs.
the game up close; the game of authority, uneasiness,

watchfulness, trials of patience and strength
the faces: chaplains, shrinks, clerks, hacks, strawberry
faces, vegetable faces, conniving faces, fearful intemperate
hate-ridden uncertain dollar faces; the big meaty faces of
those who make it, the faces of women crossing the compound, sex on legs, protected by hacks, followed by the
looks & desires & love & hate of the convicts
the averted looks of the rehabilitators, the ambulating
briefcases, examiners, official types, watchdogs of the keys
of the kingdom the mess hall vibrating like a drum, bus-
tling like a Horn & Hardart.
7 hacks protecting the virginal meat; one piece per
Sunday Mass, the Anglo service of the dead; the crooks
and racists & good men all tossed in the salad of silence
and routine, the chaplain's dead voice; food, religion, rehabilitation; 1 pot of rancid spaghetti
relief, shining like stars in a night fog; the 7 or 8 young
resisters those fireflies, those visionaries smiling their
secret smile
visitors room, vibrations of suffering   separation   impossible
glances of reconciling love   separation bridged   children
running & playing & laughing, the hack watchful as a
peregrine hawk for the covert cigarette or sandwich
the lieutenant's thoroughbred virtuous stride, a puma on
the prowl

May 17

Houyhnhnms—FABLE—Aesop   and   La   Fontaine—not
Jesus or Socrates—Parables
                    Zen and Hindu—yes
Question of what a human being is: transposed now, not
to large or small people, but to the animal world. Horses,
plain, offer an ideal; Yahoos, murky, none at all.

Swift is haunted by the question, it seems to be the only question.

He believes (1) the fauna of the natural world

(2) very large or very small imaginary creatures

(3) owners of a spaceship and the land below all offer hints.

It must be admitted, though—the horses come off best. They are nearest the ideal, even the beloved, community.

But the ideal is, as always, scored by imperfection. Whether S. wishes to admit it as a serious sin or not, the Horses have enslaved the Yahoos to the point where the Yahoos are quite resigned to acting out their masters' image of them; filthy, voracious, strangers to good order.

The author quite accepts the Horses as a human prototype. The Horses, on the contrary, never quite accept him. He is at best an improved Yahoo who could never conceivably make it as a Horse. Quite a comedown for the Englishman!

For a long time the a. is looking beyond the H., looking for the human hand and brain in this marvelous "improvement" of the horse. Why could he not search out the man beyond man-superman? The complement to his own species is obvious. Swift stops the search; he says wisdom as well as common sense faces the conclusion: there is no human genius beyond the Horses. No more is there a superman in the image of man. Indeed, the search would suggest that one stop looking for gods whose dubious claim to fame is that they produced so monstrous a creature as this one, man.

H. means the "perfection of nature" (259). Thus to the Greek, "man is the measure of all things," as to Horses, men would say: they are exemplars of brute beauty; in relation to man, strictly instrumental. Houyhnhnms would say of Yahoos: they are the very bottom of the barrel of creation, the quintessence of pig filth, cat cruelty, poll parrot cunning, dog laziness, jackal stench.

But the Yahoos would say of the world of noble Houys:

"Fuck you." Which is the slave's way of declaring his alienation from a system of values that works admirably for those in possession, but not at all for those in slavery.

We may say also of Swift's episode: yes, your Horses are all very well; but like a good Englishman you have once more verified the old saying: only the winners get to write history.

Or if now and again a loser gets to tell his story, only under peril of himself becoming a winner, or because he wants to show how the loser really *won*—another way of intimating to those who can read the seismograph: yes, they buried Jesus, and Constantine leads the tourists to the tomb!

How could Swift write a history of the Yahoos when he despised men so deeply? It would have required paying heed to the principle: *Nemo gratis Yahoo.* Slobs, even ultimate slobs, are not born, they are made. Immaculate power goes hand in hand with filthy powerlessness. Nietzsche would have said the H.'s need the Yahoos as the master needs the slave, and vice versa; at least after a while, when the relationship is so strong as to seem beyond rupture. Fanon would have said the Yahoos must eat horseflesh and drink horse blood before a Yahoo will ever be a man. Jerry Rubin: the Yahoos waste a lot of perfectly good shit on one another. Shame on you Yahoos. How come all those Horses look so clean?

The H.'s have an admirable non-violent community. They neither lie, cheat, defraud, pillage, nor kill. They are thus far ahead of men who commonly do all these things. But there is one defect in their virtuous arrangement: they hold slaves. And in the manner of all slaveholders, they do this without noticing it. Their defect would be indictable only if they were to hold other H.'s in bondage. They do not do this. To hold a Yahoo in bondage is not only not a crime in their sensitive legal system, it is a virtuous act necessitated by the criminality of the Yahoos themselves: we have to keep them from doing harm to themselves. (We destroy them to save them.)

It is unfortunate Swift did not contrive a way to voyage among the Yahoos.

"I will make you fishers of men." Yes, but by all means let's hear from the fish. Some of them perversely don't want to be fished.

(The story is told in Bogotá of Cardinal Concha in '65 appointing a new batch of military chaplains, whose chief ministry was to the soldiers who hunted down the guerrillas. Camilo Torres asked to be appointed to the men being shot at. His request was denied; he went ahead anyway, and was promptly shot and killed.)

Which is to say, for a man among H.'s, life may be humiliating. But what would happen to a man who went among the Yahoos, who were slaves to the H.'s? What would it mean if he led a Yahoo revolt?

H.'s are irrelevant. The question is: can technological man be a virtuous man, i.e., can he evolve and sustain structures that will be pro-human, even as technology makes him arbiter of death?

July 3

First thing I have to report after the near apocalypse of June 9, which still finds me weak as a bird wet from the egg: there's an inmate who stuffs the bridal moths in his mouth one by one and swallows them. No worse, I suppose, than chocolate grasshoppers.

July 4

—A long silence here is due to my efforts to get in and out of death. I shall be (in fact am) heard from again.

—Half of life they say is patience. I know that now, in my game. The other half is impatience.

—On June 9 I was taking a dental checkup, consequent on the cracking of a cuspid a few days before. The doctor had begun with a routine injection; five minutes of waiting, then he wanted to know, as I had winced under the drill, was I still in pain? I was (obviously). He filled another needle holder and injected me again, this time on the outside gum . . . Thus began, in a sense, a comedy of errors that was to turn in very short order into something very near tragedy for your correspondent. The second needle; it was like shouting the right infernal word over Mount Etna, it was a match tossed into tinder.

The dentist wandered off to allow the potion to take its course. He even called me over to help with an impression for dentures. I wandered over, feeling vaguely dizzy, unwell; comforting myself as usual with the formula of the "unchoiced," i.e., so who feels good in a place like this? Not I certainly . . . Back to the chair and in some minutes, about two I think, into a faint, into shock, into massive paralysis of lungs. An hour's tense and turbulent effort followed, to keep me moored this side of the Styx.

I was curiously in and out of the happening; detached, at times "floating above," struggling like a blue baby the better part of an hour to make it, to keep breathing. I remember the dentist picking up my hand, which was icy and blue and stiffened, shaking his head with disbelief, pointing to my feet, which were not about to go anywhere, ever; just look at this.

They were free to. So was I. When they rushed me across the hall for oxygen, I recovered enough balance to begin saying a few prayers.

Close as all this was to the final curtain, I remember it as a curiously secular event. Which is to say, there was nothing baroque, gothic, or Byzantine about it. It was strictly twentieth-century tawdry; sweaty, brutal, racing against time.

I could look up from where I lay into the impassive spider

face of a crawling wall clock, thus knew how long how long at every moment to wrap up a life, to keep it unskeining. Mine.

Philip was finally there and I reached up and kissed him and as I recall told him not to worry: it would be all right. For once, right. It was that very nearly total confidence in the good upper left-hand breast pocket convenience bequeathed to me (and to all six of us) by Dad-o. He would have reserved a bottomless imperial contempt for any invasion of "heart trouble" into the linear anatomy. Harrr-rumph! When he died, it was with sound heart and lungs, going under totally and grandly, like Atlantis or the one hoss shay.

How curious it was, a few hours later, to breathe again without wrench or strain! How curious to breathe at all! I felt as though it were the miracle of the end of days; as though every insect and lowly flower were conspiring with me in this miracle, renewed with every instant, the gentle rise and fall of the recumbent, all but human form of the universe. I lay there spent, all eye, all ear, skinless as a heart; was this a second birth? It was the nearest I would come to it in all the years of life.

They diagnosed "massive allergic shock." It was like most of life today, unpredictable as lightning or wildfire.

The difficulty, as I glance back, was not with dying, which was a fairly simple affair, rather in the course of things, like a self-conscious eclipse or the gobbling of a smaller fish by a larger mouth . . . The difficulty is getting one's customary clothing back on, getting back to life, getting enough of that sweet and vanishing air to keep one on the move . . .

So here I am on the compound, dumped back into time; as the Buddhists would say, for recycling. All is wheel. I have bowed out of the dental office. I am afflicted with gout in the right elbow and the neck, with a hernia in the esophagus. Grave medicos put heads together in my presence and cluck commiseratingly about my deteriorating frame. When my

oval ivories loosen in their sockets from now on, I shall flock
to the leaves as though tasting, foretasting, dramatizing the
onset of death.

I hear Mr. Bernstein was listening to the "Holy Outlaw"
sermon (underground in Philly) and came on a title for his
celebration at the Kennedy Center in D.C.—"A Mass for the
Unborn." But what will Nixon think? . . .

July 5

People ask: what is it like in prison? We should be about
more than supplying a weather report from within the orgone
box . . . One obvious response, perhaps an unkind one,
would be: come in and find out! But people are desperately,
inaudibly asking sometimes: please share your lives with us;
you have obviously come on something for yourselves, help
us also . . . In response to such perplexities one ought to
share even the atmosphere and pressures and madness of life
under lockup.

What strikes me is the need of a "center" from which to
deal with the issues, moods, assaults, chills and fevers, se-
ductions, distractions of such a place. To say this is of course
to add very little to one's reflections on life. What good is
the centrifugal man—anywhere?

This is our discipline and our glory. For months after coming into prison, when I was dragging my tail exhausted
through the daily round, I could only cry: preserve in us the
spirit which brought us to Catonsville . . . Now after a sojourn in the valley of death there is less need for such a
prayer. It has been granted. Or so it seems; but we shall see.

Here the defeats inflicted as though by a madman's flail,
on all and sundry skulls, near and far—here it comes close,
comes home. Everyone is an "instance" of that widespread
defeat, everyone is a walking dossier. How few men are left

among all! And yet—when that is acknowledged, how quickly one comes to add—how much goodness, kindness, longing for friendship and courtesy and dignity remain after all! Those who do not have the courage to be men long to be in the vicinity of those who have shown virtue under stress. Man resists being broken at least as firmly as he resists being reborn.

The stalemated intelligence; many of the youngers have read everything, been everywhere. And they are here in prison perhaps for sound reason, perhaps not. But they are not greatly improved in their soul's fiber merely by finding their intellect. Alas, by no means. Their eyes scan afar, they see much, it is a joy to converse with such lively minds. But their feet remain planted, like Markham's slack-jawed clod with the hoe. They are no more in control of a moral universe than was he. Indeed, if we count all the potential granted the one and denied the other, it is clear that the plowboy has the advantage. He at least has some connection with the earth to draw upon. These have never had that; moreover they have suffered the disconnection of almost every human relationship, through the cruel wound inflicted by prison itself, and its consequent stigma.

To renounce one world does not mean that one has discovered the real world. In most cases, as the event has shown, one has renounced a relative good (church, middle class, priesthood) only to bury himself deeper in the evil which that renunciation, to any real view, both mitigated and mediated.

The light of the world strikes in vain: no fire

"There was nothing wrong with our citizens; they forgot to be modest, that was all." Not something forgotten easily, especially as the plague is still in the air. To forget modesty is to embrace hubris, and therefore the destruction by the gods—whose godhead is the equivalent renunciation of hubris in the world, and toward one another.

An element of this modesty is one's will to keep a firm and lucid center at the labyrinth—where there dwells not a monster but a void; the void of will-less acceding—"to what is, in any case, inevitable; war etc." But one is mauled by the void no less than by the monster; there is no blue air there, but a chaos contra naturam.

The modesty is the simple assertion, so near one's being as to be carved on stone; that to be in prison in a time of such official disposal of human lives is the logical and right decision. And one is called to live and die in peace for such a conviction.

Having not yet brought my life under the unified spell of personal inwardness, I am at the mercy of a nearly encompassing personal perplexity and depression of spirit. This is the inward noisome form of self-waste whose ear-drowning blare is all around me, a bottomless sea of noise and distraction. I must surface somehow, but it is a long, grievous struggle—with bad health, bad advice, bad and directionless thrashing about. I am unable to take decisions which are right for my soul, for my moment, for my "others." Humiliated by indecision—too much alone, too exhausted and wasted, little changed even after the nearly fatal plunge of a few weeks ago. I do not love people to any consistency or purpose, I seek out the attractive and winning and shrink from being the gentle man with the others. Strung between two absurd poles of distraction and self-absorption; loss of height, tension, grace, fearlessness.

Little time or will for meditation, dread of the gift self-discovered in the giving, a breakup of central unity; a further scattering in a time of harvest. Pulling the plug on the spirit. The dark night—another literary fiction. I would wish quite simply to be able to live with the equanimity and surplus with which I was able to face death. To relieve the suffocation of prison with the purity of means which might make a harvest even of such waste. An ill-tempered clavichord gives out notes sour as whey . . . The mindless humiliation of that near death! Who will make of me a Philip to Philip; as he was a Philip to me?

When others declare they can "move with Jesus," what is this to me? I stand there like sticks and stones which the light of the world strikes in vain and glances off; no fire.

NOTICE TO WARDEN

Two months have passed since I applied for and won transfer from the dental clinic to the education department. (You may check this with Mr. Markley and Dr. Kaplan, with whom the arrangements were made.)

A week ago I was assigned (after many inquiries and no action on this transfer) as orderly in Boston house. Since then in spite of ill health I have been subject to special harassment by the officer in charge. His ordinary stock in trade is abuse, threat, and obscenity. He has ordered me to do work for which I am physically incapable, under threat of "a bust." He told the other orderly to "watch me at work."

My usual nights are sleepless, due to gastric difficulties already known to the medical doctor. The extreme physical weakness also continues.

In view of the above I am announcing the following. I will bear with this absurd and degrading charade for one week more. By July 10, I shall expect to be transferred to education department; if not, I shall have no recourse but to refuse to work or eat, and retire to the hole.

Meantime my doctors and lawyers are being kept informed of the situation.

July 7

I am back at Gandhi (Fischer's life), which is a little like saying: I am back eating again. I could long for many things; could long, for instance, that there were one hundred Gandhis in ten cultures, translating into local gestures the one root intuition of love and truth for which Gandhi lived and died. Alas alas, we have only the Pentagon Papers—to record the last ten years of infamy. It is clear also that the Kennedys were only a more sophisticated version of the old game, and that they assembled from the Charles River, a tough team of tinkers and engineers to do the murder game with new salt and dash. No go!

I was reflecting this A.M. on what one presumably lives by, and how this has changed or been deflected or deepened by the year in prison.

I see no reason to say or write anything different from what I would have set down on the same subject thirty years ago, when I entered the Jesuits. I am a fundamentalist who wishes to erect a worthy dwelling on a necessary base.

I live according to a meager capacity for good—whose deficits are a cause of chagrin and even shame to me. No matter, or little matter. I am determined now on a course whose direction was granted me—a gift; and whose outline is by now so clear there can be no serious deflection. It is to die in fidelity to the basis on which I have lived; so to live as to offer some substance to others.

This is a big order indeed.

Last night I watched the pale scraps of moths clinging to the young trees in the compound. The red maple was stripped bare to its bones by some errant genius; it is as though the moths flock—

July 8

The reviewers are on my back again for *Dark Night*. How come he fools around with a lousy garden or park scene when we want serious politics? Chop chop. As a Jesuit wrote: How come he reads the death of Socrates on B. Island instead of, say, *Das Kapital?* Chop chop. Therefore I append several sources of inevitable confusion:

1) The fun principle, rightly conceived and judiciously applied, issues from the heart of the responsibility principle. Otherwise fun hangs in mid-air like a clown's fart after a goat's meal. But what are we to do for those who are all work and no play? I think we will condemn them to flying Benjamin Franklin's kite strung on wire in a thunderstorm. Or to keeping his diary, the first of a dreary, innumerable series by serious Pelagians amok.

2) A man is to be forgiven if he does only one thing (or two things) well. Nature, otherwise prodigal, grants us only one apiece of Benjamin Franklin, McGeorge Bundy, Henry

Kissinger. There are the rest of us, the pollen children who in principle don't know any better. We know (clumsily) only the next step in a process we call, for want of wit, How to give your life and feel lousy about it. Or, Here I stand, I can do no other, since the concrete is almost dry underfoot.

I guess I had best put it down flat and risk the results: I had rather be sitting here on dry ice in the 90-degree heat on the scorched ground of justice while the Rusty Juggernaut revs up for another day of rounding up the guilty—THAN—flying with Henry Kissinger as he runs the Siagon-San Clemente Shuttle devising ways and means of evading the latest VC offer anent prisoners and war's end. So there. Confession: I don't know much about a human future, how to hold it, how to fold it. Henry Kissinger and Richard Nixon know infinitely less, a zero reduced to the head of a pin reduced to an *ens rationis* on whose barb flies themselves count the sooty derelict angels of their malfeasance. O come, all ye faithful!

3) I know much about diplomats and their invincible propensity to lies, abstractions, and feasibilities. I had the Pentagon Papers by heart before they were written, let alone published, I could have given them off by heart to the *Times* five years ago, while they were being enacted. We dim-bulbed Cassandras, in madhouses or jails for the duration, are on a life trip between evil in high places, good in low. They call the clue Original Sin, when they call it at all. It's the bone for which Mother Hubbard is known here and there. So it wouldn't stick in her dog's craw, she buried it in her cellar; the bare cupboard, so to speak, but the creaky stair nonetheless. We think (when we venture to think at all) of Definitive Solutions, Skeletons That Walk, and finally "The Night the Bed Fell In." We are correct.

Await everything, expect nothing

They give a few of us a few minutes on the hill
The flowers dust your shoes, climbing up, the sky
lifts like a silk umbrella, faces compose themselves
like clouds, rain near. Never was hill taken
by shoulders, against odds, so dear. You stretch out arms
to dearest flesh, human cross to cross . . .

The place of "Never Quite." The difference between the measure of one's life, simply taken, and the shape of life, *there* to be encountered. There ought to be a difference rightly; the difference ought to be manageable.

Here, the perpetual sense of being off base. You set down a tray on the table and settle down to eat, and the table tilts toward you or away and the food follows, the liquids with a vengeance. The world is off base in large things or small. A man who commands respect for any one or many reasons, is denied respect, he has no cause to show, his life does not signify.

It is, of course, in large measure, a state of things that happens when a judgment-with-muscle sets in motion a whole host of minor decisions, all of them flubbed in the course of vindicating, beefing up, pushing further the wrong Big Brother first declared was right. You're damn right he's right, the henchmen say loudly over the compound speaker. Thousands of affirmations adding up to a ruinous, injuring *no* in the minds of all the inmates. Yes, they go to the factories at the sound of the buzzer; no, their hearts knock like pendulums at the walls of their cage. Like wrecker's balls? Maybe, but who or what will fall first?

The lieutenant is on the prowl tonight. He's the one with the dark glasses and long cigar who in another reel of the same inferior film, made, say, in the '20s, would double as the lower-echelon thug doing *his* thing. Cops and robbers. Somewhere in the middle is the decent man, sometimes a guard who (as in today's episode) can't quite stomach stripping prisoners to the buff, in spite of orders. But sometimes, much more often, an inmate takes the manifold bitternesses into his soul, the amputations from fruitful existence, and bleeds in secret and has grace to smile in public—for the sake of the others who bleed too and miraculously are his brothers. So humanity of spirit cuts across the stereotypes of high, low, and middle America. Prison is really the place where the strip searcher is Death. And all of us, from the warden to myself, line up in confusion and shame, to have the cheeks at both ends of our anatomy spread wide for contraband pseudo-life, pseudo-liberty, pseudo-happiness. Simple, final; in the absence of metaphor the mind dies, and the spirit grows discouraged.

Mimeoed papers came from a friend who pursues, with good heart and deft pen, the invigoration of the Jewish community. I feel with him, having wrestled with the same hopes for years, from the pages of Worship to the secret cells of the Inquisitor. He still tries with the liturgy; Philip and I have largely given up on that. Nothing quite like a prison man to turn one from a paschal candle to a pillar of salt . . . At one time his Jewish community destroyed a symbolic golden calf, a toy bomber, etc., to celebrate a new Exodus. I could not help thinking, this is taking hunks of salt from the dead pillar to pour in the wounds of the living . . . "If you had only taken a few files from Catonsville, you would have made your point," our judge mourned publicly. Exactly. He would have been off the hook, so would we. Symbolic acts are not indictable. The golden calf, a real one, rages in the world like a bull of Bashan; the real bombers fly while the toy breaks up.

Our crime was to draw on symbols to break real laws; we really walked out of Pharaoh's land and Pharaoh's church as well; witness our present geography, witness the silence and anger of the church toward us. Jesus really broke temple laws and the law of the land, his criminality is not to be doubted—witness the evidence assembled against Him, the sentence meted out. My faith does not allow me, at the present moment, to give a tinker's damn about making symbolic use of real events. I am called to create new events in the spirit of the older ones. Jesus declaring himself Light of Exodus, Water from the rock, Temple of true worship—these are always connected with a real decision about the disposition, consciously made, of His own life. The truth of light, water, temple is vindicated in one's being burnt out, poured out, destroyed, and then miraculously re-created, gathered, risen from death by an act that surpasses the powers of this world.

It may be the vitality of the people is heightened when men, step by step, dramatize the symbols anew. It may be. Or it may be that men live and die among the dusty stage props of an opening night—grease paint, costuming, and postures—never breaking through to inhabit the real world, to run through it in non-violent rampage against those who rattle its keys and level its guns. What is more subversive than true symbolic action? or more seductive and amnesiac than toys, occasions, memories, mere recall?

. . . A very special atmosphere, a special grace, a gift of time and place and fraternity not granted to many.

Entailing, I would think in my saner moments, a special gratitude in response to predilection; as of a father for his son.

The dissolution of those childish "norms of conduct and response" in virtue of which God must prove something, lay something on the line, before He merits a responsive love.

No. Here we have, in iron, blood, concrete, stifling days and nights, denial of horizon, variety, laughter, spontaneity— the moral orgone box in which may be concentrated, for the sake of the future, those energies which otherwise are wasted and lost.

The loss of the God whose Name has been debased, whose savor is lost on the wooden tongue of the unbelieving believer; what does He provoke among high and low, educated and ignorant, consciously acute and dormant—except a yawn? We must offer Him a blood transfusion.

By refusing the ignorant gifts of normalcy which belie Him and ourselves.

In such a sense, we give Him life—by expecting of Him only that He allow us to be treated (and maltreated) as man.

Diminishing thereby to the vanishing point the line between those who believe for the wrong reason and those who disbelieve for the wrong reason; which is generally the attempt to fill up the empty space between existence and life.

False hope has been the opium. True hope awaits everything—and expects nothing. Thus I can admit my fear and dread of never issuing from the iron mines into the light of day. And live with such fear. And draw to my side as brothers all who live out that drama, and do not know why any more than myself.

And cease at length to be troubled, knowing that to be in the dark night is to breathe there, and embrace the terror of pre-dawn, for myself and in measure for the others as well. Brother, father, friend, enemy, "opposite number." But never manipulable idol. Let Him speak the first word about Himself. Let Him have the last word. Let death (recently all but undergone) be as opaque an event as life has been. He never speaks. No one was there. I believe. *Non in multiloquio.* Afterward will be the after word. It cannot be presumed beforehand.

We may come to the point where we, especially Phil (at whose Passion I am an eyewitness), can offer a larger measure of steadfastness. Maybe. If others love us, if they hate or dread or avoid us—or if they draw near. It may be they will have a sense of having struck against something living; those who with others, for others, endured the turn of the screw. Thus they also are steeled to endure, to be of good heart, in like circumstance. And that may be all. That may rightly be all.

The old doctrine of purgatory arose out of a need to make justice a subtler and therefore a "juster" proposition. It was one thing to cast sinners into hell and quite another to grant heaven to those who had not "paid up." A middle ground was necessary; people felt cheated, they felt even that too easy a "way" was cheating themselves of the fully immaculate nature of glory.

So jail was envisioned—by the Quakers no less? They thought it was one thing to whip a man or half-drown a woman or leave a malefactor in the stocks—and another to let such go scot free. Let them think on their sins, give them "time"!

So the birds come home to nest. I sit here in this steaming caldron of a New England jail, paying my debts to church and state. The present is as vivid to me as any time of pain or conscious prognosis—that outer world, a pure future. Just as someday in the normal course of things, *this* will partake of all the freaky remoteness of a dream awakened from and that world will have seized me in its talons and borne me to its nest, irrecoverable to this; as this is, by dint of steel and shotguns and justice unappeased, to that.

This A.M. being Sunday I staggered to my feet, awakened a perfervid sleep-ridden Catholic neighbor, swallowed a cup of coffee, and hastened to Sunday Mass.

In the beginning of our stint, Philip and I undoubtedly asked ourselves with the pain of the fish in whose gullet the hook still drags and bleeds—why go at all?

We were fish, but ambulatory; taken, but with a will all the fiercer for being thrown into the man's tank. We hated and dreaded a Mass celebrated (?) over the wounded bodies of others—who, if the truth were known, were related not to the man but to the first murdered ichthus of all.

Anyway, we went for reasons which remain as obscure to us as to others of our friends. Prison religion is a function of prison; rather than a relief, rather than a cry of rage or a compassionate hand or a brother's ear or a burning word of truth. It is an adjective tacked to the stone wall—religious prison is prison at its most.

You have to taste it, along with the tasteless food, the third-rate movies, the dog-eared reject books, the slam of bars and bolts. Another affront, a reminder in a series of smart blows, that one is being punished anew, that his existence is third-rate, that he is up shit crick without oars.

After a few months the rage subsides and your psyche, not recovered but reconciled, settles down, at Mass as everywhere else, to the first business of all, which is communal survival. You perch there like the half-drowned dove of the deluge, your house broken like matchsticks under you. It is possible in the strange land to sing the songs of Israel. "We will call upon You, we will live."

Out of possibly 400 or 450 prisoners some 30 attend. To the chaplain the failure is squarely on the shoulders of the men. Irreligion is a part of criminality. Which in an ironic way that utterly escapes his poll's powers is true. Jesus would probably have fled him, and his service, like a seventh plague.

The Catholics are led by a limp and spineless priest who does his job—which is precisely to be unconcerned, lazy, and spiritless. At nine, the Protestants begin under the aegis of a dominie who, for all his hair-raising foibles, is nervy and devious as a senior hack. He comes among the broken and bowed like a serpent in a starving nest—woe upon woe. Out of the Air Force by Oklahoma religion; no better melding of fundamentalist ignorance and state chauvinism could be imagined.

I have not knelt in his shrine of Baal, so cannot report on its signs and wonders.

During our priest's Gospel mauling I covertly open a small paperback—lately Eliot's *Four Quartets*—and so comfort myself. With no intent of superiority; the object, I remind myself, is survival. That noble poem offers, if not a way, a hint of the dignity of ignorance and deprivation. One is required to dwell at peace in the stews and sweats of his purgatorial fires. Yes.

We receive the tab of bread with what faith we can muster, leaving to another time and place the many questions that inevitably arise. We receive with what grace we can muster the vacuous blessing of the necromancer, who departs, in effect, until next week's burial bell summons him to his thing (not ours) once more. He has a seven-day hiatus ahead. So, in another fashion, do we. He will spend the days, as far as one can judge, artfully dodging the human cries that thicken the air around him, inaudible to his ears, as they are to the ears of all the fusty functionaries who with him stoke the engines of juggernaut.

Sunday clanks along. We eat, a kind of brunch and a midafternoon supper. There are a ball field, three handball courts, one basketball court, benches to take the sun. Now and again a movie. The loudspeaker blares out as though attached to the mouth of a great bull, in command of Animal Farm, the names and numbers of those lucky enough to have a visitor. There are two acres of ground for 780 men.

Someone has stripped the most beautiful of the struggling young trees of its bark—it shivers and gleams, a copper-haired dancer in some romantic ballet just before death. The "girls" preen and pout in the doorways, the muscle artists lift their steel worlds like Greek gods gone to seed. There is a secret hope running like incandescence through a dark place; it consumes manhood even while it graces it. Release! Do your own time! How often one hears it—disclaimed in public, honored dishonorably in secret. It breaks a man to be here among amputees and broken men; it scatters a man's parts to be the implicit agent of payoff. They do not fall away because of their crimes, as described in the indictments; they die because there is no reason offered them to be loyal, to be free of spirit, to be uncompromising of speech, to give their lives for others . . .

There are about ten basic obscenities that cover all situations. A few of the guards borrow one or another on occasion. Most eschew them entirely; the most malignantly cruel are invariably the most puritanical of mouth. An old Orthodox Jew, appalled to have bodily functions so publicly appealed to, sickly with the memory of evasion and mulled religion, reproves the voluble backsliders. To no avail.

Merton: a Buddha with sweat on his brow

For some reason that escapes me, I think of Merton a good deal during these days. Death is the kind of "refining" fact that makes a friend finally available to the concentrating soul. Maybe my own near death gave me some small insight into the equal absurdity of his passing . . . In any case, how nearly impossible it was to write of him, since his death, right up to the recent present! His memory was like a constriction in the throat; it would not pass, whatever the effort. Now I find most of that sorrow dissolved; perhaps in the understanding of our common lot? . . . In any case, what occurs to me this A.M. is gratitude for his transparent bunkum-free, almost rowdy character. Reverent hagiographers cannot quite bring themselves to assay his weight, his mettle, his free speech. He seemed to me so much a "given" that one came only very gradually to any understanding of his interior life. He acted with the spontaneity and confidence of one in command of his own freedom—so good a nature that one sought in vain, if he came to poke the specimen, for the presence of grace. Nature, grace; the distinction was not helpful in his case; prayer, sacraments, community, discipline, love of life had conspired to make him more intensely and fruitfully son of God, son of Adam.

I think he would have taken jail in stride, with a certain hilarity, an eye for tragic and comic analogies with the monastery.

I often reflect that my conditions for prayer, study, writing are better than the ones he describes in the monkery, at least in the beginning.

For him liberation took the road from monastery to the world. My own journey is a funny-bone reversal of same. I have lived and traveled almost everywhere on the planet; and at length come like an exotic beast in a net to the lockup, the zoo. I claim the text literally for myself: "When you were younger you went where you would. Now that you are grown old, another shall bind you and lead you where you would not go . . ." But in his case as in mine, there should in all justice be pause for wondering, even mazed tribute, to the One who overturns all applecarts, and makes of the debris turnovers for the king. "And when the pie was opened . . ."

I remember our first meeting. I had been greeted at the airport the night before by the taciturn brother of Abbot Fox, who drove me the fifty or so miles to the monastery; as I recall we drove without a word, except for a few inanities I offered to dislodge the glacial silence. When we arrived there was a late cold supper but no Merton; the great silence had begun. In my room was personal note of welcome, word he would see me in the A.M.

He came himself to my cell, that short, electric, stock-taking hull of a man, concentrated muscle and passion like Picasso, the best possible body, inhabiting space ideally like a fish or bird; enough manhood for others, not too much to endanger survival—a target, but a moving one; a signal, an electric one.

He was solicitous as a woman; I was to see later, as he underwent more from his Order, how murderously accurate a mind he had when justice or love were in the breach. Zing!

He could launch a very nettle cloud of arrows. But I came to realize how his friends could serve him as a straw target or clay pigeon; he could be harsh as he wanted with regard to third (religious usually) parties, because the game stopped with us. His "above all, charity" was just that—above himself, therefore encompassing. He would not misuse his considerable forensic gifts in drubbing the demons out of churchmen.

His charity had a sublimely textured, almost tactile quality. He really loved the brethren; those who were light-years behind him and yet had the power to muck over his manuscripts and periodically make his life miserable; or who were intelligent in this or that discipline, superior to himself—and who turned against him along the way. One never had the sense in visiting the monastery of seeing the sheep of God trotting after a sheep dog. He would have yelled out in anger at the thought, snapping away at the heels of the disciples; like Gandhi he had the strength to seek opposite strengths to his, not befitting mirrors. He liked Philip's relationship to me.

(I am writing this cross-legged in a patch of clay that in better days was probably a prison lawn. Now it gapes and blows like a parched face. I am assigned to education but prefer for the indefinite present to do nothing, zero. This requires that I put into practice my all but lost art of melding with the universe. I have only to think "park bench" or "pigweed," and the hacks go blind and pass by. Well trained for survival in boyhood, I have survived while others, teethed and clawed to the hilt, have gone under.)

Merton is removed; we are still very much in the vicious thick of it. He cannot defend himself—even against his friends. Somewhat in the same sense as Jesus, helpless before Paul . . .

In any case, Merton cannot say now what we meant to him; when we try to say what he meant to us, we must be conscious of the difference. Even those gifted with the strongest faith do not hold a very substantial dialogue with an icon.

What an interesting prisoner Merton would have made! He had an unquenchable child's curiosity about the world; the types, crimes, conduct, inner-compound perfidy, humor, pathos would have called out his best response. I am consoled to think that in main outline, he would approve and go along with the direction our work has taken—long-term change, patience, good humor, the discipline required to keep footwork fancy, just out of reach of Gargantua.

His wait-and-see attitude toward human change was the very opposite of sitting-duck quietism. Which is to say, he was a passionate, thinking man in a burning city—and he had to decide what to do. He did not think he was called to be a universal fireman; I think he was never able to get excited about saving anyone's grubstake. He wanted with all his virile heart to save lives from the conflagration being programmed by the Brooks Brothers Destructors. That was mostly it. That was what made him both serene and urgent; a Buddha with sweat on his brow.

We were a spur and a question mark to him, as he to us. We were moving from different directions, by different speeds, fits, starts, under the northern light, toward some unimaginable dawn. He got there first, aided by a thwack of doom. But if ever the doctrine of differing Taos was fruitful and exact, it seems to me it was in our case. Almost everything was up for electric grabs when we met—and yet there was a common touch and meeting ground that saved us from the corrosive hatreds so typical of the times. We met, the differences were in the air, they were even the most fruitful things of all—we went back to our lives refreshed, home base made sense because we had ventured very far from our suppositions and even the range of our hopes. That is the most solid and reassuring aspect of our friendship and remains firm in the sensory part of memory—even when much else is tempted to destruction or hagiography or adventuring. We were Catholics together—we had a common *pays, patria* to stand on—so we could never quite betray that one who loved and mothered us in her own image.

All this was overt at the altar and implicit in everything else. It still is. I know he lives, and loves us. And his energies are ours for the asking, at our side.

July 13

Our present resolve, Phil's and mine, is not to answer our critics, especially the Catholics, even were the opportunity granted us; which it is not. It is far simpler and more peaceable, we judge, to remain silent (in print); but I wish to make the following points, if only to clarify things for myself.

1) Much of the to-do about us, in spite of "religious" language, has nothing to do with the New Testament. It has to do with members of a given national culture thrashing about in the net of public "policy," casting around a ruinous and lethal military method arguments purporting to be religious, language borrowed from religion.

2) Practically none of the critics have any sense of what is really revealed by Calley's trial or the Pentagon Papers. They seldom or never refer to the war. There is no hint of the compassion one would think to be a normal Christian or human response to the fate of so many today. So they judge us in a vacuum of their own making, as though our "escapades," "capers" were born of a boring clerical fantasy instead of an urgent sense of responsibility toward the helpless, wounded, defoliated, enslaved people.

3) At least one of our critics is motivated by an active cruelty. He rejoices openly in ill done to fellow Christians— while they are imprisoned for non-violent resistance to the state. In such a way he removes himself from the right to a civilized exchange with brothers.

4) The dialogue should continue in the lurid actual light of the war. Only those who are aware of the war and have reacted in some real way are worthy to stand in judgment on us. We are not obliged to take the armchair abstracters seriously—or emotionally.

5) We will discuss, and gratefully, certain careful reservations adduced by G. Zahn against our position, actions, language. We respect him as a man and a Christian, because he has tested his life in the arena of non-violent response. He can distinguish principle from tactic and proceed accordingly. Moreover he is no more wedded to the American state than he is to the German. He is wedded to the truth of the gospel, as his life of Jägerstatter makes clear.

6) Our critics in general have no real position on the war. Indeed, they would be ignorant of Newman's use of the term "real," and its implications for rebirth of spirit. More, they have no sense of what it means to be locked up in prison, able to hear what is written and said, but like the conscious dying, unable absolutely to respond. Some behold this unique muzzling of the opposite number with a kind of fervent glee. It is so easy to "dispose of" the troublesome who, in any case, are already effectively dead. And whose most personal and even sacred possessions are already public property. This curious analogy between treatment of the enemy and treatment of us offers a sinking but at the same time a liberating sense of recognition.

7) It is essentially untruthful to enter into dialogue (were dialogue possible) about essentials. At this point. This marks the difference between, not only the young and ourselves, but many of our critics and ourselves. To many, the necessity of action at all, absolute adhesion to non-violence, discipleship of Christ, the enslaving character of the warlord state—these are negotiable. They are up for grabs: one can be a virtuous man on either side of the question.

8) But not we.

9) It is thus necessary not to be gulled by Catholics who,

pleading a like tradition or an equal experience, are in reality precluding by debate our conviction that (a) debate be
deferred to second place in favor of resistance, (b) debate
proceed from acceptance of the assumptions of 7) . . .

I wish to be able to learn in the months ahead the meaning of my near death a month ago. It seems to me I must
work through a natural sense of horror which arises when I
consider how unexpected, gratuitous, and brutal was the at-
tack. Presented, as it were, without meaning—as though indeed it could have no meaning, were meant to be absurd . . .
to render my life absurd. The ineluctable dead end of prison
itself—to strip man and his life of all meaning, as a dead animal is rendered of its juice and flesh.

Reading Fischer's Gandhi in the prison yard, I reflect on
his great "fast unto death" in '32. On his mysteriously correct
sense of the time to act and the time to be silent . . . and
reflect on how clogged and drugged my own life is, like a rat
in a drainpipe, unable to go backward or forward, im-
mobilized between yes and no. An uncertain note . . . Did
Gandhi ever feel like this, and suffer from it? I think of the
difference between his dignified deliberate willingness to die,
with all India holding her breath, and my lying on a prison
cot one month ago, gasping like a wrung chicken for the air
of all four winds after an absurd medical mischance. What a
distance we have come!

P.M.—I was so shot full of pain, cortisone, weakness, and
malaise of spirit that I wept tonight for some fifteen minutes,
calling upon an absent one, so near a nobody as to be no relief, no opposite number to the *horror vacui.* Dried my tears,
which at my age are hardly even wet, and went down to our
class on the lawn—to work through two hours of that struggle
toward rebirth that vindicates, so rarely, the name "education." It does not frighten me even that I find it impossible
to keep a more even keel in this place. I know the Psalms too

well to expect to go about in an iron mask. And my personal resistance to personal death is much lower than when I came here—too much has happened to maintain that constant good humor I once could rely upon—for myself as well as for others.

Someone brought me a flower from Block Island.

We are still fighting, on many fronts, the battle of the media—saving, when we can, the lorn media masters, committed unto gnashing of teeth and the undying worm to the word that (they say) saves.

July 14

There is a poor mad young fellow. The same one who danced under the moon a few nights ago, now runs around and around the track, to the shouts and hoots and catcalls of his fellow prisoners. They are like captive Jews aping the Nazi captors—even the bloodless cry out for blood. I was going to shout out something, but the boy gave up his trotting and the matter subsided. What is this need, dark and deep as a bloody fountainhead, for a scapegoat, so that those on the bottom can stomp on someone beneath them?

July 17

Our usual Harrisburg trial meeting poignantly enriched by the presence of Eqbal, his chastened, gentle grief, our mourning together for his brother. How close death edges in on our designs; suddenly the table is tipped with a crash on its side, all our fine plans foundered. All that promise gone under. And who is to say from the depths of his violated heart how the riches of this loved man are to be duplicated? They will not be.

I think this admission makes it easier to go on, a clearing of the decks. Eqbal: "He would want us to get to work." Picking up the pieces after the death of David Darst or Merton was something of the same slow, wearisome walk into a vacuum, to fill it somehow.

We progress slowly; there is an enervated sense, in spite of the best will in the world, of a loathsome *déjà vu*—the beast has rounded on us once more, we are in the net.

I think of how a discipline keeps us from fraying out completely. It would be so easy and disastrous to take the downhill way of mutual grievance, dislike. It is because we are trying to cling, even by the fingernails, to a tradition, that the command to love one another conquers. This may sound on flat paper like a report from Flatland. In reality I am reporting an achievement as rare as it is sovereign; the hatreds and divisions among movement people are by now a matter of sorrowful record.

Up and down we go, feelings high, hopes low; a fever chart of people in the high fever of moral conviction.

I long for affection and am grateful when I sense discipline, direction, good humor, control. In myself, most of all.

I can now imagine what it is to die. Which is to say, in principle, I am in command of a crucial alternative. Or so I would judge . . .

They will be asking to the end of my days—what was it really like? And I will be unable to tell them. It has to be tasted; like aloes, like brimstone, like the taste of the needle of death—loneliness plunged to the hilt, the taste of common desolation, the punishment that seeps about like the smell of a Dickens graveyard, the look in the eyes of the bereft, the clinging of bodies to one another in the visiting room, the hunger for life's essential (which is the life of another), damage, blunting of decency, the blare of loudspeakers, the food line for the colorless, tasteless chow, the pack of guards guarding the pork chops, the sick in the hospital, prison within prison, the wandering old facing their first days and nights alone, alone, the mad boy wandering, running about like a scrap of paper blown in a feckless wind, the high priests of purported professionalism, the chaplain's fat, rolling gait on his way to a fouled nest, the web of connivance among old-time powers, holding on, holding on. And in spite of all, the good humor and camaraderie, the peerless unkillable young eyes of the peace prisoners, the clouding over of brows as evening comes on and silence takes over, and hands ache with the touch of an absent hand, the resolve which the day had made easy, to be courageous, to support others, to be cheerful and self-forgetting. The silence among us as we flock together on the empty ball field. Johnny's guitar orchestrates the unbearable (but always borne) loneliness, absence. The bad news stuffed in our throats like tar and feathers from the world outside, making mockery of our hopeful sacrifice. The taunts and lies of power on the tube, naming us fools where we sit, the guns and mad looks aimed like smoking missiles at us, at us. The church that goes by us like a Sisyphus stone, the stone in our guts. The year that seems at times a day, at times an aeon, measured in lives, in deaths, immeasurable, a surreal simulacrum of normal times, times of beauty and communion—times chosen, breathed, tasted, time of our best gifts, our foolish necessary laughter—the hand clapped hard against the spontaneous mouth. Yet, yet, such growth, such great changes, such turning toward one another, a fraternity most of us had never known before, born of peril and misfortune, the other discovered as the one who matters, whose life stands there, invitation. O this is how it was . . . We have died—into what? we can no more say than the bleating infant can sing of its birth.

Some, mainly academics our age, mainly Catholics, embalmed in their mind's saffron smoke and juice, frankly dis-

agree, discursively descant, balefully sure of the danger to
throne and altar offered by two clerics breaking big rocks into
little rocks for the greater glory of Caesar.

There are the public defenders. Jewish.

The Media Makers and Breakers. They sniff in the green
marrow of walking men, the decaying odor of the primal
buck. You may make tolerable good sense to yourself, you
may be fortune's cookie with good luck warranted by a
phalanx of guardian angels—but
   we will make purée of cement of you, bud,
   and recast you in the image of
   the great image.

July 18

It came to me this A.M. at Mass that I have been too slow
and sluggish in writing of Jesus Christ. I am undoubtedly allowing to appear in myself the blast effects of the ten years
just gone, which have made the church querulous, ill spirited, and rent with division. The shock waves have passed
from church to Christ, from the visible search for a scapegoat
to the entrapment of the mystery. We are now at a period
when a bitter triumph is to be celebrated; the Man of good
news is tarred with the shamed legend of long ago, freshly
touched up by the hands of Christians; He is become bad
news.

At least once, there was a certain understanding, a welcome, peace in the dwelling. And always a few who could be
counted on, to the bone; to die if that was called for. And
of course anything short of that, the ordinary fidelity that
gave character and style to life. Then the larger numbers of
intellectuals, artists, clerics, popes, people of every station,
of whom no great thing was to be required, but who remained
affected to a degree by His presence, example, words. The

variety and range of people so touched is not to be under-estimated by a sane mind. Apart from Him, apart from belief in Him, apart from the rhythms of work, play, worship, family, and professional conduct upon which His glance rested—apart from all this, such lives would differ from their present coloration, self-understanding, their feeling toward one another and the world, the fears and quiet which racked them on occasion, the areas of health and illness which made of their minds both swampland and solid ground—apart from Him, simply put, their life would differ from the common Christian Western life, as, say, the life of the casbah in Tangier differs from the life of a Trappist commune. Really, a matter of two worlds, the life, death, rhythms, verges, horizons, range of hope and grasp of life, tastes in the mind and mouth, cultural nicety and crudity, fierceness, gentleness, insight, blindness—

You would have to see it in action, deal with it in fact. There was a goodness palpable in the air, a call to surpass, a time of seriousness and sweetness, when these things were violated in fact and ignored in principle, which happened in so many places, for such long periods, as quite to submerge, wantonly murder, the meaning of the gospel. Such times, such sins, such attitudes were in fact doubly cursed—standing as they did against the law of humanity and the law of the Savior . . .

July 21

Overheard on the compound: "Will the liberated woman have hair on her chest?" "Only in cold climates."

I am reading the 2,500 pages of testimony in the trial of the Flower City people. What a wasted piece. It should be billed as the trial of youth; it shunts to one side all the trial lawyers and their briefs and cases and concentrates with what verve

and humor on the story of what happened to FBI offices,
DA offices, and SS offices in one night through a group of students, all of them loaded with talent and passion for life. I
shall have to urge with what I can summon that something
be done to get all this into print . . .

A poor gray-haired wraith drifts by as I write this, sweeping butts in the yard. They have him on Thorazine three
times a day. He will look in ten years or so like some of the
debris he sweeps up today. Wife and seven-year-old kid.
"Seventeen months gone, twelve to go; my mother said to me,
it won't be long. I said to her, it won't be long *for you*: but
did you ever try to hold your breath for twelve months?

"My toothache's worse [continued] than your earache because my toothache's *mine*."

"In the public prayer of each evening [he lived among the
untouchables of Delhi during the height of the troubles] he
[Gandhi] asked: 'Who would object if we read from the
Koran?' Several raised their hands. So he withdrew from the
meeting. The second night he raised the same question, same
objections; again he refused to pray with them. So on the
third. On the fourth, no objections; the 'priests' had withdrawn. Gandhi said: 'If all of you had objected I would have
gone ahead and risked dying at your hands, prepared to die
with the name of God on my lips if you so wished. But
I wished to avoid a clash, since you were divided. In the end,
non-violence prevailed.'" (Fischer: *Life of Gandhi*)

July 24

Conversation: so this fellow says to me, I have a message
for you. I said, looking him up and down: what's this message
stuff? You have a message. I don't see any uniform of the
postal department. What's this message stuff? He says: you
know So-and-so. I say: I'm sorry, the name doesn't ring any

bell. He says: I also had the same district attorney as you. I said: funny, I don't remember anyone, anything. Look, don't try for anything, don't try setting me up . . . Who's trying set you up? . . . Look, you need anything, coffee, cigarettes? No? Well, let me tell you, don't lose any of that human quality you have, by which you came to see me, with your message. Don't lose it: without it, you're nothing, nothing but a piece of shit . . . He went off, quick. You see what they try to do, how they want to set you off? Father, I never saw so small a place filled with so much garbage . . .

This is education too, the way crooks don't know nothing, hear nothing, say nothing. Really the most wearisome, worn-out game in the world. Contrast: the open-heart spontaneity of the young resisters when they meet here by transfer.

Suzie Williams: My next witness is me, and I won't be able to ask myself questions, so I guess I will just talk. Court: Do you swear to tell the truth? Suzie: I don't want to swear, but I will tell the truth.

"I guess it would be helpful to you all
        to know something of my background.
I was mostly raised on a small vegetable farm
        in southern Vermont.
We grew strawberries
        And I went to school there.
        It was a good time
And I think during that period of my life
        I got to appreciate something
            of man's relationship to this earth.
It was a happy time too.
        We worked in the strawberry and vegetable fields in the
                summer,
            myself and my four brothers and sisters
        and in winter we went to school
            and we did a lot of sliding on the hills there
                in the snow.

Vermont is really a great place to live."
(Suzie Williams, Flower City Conspiracy Trial,
November 24, 1970)

COUNT!—If sleek divinely inhabited Jovian hyacinthine-locked black bulls of Bashan could ever take cognizance of their worth—

—If the vestal virgins could be even more jealously and fervently guarded; even as they themselves, by fiery virtue of the indwelling spirit, guard the sacred flame

—If Dobermen were men, or vice versa; but in either case, the resultant fauna displayed qualities of greased lightning and omnivorous, stupid single-mindedness in pursuit of the runaway tin hare—

—If the crown jewels pulsed with pride in the dark, a phoenix nest of unimagined splendor, tasting, savoring self only—

—If count were indeed countdown—

—If all things, as a few benighted hairy Greeks believed, converged on man; if the ugliest of all Greeks were indeed correct and it were better to grow numb in the knees from self-imposed hemlock than live on as Big Mister's sedulous eunuch—

—If if if; we grow iffy, we shall wear our trousers spiffy as they count us, as they count us in the dark.

A bit of a go at our minister of religion

A diddling to do this A.M.

I decided while serving the Mass to have a bit of a go at our minister of religion. In the following matter: A Vietnamese friend had asked to have his child baptized by me, here in prison. The lawyers had been invoked. F.D. had effectively crossed the wires, confessed his powerlessness, transferred calls, invoked higher authority, etc.; the affair in a matter of days was so thoroughly gummed up as to trap feet-first the most adventuresome spirit. This is all according to a skill thoroughly developed over years of evasion and sucking up—to the point where some thirty dispirited worshipers out of some four hundred Catholics assemble for the limp dominical mysteries each week.

I decided something should be said. After Mass, collared our man. Why was the baptism impossible, why was I not consulted, why was the buck so consistently passed?

Response: the bishop didn't want the baptism here.

But why has the bishop to intervene in the simple matter of a baptism? Why could not the decision be made by you?

Then it was out; I would not in any case allow the baptism here—it is not a worthy place for a baptism(!)

Neither would Calvary be; called the place of the skull, where malefactors died.

The best feature of all this was the discovery that our man, who appears benevolent and soggy on all occasions, before all comers, was rendered angry by this little encounter. He reddened up like a turkey, invoked canon law. So thoroughly played the third flunky to the grand U.S. inquisitor general as to make one revaluate any prior conclusions regarding vital juices. No, he stood there at the mouth of his threatened lair, making fierce noises.

It is hard as hell. One never gets over it, used to it. The depraved genius of a system that can seek out and hire such a specimen, give him "job security," entice him into laziness, duplicity, install a knee-bending device before the absurd authorities—and call the resultant disaster a chaplain to prisoners.

I am sure Gandhi would not have written the above lines. But was Gandhi ever so provoked? I am sure he was . . .

The day's Gospel dealt with the need of persistence at prayer, and contained the great promise, knock and it shall be opened to you . . . The figure of the children in the ditch at Mylai intervened and I am all but turned to stone. To whom do you cry out when God is dumb?

But I am also sure Gandhi was a man of bottomless resources of spirit. I am not.

And the thought of the frustration of the simplest gesture of reconciliation (baptism of a Vietnamese baby by a priest in jail for war resistance) arouses me to fury, anguish.

We really expect that in wartime, such a war, such a scene of death abroad and breakup at home, liturgies can be controlled so as to express either a tyrannical fear or an indefinite good life (ours because we are in possession) or a vaporized sense of self-justification as "His people" . . . Thus

the anger of Jesuit authority also over the disruption of ordination services in New York some weeks ago. Phil was right
when he wrote, five years ago, that the American church is in
a worse position before history than the German church under Hitler—here, information as to the truth is not withheld
from us, and the threat of reprisal on us for speaking out is
practically non-existent. And we have not spoken out.

Listening to the A.M. sermon: this man chops a bird of
paradise into stew meat.

Fischer on Gandhi and Nehru: "The first was no problem
to himself, the second was."

About all one can hope for, as I write a friend, is "to put
something on record." We are all stuck in the cave together,
with the water rising. At such a moment, someone grabs a
sharp stone while the others hunker about in despair, and
draws the immortal bison hunt—what we were like, what we
did way back then before the deluge—for the spelunkers of
the future, whoever they may be, whenever they may come.

Meantime we and the Vietnamese huddle in the cave together—we are wasted together, some are giving in to despair,
some of us. It is already under way.

July 26

Jail intensifies at times, almost beyond bearing, a sense of
the futility of what goes by the name of "meaningful living"
outside. Jail: the drama of the meaningless! For 780 men
there are only perhaps forty or fifty jobs, which could be considered, even by the charitable eye, as benefiting the agent or
others. The rest, beginning with the hack jobs, is a bottomless pit . . . But the atmosphere of spiritual dampout puts
sharply the question of the worth of *any* activity at all today
—including the keeping of a diary, the attempt to be truth-

ful about life which tends to curve, in large or tiny circles, into the same old circle of absurdity.

July 27—Parole hearing

Tomorrow the grand viziers decide our fate. Good hearsay has it the folderol will take them most of the day. I find the prospect of so little wisdom expending so much time in so small a cause—delicious, exquisitely so. In case of either possible outcome, we win. This is the heartening conviction which steadies the heart. I can truthfully say that if I am to have the lock turned on me for another half or full year, it is OK. The conclusion is not come to without a wrenching of the spirit. I had naturally rather be in fuller possession of a portion of the fifty states—a condition of freedom which I find inseparable from a full use of my capacities as a man and therefore infinitely precious to me.

Peter Riga sees blood on the hands of the bishops for their connivance in the war. He asks for their resignation. These are brave words, so near the truth of things as themselves to draw blood. But is the same criterion to be applied also to priests; if not, why not? Alas, there are no equivalent Pentagon Papers to "break" for those who would undertake the thankless job of searching out the sources of decision. The sorrowful fact is probably this: the sins of our fathers in the faith are sins of omission; their consciences have been stifled by the grubby catchall culture, the "run for broke" mentality that made them footstools at Caesar's throne. Dante would deal with such men with a backhanded mercy.

I do not know whether it is morally useful to search and destroy those leaders who have admittedly been derelict, in this negative, tawdry way, blessing business as usual and calling it Christian life. After the exposé, the resignation, then what, who shall replace such men? And who in the flock is so innocent as to pick up the first stone; who has been a Christian son of such quality as rightfully to demand a charismatic father?

July 28

Be it known this is the day when the D.C. Imprisoners meet to take counsel on whether or not to spring us. I put this down because it is another delectable occasion on which 1984 nudges closer. Are they rehabilitated (recycled, new bottles for broken); are they ready to rejoin the good warren of good Germans? Can we control them well enough to keep the peace on the one hand, and on the other, to get them pointed in the direction of other prey?

Our newsprint hassle with Nelson (of L.A. *Times*) et al. pushes us to think more consistently on the relationship of media to actionists. We have not done very well so far; Nelson's outbreak is only the least bearable in a series of idiocies, betrayals, etc. that pretty well swamp the thinking mind. Now with Nelson the last leg of the colossus is toppled; this is the guy anyone would trust the pearl of his repute to. Ha. Even so good and canny a man as E. must be shattered.

We shall have to stop indulging in the fantasy that the media are going to mediate our existence to the people. Only in the rarest instances. Mostly they sell toothpaste and beer and level us off to a blur that will make the "other commercials" more palatable.

Most of them do not see their lives in any but a parasitic role. They want to be first on the scene, but they miss the action in principle. Thus their "profession" becomes as destructive in the long run as, say, a merger of morticians.

We have to control the news about our lives in the way we control our lives . . .

August 3

A wearying, poisonous monologue is going on a few benches away as I write this. The protagonist is ruffled like a turkey cock as he discourses on stool pigeons and custom-made television sets, fast money and mobile women. He is a veteran of Dachau; his old age is crowned with the dubious honor of matriculating into second childhood at Danbury. *Proh dolor.*

Re: a priest now sitting in Congress; I see no need to put off the raiment of Christ in exchange for the emperor's clothing. Run *from* office—whether in church or state . . .

P.M.—Sometimes it seems as though a whole lifetime is crossed in a few moments. It was so when I was seized at Block Island a year ago—it is now so again. Tonight we were summoned to the captain's office and told I was to continue "to expiration," Phil another sixteen months "toward a progress report." So be it. Many things are clarified in one stroke. We are a threat of some proportions to a powerful group which is determined to prosecute the war . . . Now we can settle into the next stage of things. I must say my soul feels more in conjunction with the stars than if I had been released, filled with a sense of unfinished business of the war, the sufferings of people here and abroad. A measure of peace descends. It will be a great privilege to continue to live and work with Philip, with the prisoners; never dull. The ruling is so rigid and so in despite of even primitive feeling (my health, etc.) that it places us in an advantageous position, a place of initiating choices of conduct; a mere six months set-off would have kept all sorts of hopes dangling about.

August 6

With respect to the church we have a peerless chance to raise questions with others who believe and struggle and hope for some way into the future, together. And to offer some sufferings, as the common cup goes around.

I feel at peace, a strange feeling, one to be grateful for while it lasts. The penance of life here is incomparable in the bonds it offers us with the other prisoners.

In no sense has a final word been spoken. There is a highly inflammatory decision which the community, as well as myself, will have to absorb and deal with.

The common life here can be embraced at a new and deeper level; what it means to be a man for others, to be at the mercy of an authority which is more desperate even as it grows more sclerotic. To speak the truth to such power.

I pray tonight for strength for Philip as well as all other prisoners, who are in the hands of Christ, even as we are.

I am now freed by this decision from the cowardly remnant; expectation of a "normal existence" in the face of brute abnormality. My generation may yet be redeemed.

What then is freedom—and how may one be free, in a bondage that has brutally chosen him for itself?

August 10

I think of Mother and the great gift placed in her hands —to live by a faith and love which are marked by some semblance of the suffering of Vietnamese mothers. The price of peace, which is bound to be at least as great as the price of war.

August 17

Events of the last weeks set up a humiliating and vivid contretemps in my bones. To decide to join the others in the protest and fast is, as I well know, equivalent to accepting a further disintegration of health and shortening of life. On the other hand, not to do so sets up its own perplexities—at one time I decide, here is my stand, and breathe deep as I know how . . . Then I hold back (mainly on word from others) to see if there is not another day on which one is called to fight. Can one, morally speaking, decide that the simple cold project for the next fifteen months is survival, given the state of my health (wretched at best) and the needs that lie ahead? There are very few willing to resign themselves to the idea of my death. Or indeed able to offer much help in this cruel dilemma. Do the times allow one to conclude the "long haul" of breath is still the first consideration? Or is my life in effect to be considered wound up, given, finished, not in a despairing sense, or a death wish nakedly considered, but as a simple matter of fact, in a gesture finally entered on; nothing saved, mortgaged, begrudged? What is the correct "sense of time" for a character like myself, time considered as consciousness of "the world, the way it goes"? . . . These thoughts undoubtedly wear me down further. There is in addition no news about the others now under solitary lockup from which to judge my own best course of action. A way on the one hand of sharing in the common fate of prisoners, many of whom are cut off for long days and weeks from news of their families. They must deal with rumor, mood, surmise, blackest foreboding; so now must I. Another inkling —after having so much attendance danced on me for so long.

August 19

Poems that never got writ:

A young Panther. In the dorm he staked off his turf with masking tape, exactly 20 inches around his bed, then carefully waxed that territory, roughly the space of a grave; living space, so to speak.

The face of John Bach, that radiant good angel, blowing a kiss to me in the yard from his barred hospital room where he was on the fast. His parting words to Phil and me the night before the big day: I love you both. Who would dare such words, who could MEAN them so fully? It was the befitting character, the wine to the wineskin.

TIME is the mercy of Eternity . . .

August 20

The fasters, including Philip, shipped out to Missouri in chains. I have been so stunned by the events of the past two weeks as to be quite unable to put a word to paper. How difficult it has been without Philip and the other resisters! As though the heart had been torn from the breast and a blank body left to make it as best it might . . .

There is the most perceptible change in the atmosphere of the compound; people less able to sing and play, a sense of *mauvais esprit*; people who failed to come through look at one as though they knew it, the how and why; the unfaced questions multiply in every direction . . . Being unable to face this resistance with the others, they convey a drowning sense, more and more at the mercy of the enslaver.

And yet what chances one had asked them to take! And is

it to be wondered at that they "could not quite . . ." Cruelty at the top, triviality at the bottom.

I go about, both numbed and quickened by sorrow, by loss. Eternally necessary to pay the price of commencing again.

They have upped the ante once more. Above all times, NOW one cannot allow himself to become a blank-faced complainer. One thing to be said for being an underdog: it is all a *déjà vu* experience; yes. Bad health; so one takes it in stride, sure of the outcome.

The extraordinary issuing forth of friends from the most unexpected quarters:

—The old man who fasted and went into solitary "because the priests were there, and we go with them." Even when they summoned their creature-chaplain, the man would not budge. By "the priests" he meant "the priests who were prisoners with us" . . .

—Matty the factory hand, scarcely known to us, went there "because he respected us" . . .

—Steve and Danny, characters at the edge of the class and of our friendships; there at the countdown . . .

Tons of tuna, walleyed, near to tears

We are in another rhythm entirely, awakened by the roaring departure of virtuous men (in chains) some ten days ago. As though with the capture of the white whale, the seas closed with a sigh of relief, wide as Europe from North America. The closure of the jaws of the mediocre; the crooks and cowards are in charge once more; in charge, i.e., literally of nothing. The place loses the electric quality of a hot smithy for the forging of new men, and wears once more the fishy look of the inhibited and shark-infested sea—tons of tuna, walleyed, near to tears . . . We have lost character, experience, the taste and tang of quality. One begins again the long uphill patient climb of working with the broken, setting bones in hopes of making men . . .

Elitist? But the elitist could not summon the heart to go on with a task that simply must be continued—as Philip knows better than I. The road is a long dust cloud, along which one trudges patiently—now and again the cloud lifts and there is a clear moment, a savannah, a prospect that brings ecstasy or tears. But only a moment.

August 28

Mostly taken up with writing Philip each day. Fast is three weeks and one day old today, and no end in sight. An alternative in sight. The boys are winning the conscious and loving struggle. Word from them continues cheerful, filled with the kind of indomitable *esprit* one would hope for in those who "wish for something better today and live as though it were possible."

August 29—A declaration on the Danbury fast

Today we celebrate together with eleven men, prisoners, friends and brothers. Eleven men, prisoners, are sitting down to their first meal in over a month. The celebration, the men involved, all are instructive; most citizens would affirm that prison offers very little to celebrate about. Moreover, these prisoners are worthy of note for a peculiar reason; they have an (unrehabilitated) habit of getting themselves into trouble. One month ago they started a fast in Danbury prison, distributed leaflets saying why, and got themselves thrown into solitary. When they persisted, and other prisoners joined them, the eleven were snatched out of Danbury, across country by air, and under heavy armaments; almost in fact as though they were named Tom Paine or Paul Revere, caught in the act of distributing the Declaration of Independence.

It was that absurd. The pamphlet that launched a thousand marshals advocated nothing like the overthrow of George III, Thieu, Parks, Hoover, or other peerless benefactors of mankind—the leaflet merely called attention to the duplicity or non-accountability of the federal parole board. It also linked crimes against domestic prisoners to crimes against Viet prisoners, recalling the nefarious Tiger Cages of Con Son, seeking to join hands with others across bars, barbed wire, and free fire zones, to assert a solidarity of pain in the search for redress. There were no threats, no hints of violence. The eleven merely said: we have grievances, we will not take food until our grievances are taken seriously.

Taken seriously they were, at least by some. A month went by. As they went on fasting, their friends gathered, measures were agreed on. Violence, before which America is perennially ready and able, did not occur. Non-violence, for which America is perennially unready and unable, continued. It became clear that the eleven were going to persevere in the fast in spite of a great show of force which masked a great measure of fear and dread. Facing the eleven was the fear of the armed bully whose knees turn to water in the presence of the unarmed Man of peace.

I was, one might say, more than remotely concerned in this matter. My brothers were fasting. More than that; they were fasting for me. We had decided to use my case as an exemplary one; not because my refusal of parole was more outrageous than others. In fact, the faceless, unaccountable powers of the parole board had dealt inhumanly with a thousand other prisoners in the last years, refusing parole to many and granting it to few with the mindless abandon of little men with big salaries, big power, and small conscience. But my case was special, because my name and crime were known here and there, and might stir the public to take action.

It seems that something of this hope has been vindicated. Eleven prisoners—bullied, segregated, harassed, transported —stood firm. At length their non-violent consistent purpose has moved the public, at least a little. It has moved the Congress at least a little. One may hope that soon the Congress will declare in effect that the human rights of prisoners are not suspended for the duration, that twenty-two thousand federal prisoners are no longer to be men without a country, men without a Bill of Rights, men without hope.

There is but one more thing to say. My brother and I did not come to prison in order to reform the prisons or correct the injustices of the federal parole board. We came to prison as an act of resistance against the war. And our government was acute enough to take us seriously. It sent us to prison for a number of years. For continuing to resist in prison, for refusing to become a cheerful robot or housebroken "model inmate," my brother has been named in another absurd and tawdry indictment, and both of us have been denied parole. We could hardly have been paid a greater compliment. We are dangerous; dangerous to the war-making state, dangerous in our unbroken purpose, in our non-violence.

We wish today to link the fast of the Danbury Eleven with the continuing struggle of all who resist the war. The fate of prisoners, the fate of America, the fate of Vietnam are joined. Human rights will be denied Americans as long as the rights of man are denied the Vietnamese. The political charade of Saigon will be matched by the political charade in D.C. Thus, the ironic revenge of history; the war comes home.

We wish only to bring the peace home; to bring the peace home to men's hearts and minds, home to our churches and universities, to our economy, to the White House and the Pentagon.

Resist the war, remember the prisoners. End the war, free the prisoners.

September 18

ATTICA, CHRONICLE

of cancerous inhibition;
dispassionate religion, dumb schooling, slave labor.

They wore the Mass vestments in the yard. They cut slits in
      blankets
and wore them like ponchos. It was a moonless, lurid scene
cut from a Civil War sepia photo. In the cellblocks,
in/out, up close. Hostages sat, with food and
drink, surrounded by guards. Wall to wall, armed,
the prisoners, facing alternately in and out, kept vigil.
It was a supreme American moment. It was the war
brought home. That déclassé word, violated by American
arrogance in a thousand bloodbaths, was given
its pristine value back.
Item: chaplains in the state system receive fifteen thousand per
      annum,
use of a house, a housekeeper-cook. Their pay scale is above
that of a lieutenant guard.
An economic analysis of the corruption of "guardians of the flame"
would be in order.
The authorities acted their part. The prisoners acted their part.
Which is to say, those in charge were faithful to the cold war ethic:
      lie where
you can get away with it, tell the truth when forced to.
The hostages' throats were slit. Saw them being slit.
Maybe saw them slit. Maybe mistaken.
No they were not slit.
Yes they died by bullet fire. Yes it was so testified by the coroner.
But we had to do it blah blah blah. In any case the governor
told me to do it, I only passed his order down.

We are rapidly approaching the point where the following
will be a *"feasibility schedule"*

    SCHEDULE: 10:00 rise 11:00 eat midday meal 12:00 read
and answer mail 1:30 leave with friends for a P.M. manhunt
(open season in some states, continuous) 7:00 P.M. return, put
carcasses on ice; drinks, dinner 9:00 a few hunting companions
in, recall events of the hunt, over drinks 12:30 retire (make
love; optional), asleep by 1:00

September 24

Literally being pressed into new form. You may take Mr. Skinner's word for it, or Mr. Krīst's. In any case, it's happening. Which accounts in mysterious part for the near extinction of yrs. truly last June. It needs to be said—I had been without air for too long. I was asphyxiating—too little space, too few humans, too much guardsmanship.

So I couldn't get breath. I was denied breath, an instant of truth; the universe refused to conspire with me as "another member"—I felt those arms reaching out of mother joy, to snuff the flame, to enclose me in a final dark love. I was worthy: I was ready.

Now the work is largely a formal reworking of the meaning of that failed embrace. I was cast back in midstream, literally to "do more time." The prison image meets the world, and it is *it*.

September 28

False death or true.

we come to a birth day . . .

Henceforth the cat can look at the king, the king decreed grandly, waving his scepter about like a thrasher. I decree it, I even like it. Therefore I allow it.

The cat looked at the king, askance. To be allowed to do so. He arose and padded gently across the room, head down, tail twitching like a thrasher. He was searching his mind, labyrinthine as the corridors of a pyramid. Who said it: the kings of the earth are cat food . . . He half concealed a smile;

lascivious, golden. He bore his smile along the imperial rug like the hint of a sunrise; out the doors, and up like the sun.

September 30

An abortive, angrifying interview with two bureaucrats yesterday. I spent an angry off-again on-again couple of hours (with myself) afterward and last night before retiring.

Seeing, and appalled at the sight: the anger that threatens to take over on occasion; knowing, seeing the narrow limits of non-violence in me. Sensing too a breath of exhaustion that seems to dump on us from worsening policy, befouled power . . .

Coming off so badly in such an exchange, which tightens up the throat and chokes off the breath; literally one seems to have no available equipment for dealing such cards. A kind of vicious circle closes in. All the resonant appeals of the good charlatan are made—then the rhetoric of Skinner or Esalen is invoked . . . Why so hostile, why so silent? Which is not our way of dealing with those we trust, but we simply have no equipment for dealing with those we cannot, must not trust . . .

Mail came loose again yesterday, a great spate after a week or more of drought.

They were certainly taking soundings for future use; inevitably against myself or others.

I feel more and more acutely the impossibility without grace of acting as a human, surrounded so by these incompetent connivers. It is necessary so one is not forced into their mold (creature) or into some counterploy. Which would only ape them after all (rage, violence).

Sometimes the silence of Jesus is a clue. Am I still too concerned to win, to make it, big or little? The chances are very great we will not make it at all.

October 5—Phil's birthday

Great absurd weird perturbations lately—sense of being used and used up by those who are becoming dependent on me and making me an "excuse" for not entering into the life here. A feeling of being trapped in a complex of relationships for which I have neither patience nor good response nor valid equipment. How I wish my soul could be seen lucidly, somewhat like one of those plexiglass male models of the medical exhibits. So I could know why at fifty years I can be put off and spun about by such childishness . . .

The psychotherapists, psychologists, and others are taking their pummeling from every group that puts its head above the tombstone and calls out "liberation." There is a powerful analogy with what has happened to myself in the church here. *Nulla salus* yields to the pressures of an awakened sense of other styles, one God. A parallel secular pressure for movement—*extra Freud nulla salus*. One sees the narrowness of the claim in the people to whom it is finally addressed—and those too bound to be the counterpart of those who announce the "narrow gate" and keep it intact. Only a few geniuses can both concentrate human energy and encourage its extension. This is an abstract statement of a concrete inner fact; they die in the dramatic moment itself, i.e., to grow toward mankind and God and to be faithful in a double movement which amounts to the most determined attacks on the old gods and their men . . .

Freud should have stayed in his own back yard: which was the soul of male white Europeans. Or to have ensured he realized his limits, he should have set up demarcations—so it would be clearer who was sinning in the claim of universal application. Now as it is, the women, among others, have him up the wall. And rightly so.

Maybe the Marxists are right, and old Ezra P. and the thing that brought the church down, usury and sale of sacred things, will do the same for the headhunters.

Some facts about the century:

1) Rather small percentages of men and women can be drawn into the killing of enormous numbers of people.

2) Governments of the right and left escalate older, anti-human qualities much more speedily and effectively into decision making about who lives and dies; the nub of the matter.

3) Churches live on, mainly as inert models for newer secular forms of control, newer gods, new kinds of saints.

4) Technology proceeds apace to make, on a universal scale, a sow's ear out of a silk purse; the despoiling of creation.

5) "Liberation movements" in the main are translated quickly by the cultural powers: "I want in." The scene is generally a trough where goods, services, poisons, excreta are dumped.

6) Liberation implies transformation of the soul of the slave, and thereby of the societal picture. This is quite possibly the most neglected idea of the time. Its truth may be judged by the fury it inspires in the right and left.

7) The meaning of Christianity, as self-understanding and continuity within a tradition, is very much an up-down thing, like the visibility of a wounded porpoise. (Catholic ultra-resistance seems to have a lead in this regard. A plain life span since 1967.)

October 6

Foggy days here and very little hint of Indian summer. The food cart, the garbage cart, the tool cart drag along in the gloom, indistinguishable as Platonic ghosts. Cannot see the opposite end of the compound, lights working eerily, it is wartime, doomsday; the vanishing at length of the vanishing species? At any rate one knows in a new way that he is here, his life is here, his bones are here—and everything in the machinery is designed to let him know—here or nowhere!

Every day one takes up the day anew, as though it were the first day of all in its somber, wounding self-realization: you are here; for the duration.

Not new, but infinitely stale, stereotyped, in conversation, faces, clothing, food; you have been here, you will be here. I.e., denial of a true present, pummeling into one's substance, like flour and milk into yeast, the bland continuum of past and future. No more present than a knuckle mark in dough, to be breathed out again in a minute.

I write for the same reason I confess, or reflect or read or keep silent: to guard my sanity.

The understanding of limited gains

Leads for a discussion:

1) The fast and transfer of the Danbury Eleven accomplished limited gains; people at least have become slightly more conscious of certain ills that afflict them: parole, censorship, arbitrary punishment; also the war.

2) With the advent of Mr. Qici it seems clear we are faced with two of the most intransigent ministrations on record. No getting away from it, literally.

3) The nature of the prison also makes it enormously difficult to envision, let alone to bring about, change. Short terms, snitches, self-interest, apathy.

4) Need of change, in the men as in the institution, seems evident. The two are closely related. The men generally accept their plight as inevitable if not inescapable; they are given to random violence, dissensions, drugs, machismo; they brutalize one another, missing the torrent for the breeze.

5) What can we do? Experience of the fast drew us together; this continued fruitfully at Springfield under conditions of great uncertainty and even danger. People drew together. How draw others in? My feeling is a further step is

necessary, lest we begin to drift and lose the gains made.

6) Relations with the committee ought to be strengthened and continue.

New, small, continually probing groups ought to be formed and go forward. Discovering what people are willing to prepare for on the outside—a true future (member of my group, after intense Gospel discussion on the material world and detachment of heart, in which he took vociferous part, explained he needed $350 for bedroom set for his seven-year-old daughter) instead of continuing stereotyped past . . .

7) Understanding of "limited gains" possible; this helps dispel discouragement and prevent illusion. There are going to be great losses this year, but no great gains. Attica is a case in point. The foregoing is so true that modest language and thinking about oneself and the movement is the best criterion of sanity . . . whereas random big talk almost invariably marks the self-deluded, undependable.

8) The action of the fast is possible in such a place as this only about once a year. We know how carefully it was necessary to prepare for it. But to prepare ourselves and others for life outside is by no means a delusion. Since life outside is going to be the burden for most of us, most of the time.

What then to prepare for, and how?

Everyone from Paul of Tarsus to Trotsky to Cleaver used jail for intense study, meditation, preparation.

October 13—Matthew 12:43

It might be called false conversion or foreshortened conversion; or conversion by fantasy or self-duping. The spirit ironically comes out of a man, and says to himself, I will go back to a house (a "dwelling") . . . He is an it to—*him*—to *it*? How designate a spirit that needs a man only as a man needs a dwelling, or a turtle a shell, or a bird a nest?

The epiphany of false spirits; the "object" quality of the men they possess, in order only to objectify them. Whereas the Holy Spirit makes a man "spiritual," in the sense of fully realized, impregnated, truthful, peaceable. This spirit of evil makes him into a more or less clever, expensive construct; a shell, a warehouse, for the sheltering or protection or amassing of objects. We would think today of the perfect "piece" of real estate; the unrealest element of which would be the entirely wooden man, the ridiculous rich homunculus jangling his keys about his premises, guarding his person like a thing, his things like persons.

Melville wrote shortly before his death at Attica of the freedom of walking about minus keys and money, for the first time since his boyhood. Only keepers have keys and money here, we others are as outside the "economy" as Trappist monks, we float in the air like poltergeists.

Trouble is, owning nothing, most of us do not yet own ourselves.

The parable has something of the lurid mystery of a Fellini movie script. This spirit who inhabits a man wanders the world, holds debates with himself, contemptuously and coldly weighs his loss and gain, decides on a return, making his solitary Jonah into a kind of commune of devils . . . He has lost more than he gained by leaving; it is the dark replica of the plight of the prodigal: I will return to my father.

Seven is a symbolic number; an infinity of demons returns. Everyone wants in on a good thing. The commune quickly becomes a disaster area.

We hear literally nothing of the man whose fate is thus sealed. He is outside the debate, outside his own history; a dead nest, occupied last year by the builders, this year by the predators. He is no more in his own hands than the boarded-up house of a dead owner.

Or he is "occupied" again, somewhat like a house. But the occupation is like a squatter's act—an act of possession. No house in history was ever "possessed" in the way of a man given over to demons. Do we need examples? Of the seven-fold, endemic numbers, the giving over to dark forces of power, cruelty, lust, fear of life, inner and outer violence at once?

Technology has made it possible to (1) keep one's house (life, soul, style, mode of action) in spurious order (we speak of "timesaving devices," "exalted standard of living" "law and order,") and (2) wreak an abstract, crafty ruin on others, with the clean hands of a prestidigitator.

The spirit, please note, has not been "cast out" of the man —this is not a wry parable on the regrettably half-finished work of the thaumaturge. No, he simply "left," out of rest-lessness or boredom, a desire to take soundings . . . The man, possessed and depossessed, is thus ripe as a dry stick for the fiery moment of repossession.

It is a parable of, among other things, the fiery fate of the morally indifferent. Who imagine they can take in a devil like a house guest—one who will have, let us say, the civility to enjoy, enjoy, depart on time, neither presume nor be obstrep-erous or drunken, respect amenities, we would say. No, there is a far more serious project in view. He is no guest at all, but in his secret heart, master of man. His coming and going is meant as a contemptuous sign of literal possession.

The parable is marked by a kind of irony that comes from the deeps: the other side of conversion. The conversion that ends up worse for the poor convert (the "converted" dwell-ing; apartments for seven devils instead of one).

Man has spiritual space for the infinite; he can offer lodging to the Holy Spirit. He also has room for the pseudo-infinite, the "seven" devils, the world totally within, totally possessed and possessing.

"This kind," Jesus said on another occasion, "is cast out only by prayer and fasting." Before such a program making such close and rigorous demands, this man, the shadow man, is man-object, the stick whittled into a man—the Pinocchio —swings wide, is opened and closed, is spruced up and ready for more. But he will never choose—whether God or a brother. So he ends up being chosen—by demons.

Jesus, ordinarily serendipitous, is also distressingly chthonic at times. He seems to have lived both with the demons and with the Father. The second He commonly speaks on, about the first He is wisely parabolic. But of both worlds it could be said simply, He knew what was in man.

But what *was* the man to do if he was not to become the mere dumb corpse keeping house in the interim between death and burial, the house full of mocking hirelings, mourners making hay of his nearest and dearest things? . . . "Our fight is not against human foes

> but against cosmic powers, against
> the authorities and potentates
> of this world, against spiritual wickedness
> in high places."

The fault of the man is implied in the meandering freedom of the evil one, going in and out, wandering about . . . He is complacently at home even away from home.

There should have been a "resistance," a casting out; the call here was for a form of violence that would have made the dwelling into a man, the man into a last-ditch resister.

To will the way and follow it, he would need "another." There is no gainsaying what the Lord has said. "Not peace but the sword" . . . "Your faith has healed you."

We have prisoners passing through the great tank here day after day, in various degrees cowed, enraged, broken, shaken awake; most, almost all, of the same mind at departure as at their entrance. They are the closest, most tragic evidence of the inability of two supposed "forces for good" to bring change; the powerlessness of the prisoner, the power of the state.

Here one could perhaps rush in, papal flags flying, to announce the church as *tertium quid*. What folly! With regard merely to my own "crime," the church, casting Christ out with exemplary promptness, converted herself to Constantine, and then as a gift for the baptism-wedding convened at Arles in 316 to make pacifism a heresy. The wedding meats supplied the funeral feast—the burial of Christ, the burial of Dan at Danbury. Against which: our lives are not grave robbers; but in us, He is risen. Even in us.

The prison is thus the mausoleum not only of the pretensions of the state—to "improve things." Obviously burial is a kind of Draconian improvement on the rotting of corpses aboveground.

The prison is also a bitter reproof to the church, to her claim to exorcise in His name. The so-called keys of the kingdom turn these locks also; not to free, but to enslave further with that heaviest of declarative forms of guilt: the invocation of the will of God.

But in a true sense, the church is beside the point here. Because she has so declared herself. (Make it new! [Confucius])

The violent analysis of social ills, the inflamed rhetoric of blacks, of the poor, of the Third World peoples—now also of the women—must be seen as a dangerous, necessary preliminary to the kingdom of justice—it is language of exorcism. Its use becomes expedient from the moment when the possessed peoples awake with a start—we are not autochthonous, we are colonials, slaves, the possessed.

The "other" is always a demon until right order is restored. He can never be simply brother, white, man, friend. YES. The language testifies to the root and marrow nature of the invasion, rape, possession. Only demons could do such work; or demonized men.

October 14—Where the seed falls

There is no doubt of the seed's goodness. Of its fate there is considerable doubt. The analogy is both precise and mysterious—God is at the mercy of men. We have heard so much of the opposite—man at the mercy of God—that perhaps we hear it no longer. Is it time to go deaf to one truth, to be able to hear another?

Here it blazes out—we are the glory of God.

The seed perishes in all sorts of ways—wantonly, by chance, by conflict with stronger forces, by bad weather and bad will.

The seed prospers in only one way—the exact, chancy, rare convergence of good things—weather, soil, sun. It is the most unlikely combination of happenings; but the rarest in the abstract is also the commonest in fact.

"Man is consubstantial with his faith and his father" . . . (Bhagavad Gita)

Let the analogy hold here also.

In Jesus we love His love for the moral universe, unfolded or outspread, but always free of the crippling rusting disease that brings the seed to death before it has well come to life.

What chance does the seed, even the best seed, have in a place like this? It falls on cement and concrete and iron. The stony faces of authority, the slack, defeated faces of so many inmates—the sense of being broken in a broken world. Truly nothing from ground up could flourish in such an atmosphere. It is foreign not only to what I most cherish in the church but in men at large as well. A special death, a very special account to be paid.

October 16—Matthew on relationships, 12:46

It is not terribly helpful or to the point to say: He wants to "elevate" human relationships. A statement more germane to his mind would say: He wants to speak the truth about human beings, because that truth is so necessary to them that they languish or perish without it . . .

They perish in the old static, unresponsive, irresponsible

way of the blood—of "nature," so called—which is a trans-
ference, shifting of the truth, of responsibility, to an abstract
Platonic entity . . .

We perish because we make of the bloodline an absolute,
a value beyond question. The "elevation" is in the paradox; it
is not an elevation at all but a penetration.

I don't want a mystical veil cast over something that is
quite plain and earthy, language about which ought to be
plain-spoken. We die of one another. Or we live off one another. There is not much difference, in process and effect.
There are few who can bear the weight; a love of which we
are the dark heirs—in our blood. We are stuck, for once,
at the point of time described in the Gospel.

They think in the big house on the hill such a union is
bound to turn out well: it has so much to recommend it;
friends, income, "security." Maybe.

It had, when the chips were down, only small appeal to
transcendence: to a "third party." It ended up part of a public display—"for the family's sake." In private, which is to say
in reality, pure horror.

Now He is making a claim about Himself and us. In the
first instance, doing the will of the Father forges a link between ourselves and Him. "Brother, mother."

What of the rest? It follows from that. Men and women
learn in the movement of that life to get moving with one
another.

Look what a man might be, and be healed

The bishop came this A.M. I read the Gospel and received communion and generally helped out. He preached on his recent Rome trip to beatification of Maximilian Kolbe. No reference to prisoners. I asked before Mass to meet with him and inmates. First of his sleights of hand; he had no time. The chaplain had let the sleight out of the hand yesterday, remarking that the bishop had several hours before next appointment which he would spend in a rectory nearby . . . After Mass I was corralled by the chaplain with an invite for Phil and me to meet with the bishop over coffee. It was to be held, as it developed, not in the chaplain's office but in the officers' mess hall; warden, guards to be present also. I refused as politely as I knew how; explaining I could not come unless all prisoners were invited. So it ended, he going his way, we ours—to walk the compound for two hours in the rain.

Camus's "stranger" says to the prison chaplain, refusing to make confession or "prepare for death": "You are one of them." Again, the young resistance Frenchman about to be executed and making a desperate escape plan is betrayed by the chaplain, who becomes aware of his intention. Camus seemed to have been hyperaware of the deep, even awesome complicity between church as power and state as power. Both ultimately join in a classic handshake; same ends, same means, same recognition of troublesome characters.

I feel quite at peace in our conduct of this A.M. Jesus, hardly conscious of a *détente* between Himself and the Romans, was less conscious of "founding something" than of being someone—there were only a few years, it was necessary to stand somewhere and die for one's stand . . .

The sermon was on shrine visiting, Rome, Poland. This bishop went off to honor the dead. The question arises where he would have stood at a contemporary Auschwitz (Danbury). Our prelates whitewash the sepulchers of heroes whom "your fathers" have created.

One does not want to wax arrogant or sanctimonious about all this. The church will fare, within a given culture, about as well or ill as that culture. With respect to enemy cultures, it will generally counsel enmity; with allies, friendship. This is almost a cruel necessity of things, since the immanence of members to both church and state initiates the danger of bad war and worse peace from the beginning. The one who crosses borders, crosses into enmities, will be an exception, an object of disbelief, unease, to both parties.

I felt the dust of falling objects, walls, masonry, in my nostrils. So much tumbling down, so much rendered ridiculous by the press of change. Men kill the heroes, men keep their tombs—and call themselves churchmen. They have a rhetoric compounded of unction, hypocrisy, Bible. But the real and lurking security that gives breath to their words is in truth real estate, money, the more or less conscious ties among those who share power, common need, common view of life; and whose determination to keep these things intact is never to be despised or underestimated. Most churchmen would die for mammon with all the fervor and conviction commonly associated with a baroque painting of the expiring of St. Sebastian.

But maybe, you see, nothing real is falling apart—only the mortar crumbles. The foundation stands, a little painting here and there is all that is needed. I am really thinking of the *peccatum perenne*, the self-renewed, self-blinding arrogance which the world, that world in lamb's clothing or shepherd's clothing, still exacts. In which case, one is not witness to anything as invigorating as the death of a bad thing; all is cyclic, the same hyperidiocy is already latent in the veins of some unknown gauche schoolboy who in thirty years will preach at the White House and oversee his current overseas armies. Blessings!

One does not know. That is the true element of ignorance which makes for freedom from obsession. It is simply good to be here, at the foot of the mountain on which the Man stands for a moment now and again, in one's friends, in Philip, in the young resisters; saying: look what a man might be. And be healed.

December 3

I have been thinking a great deal, perhaps too much, about my chances of surviving this bit. My near taking off in June seemed to precipitate this; then the certainty of another year, my daily battle to keep my head above water . . . Today I had a bowl of chowder; there must have been onions or spices in it, for I was sick as a dying dog all P.M. I've come to the following formula: right now I'd say 60-40 against survival. That for the next three months. Then 50-50 to six months; 60-40 for, next three. At ten months, 70-30; eleven months, 80-20, etc. I think this is realistic and will not create false hope.

Very important to keep this diary up—even though uncertain when or how it will ever see the light of day . . . Someone sent me a photo of a thirteenth-century Limoges Eucharistic bird, to keep the sacrament in. A flash of recognition; I had seen the lovely thing in the Metropolitan Museum in New York. I thought it belonged on the *ceiling* of my cell—no one as far as I know has ever yet put a picture on the ceiling—we'll see how long it survives there; the Spirit is on his own . . .

The time weighs heavy on the chest, like a branding iron.

Never elsewhere or else when, such an oppressive sense of time. It is simply looking around and seeing that one's world is compressed into a small patch of sky, a few trees, sordid walls. What then? Time does its worst.

Tonight I passed the two little barren trees; it was cold and still and the trees held a weightless burden of sparrows, who shifted like leaves in a wind, as though I were prevailing as I passed. Strangely they would set up a chattering and mewing as I reached the far end of the path and began returning. A kind of delayed plaint or warning. How do they survive through such nights as these? But how do I survive through such days as these?

The grass after one punishing snowfall is as green as August.

December 8

Some kind of a duty remains. Duty to whom? It seems immaterial to whom; to myself, to everyone. Not to lose out on the moment, the face, the spoken idiocy, the saving abnormal. A junkie insists on reading a poem which is an outlandish Ferlinghetti takeoff, inferior and childish. He plumps down next to us at supper, interrupts our lousy food like a cop's glove over insect traffic, and *reads* it, page after page, the whole thing. We sit stupefied, angry, then slowly reconciled. Good humor again. The health-giving funkiness. In the winter of our discontent.

They rip out shelves (we had one shelf for books and extras) today, they tear down pictures from the walls. Some nameless, brainless big shot is arriving by mainspring from somewhere; evidently virginal walls are his fetish.

I am stupefied and exhausted much of the time, a very complex animal run to ground, pretty well used up. Yet I have intense periods of good writing, reading, reflection, and seem to get a good deal done. Then back to home base, inertia.

Losing a sense of mutuality, overflow, good joy, capacity for sipping to the roots of one's buds, the funk and variety of the earth basket. Yum yum. Old age is irritation, news is olds, goods are bads, services disservices . . .

A Separate Reality; Further Conversations with Don Juan. Disturbing, haunting, a trip in truth, to death.

I occur to myself as hanging around, more than half expecting another smash which may well finish me off, more merciless than the last.

So I work each day in the ratty, dusty library which is no more than a dustbin filled to the brim with the castoff books of those who have "first grab" at everything—colleges, the military. The old books are stamped with the proud names of the front liners; then across the same page, a large notice—*Withdrawn!* or *Canceled!* It is like a military euphemism tattooed on the body of a dead Vietnamese.

They are punching through concrete walls to install air conditioners for the bureaucrats; and the guards sport new slacks and gold jackets—they look like sides of beef dressed for church in a Brecht horror show. Not one cent has been spent, within memory, for a book or periodical in the library.

December 9

Come to prison, nothing less will satisfy the heart of a man who wants winds of surprise blowing into his soul, blowing down the old guidelines and scarecrows and fence posts and traffic signs and outhouses.

Explain, God or man; admitted to the *in camera* sessions of the Harassburg defendants. We spoke on Paul and his ideology as in-forming efforts to form and enlighten consciences today. Why was I allowed into their company after months of exclaustration? . . .

Story of the sordid "U.S. attorney" who arrived here in jail, preceded by blasts of the shofar proclaiming him a hero condemned to fifteen months for contempt of court against a savage New York judge. Someone got the real story; he's a twenty-three-year-old embezzler with a genius for moving big sums of money like iron filings in his own magnetic direction. Has no law degree. Took the rap for himself and for his father and came into prison alone (every truly religious vocation "to desert life" is charged with the aura of solitude). Someone confronted him with the above facts drawn from life. Too much. Hours later he stamped up to the hospital asking medication, claiming depression—admitted greedily to the strip cell where the piranhas make you into short ribs in the shortest of times . . . Moral: boobies count dollars before they're hatched . . .

The constituency of our Gospel group changes continually; *plus c'est la même chose.* I.e., come or go or come anew, we are all criminals, we all dread the truth, we would like to be numbered among those who "say they will not go into the vineyards, yet go . . ." We may be among the prostitutes and publicans who enter the kingdom first; but only if we cast off the sentimentality of our sin, our romantic heart of golden self-regard (we have hearts of gold only in the sense of golden calves), and are converted to the truth indeed.

The lawyers wanted a statement from me, something to the effect that I wished to be released so that I could rest, recoup, rejoin the Jesuits as an active and productive member ". . . take my place in society once more as a productive and law-abiding citizen . . ." Quite apart from the odious stereotype of the good German, the vision nauseates me and sets me running down the road hell-bent away from the noonday devil, the virtue that kills.

December 10

Implications of Fred Hampton's "Why not live for the people, why not die for the people?"

Sometimes our Gospel group study approaches the education that might be ecstasy.

I come from them exhausted; but what a depth, how mysteriously our spirit touches hands . . . I suppose it can be only to enable us to face the gray sludge of dawn once more; in this sense ecstasy is always "orienting" at enabling. Now and again (so rarely) the element of struggle falls away from one's life. The doomed ending is ended. Not to have to draw the sweet breath of the world in struggle, as I so often must. Can see, as this evening, in the looks of the others, that words are not a struggle, either in their seizure upon taste and mind, or in my offering them, light-handedly. Like the dance that "works" in the perfect ease of its midplay. Or the poem, informed with the full confidence of its good outcome, even in the onward rush of half completion.

Read: Yeats—Words upon the window pane . . .

December 11

Comes another Irish charmer, a big-toothed crook, seven years for smuggling—*people*, i.e., a Greek into a port of New England. Nothing is heard of what happened to the Greek. The Irish are no longer "ethnics" in the sense that Puerto Ricans or blacks are. They are like the full members of the frieze cut, bold relief, into the pantheon, like the Jews and WASPs. You know it by their magnificent dentures, by the shortness of their term, by the Byzantine quality of their crimes. They've made it—into America, and America is merciful to her sons.

We are being pressed into a new existence, between millstones. Take the news calmly. It's really no news at all, except that it's happening to you.

Part of the struggle is being sick, weak all the time, dragging around with a corpse tied to one's tail, only just making it—a shell without its snail.

Part of the struggle is to be an anti-pro-sick-man, to live in and out of this weirdo-do simultaneously, an awareness of spirits including the shadow of Big Smoke Death and the Moths in the Stove Pipe.

Yet at the same time—trip, exodus, ecstasy; standing at distance enough not to be a lifer; which is to say a deather.

Insist with every cat's gut in my quiver on doing it all; and letting the regrets go like fluff from the belly button.

December 12

BE IT HEREBY NOTED: eleven prisoners today break bread once more

Today, December 12, completes another phase of the struggle for life, liberty, and the pursuit of decency. We must not fail, however the nation reacts, to take note of the extraordinary meaning of the day. Eleven prisoners, having denied themselves food for over a month, today break bread once more.

Prison, one would think, is already big enough, bad enough to deter the faint of heart, to keep the stouthearted firmly in line. Enough has come down, why ask for more? Or to put the same question another way, prison food is no picnic, granted, but what sort of sane alternative is starvation?

We must go back a bit if we are to understand. Prison, the lockup, has two things in mind for prisoners—neither of which is by any stretch of fantasy connected with rehabilitation. One: prison is designed to keep a man from thought of serious change. The world of men and women, of family, of love and friendship, of war and murder, of hope and resolve and community, is "outside." The prisoner is in cold storage, his soul is on ice. If he is a political prisoner, he must live with a double absurdity: with his act of criminal virtue, with the impossibility of purging himself from virtue as though it were vice.

Infantilism is the way to success as a prison inmate. No choices, no connections, no way out. One is literally the kept infant in the state nursery. He is asked to regress into the instinctual world of the infant; his choices range among popsicles, inane recreation, castoff books, tedious makeshift work, the toys of boys. Safe in his playpen, he can play at being a man: he can earn a living (a slave living, wages), he can visit his family (a cruel supervised mockup), he can go to school (two weeks' plumbing course) or browse in a library (Air Force dog-eared rejects). That is to say, once his manhood is amputated, once he is safely stripped, swaddled, and suckled at the iron tit of Holy Mother State—then he can begin the artful dodge of the manhood game. The prisoner can keep trying.

The point here is not to go over once again a ground already covered. Judges, district attorneys, marshals, wardens, guards are all too conscious, in varying degrees of complicity, of the cruel dead-end nature of the game. The majority of these functionaries know several facts which should, were rationality in command, work for reform. They know (1) the prison system produces criminals and multiplies crime and (2) the prison system is cracking wide.

Number two is our present theme. Once again we have the Vietnamese to thank for the cracking domestic structures. The war has brought a new kind of prisoner on the prison scene. He is youthful, intelligent, morally "together." He has the inestimable advantage over his fellow convicts, over his keepers, of having come to prison for non-violent resistance of public violence. So he is unscarred, unready for deals, outside the dollar game, skeptical of Big Brother and his big stick.

He is almost invariably white; a consideration of some import to our discussion. The fist of authority pauses, likely in midair, when our hero breaks the rules like bones (to suck the marrow, he would say). "He's one of us"—a deviant, no doubt, a troublemaker; but still white.

And what if, in addition to all this, he's a priest as well? A priest? In prison? You mean? All those comfortable arrangements, all those mutual aids and props and concessions and breaks, those winks, those pressings of flesh (secular) to flesh (sacred)—you mean that's over? You mean the Catholic church, that big landowner, gun blesser, gilt investor, slum keeper, sin forbidder—you mean the cardinal may have to say to the President, next Sunday meetin' time, something like: Mr. President, please don't take those imprisoned, hunkering, fasting, non-violent Sermon on the Mounters for us, indeed don't. Because we're four-square with you in principle; naturally we don't like war, no more than you, sir; naturally you don't like bussing, no more than we, sir; naturally we're wondering about our schools and your plans—reminding you with all due respect, sir, from our schools come more and more loyal stand-up Catholics . . . to stop the bussing and march to war . . .

December 16

As though moving on two planes; the one post mortem, dead to the world, ignorant of the world, coming even to scripture in a non-discursive, almost uncaring way. At one's worst when determined to win a point or prove anything . . .

Other level, still experiencing the world, including and beginning with one's own body. Especially in my case, by way of weakness and anguish. As though nothing had been learned or achieved.

A dream this P.M., suffused even on awakening with the unpleasant taste of life under the garbage truck. A quick call to visitors' room; some encumbrance, all my pitiful junk somehow to be gotten rid of quickly; showing up before the hack with "things" still in my pockets, his raising hell about it, visit further delayed . . . Philip present for meeting, evidently with friends of uncertain vintage; could not remember names, only half remember faces . . . a kind of sweaty screwed-up image of death, quite befitting the time and place . . .

We aren't allowed the natural light of twilight or dusk. Their way of depriving us of those hours when sorcery and dissolution and "making" are briefly at their strongest. They flick on big Babylonian eyes to keep out the forces that would bring on clean life and clean death and the seeing of both, eye to eye.

You think you're hanging onto the edge of something with the bloody tips of your soul, you say to yourself: what if tomorrow or the next hour or even now walking the eternal squirrel cage you were to say to yourself—why not chuck it all; what's it for anyway? Couldn't one simply say, no more, no more, agree that no one can live like this and not be reduced to a bushel of bloody feathers?

But you don't do this, yield to this. It wouldn't be in consonance with one's own soul, which, bloody or nicked or stupefied, or all of these and more, is still in some strange way in command, on its feet; more, conscious of the strange congruity of the whole scene, the ingathering of wasted absurdity, crudity, pinheaded violence, all of it.

The less words mean the more logical it would seem that silence is the ordinary mode, both of inner and outer communion. We are approaching the point where this law seems to be sensible.

I am in no wise cured
I would be carted out of here, dead but not inducted.
        Look to the lowest (at least with the edge of attention)
            if one would discern the highest "they said he loved
                            them. You tell us."
OLD BADS? ————————! Good news.
Welcome Lifer! (Christmas)
opposite of "doing time" is writing poems . . .

Sexist crime of the week: Big Bro got an anonymous note that one inmate was a homosexual. They called him in and locked him up "pending investigation." He spent a week in solitary; nervous and shaken. You feel like screaming, but that isn't particularly helpful. What is needed is the icy good sense to decide (1) to be furious is *dignum* and *justum*, (2) to be in purgatory is still to be responsible, (3) you have to have a capacity for anger if you are ever to come to love.

Everything that really happens to me happens quick—most of it ruinous. Downhill, lately, all the way, with long slopes to drag around and take it in; no view but down.

December 17

Sometimes the "sense of rightness" wells up in me. Take it for the fruit of a great deal of suffering and wandering among rights and wrongs, rather than the instant flush of the consumptive Jesus freak—dead before alive. A metaphysical reality, not a narrowly ethical one. Right with the stars, right with the dimly perceived reductive state of the most splendid scattered richness of things outside. Right with the lives and deaths of those who must die at our hands or live only by fleeing and hiding from those mad instruments.

I say thank you and my fears for a while at least are conquered. I feel at one with the righteous conquest of the wrongs and illnesses of creation, by that healing, compassionate rightness which sets all right, an act of sovereign healthfulness . . .

As the smile of 7 A.M. sets all the sordid grayness of the world aright.

As the noble sadness of John's Gospel is somehow mysteriously in tune with the local right note in the universal symphonic tragedy.

Weak and childish today and yet *gratia victrix!*

The "bad feeling" about being here, a sort of black necessity whirring away at the edge of consciousness like bat wings, a stinking sense of futility and helplessness, the smell of bats and belfries and graves . . . Something that comes over one suddenly, without warning, and seizes the heart like a physician of the dead, and declares it a dead organ, after putting it to death. Induced by the face of a guard, the blare of the mad trumpet that summons one to a visit as though to his execution. A meeting of all the causes of the unmaking of men, a sour, fetid mix lying like a gall at the bottom of the soul—unassailable, undigested during all the months. Turning one sour, short-tethered, a stranger to his habitual good sense and sweetness.

But I am a prisoner. Taste it, like bat's blood. Marked with it, as with stain. Accept it in the soul, live with it, sleep on it, awake to it. Yourself: stranger, plague-stricken, apart.

Sound of lockup. Good night, another bad night.

December 20

Dear Jack—

I have pondered for many hours some few words of greeting and encouragement to our friends as Christmas approached. Not an easy task, I assure you. Another Christmas, and we seem as far as ever from the hope of our hearts —peace on earth forever delayed, forever pushed aside by the cynical and self-seeking powers of the world.

And yet there remains hope. There remains hope—which is very nearly the only thing worth talking about. When I say hope, I mean that we have available the breath and energy needed to approach the truth of things and to embrace it; to cast out the devils of fear, inanition, and doldrums that hold us in bondage. I mean we are graced with a moment of recognition. I mean we see something like this: the world, the world of the poor, the exploited, the victims, those who live and die under the latest outrageous bombings or border crossings, those in hospitals and prisons and refugee camps— this world does not lie under the dominion, the curse of evil. I hope it does not. And in that hope is my victory. I hope that this world lies within the providence of the One who, on Christmas, lies within the world, a child—poor as any, exploited as any, a statistic in the ledger of the powerful— a Jewish infant, hunted down, we are told, from His birth, by the first of a long dynasty of Herods. Need we say more? I hope in this child. I hope that you may hope in Him too.

But what do we rightfully hope for from Him? For I think the content of our hopes may be of prime import. What we hope for in fact separates us radically from those who place their hopes in armaments, in money, in worldly power—in all the vain trappings and weapons which are so strikingly absent from the birth of this child.

What do we hope for from Him? We may *not* hope that He will take up arms against evil men of power, or that He will somehow equalize the lot of rich and poor. Or even, closer to our case, that He will spring the locks and bars of prisons; or that He will end the war, will restore exiles to their families. We are *not* allowed to hope for an act of God that would amount to nothing more than an act of magic. It is indeed possible that all human wrongs would be put superficially to rights, and yet that evil would remain strongly entrenched within men and their institutions; the poor filled with envy, the rich with lust for enslavement, the whites with racism, the belligerent with thoughts of violence, and so on and so on.

In all such areas of change, one can only say that God refuses to act. He refuses all false hope, since such hope would redress nothing, heal no one, change no hearts, bring none to repentance.

In all such areas, God wills to remain—helpless; to make no difference, to interfere at no point, to force no issue. He is literally as passive as an infant before our freedom, before our folly, our evil choices, our arrangements of convenience, our endless skill at self-deception, half measures, mitigation, power politics. God is a stranger to such a world, He moves within it innocent as a babe.

To come to true hope, it is necessary to cast out false hope. To come to true God, it is necessary to cast out false gods.

In this sense it may be a good thing to be in prison as Christmas approaches, to undergo with other prisoners and for their sake a change of heart that corresponds to one's change of scene—to exile from family and friends, to being placed bodily in that scene of the first Christmas, close to the burning heart of poverty, loneliness, shared suffering. Thus one may resign his freedom in the world for the sake of an unborn freedom; in order to invite others to hope, truthfully, fearlessly—in the image of that God who this day voices His hope for us.

His hope for us. Peace on earth, to men of good will.

We will not use the weapons of this world, even against those who glory in the weapons of this world. We will not be tricked or sweetly reassured or brutalized or cajoled or nar-coticized into accepting violence as the inevitable course of things—for Americans, for Christians. We will not be content, in Danbury prison, or anywhere in the world, to live at peace with the enslavement, the dismemberment, the impoverishment, the death of our brothers and sisters. Thus far our hope in God, who has first hoped in us. For a sign of hope in us, for a sign of hope that we would be human, He has Himself become human—the simplest and most blindingly logical act of hope. So we respond; we will live like men, or we will die like men; the difference being a small one, as long as the substance of our humanity, which is to say, our hope, remains intact.

Thus do we hope. It goes without saying—our hope includes you, as yours includes us. Together, in prison or out, peaceable, courageous, aware, as we strive to be, even we may be called the hope of God Himself in the world.

The larger issues remain—grievous, overmastering: the war, the anxiety, the unknown. It seems as though men will grant the child a filthy corner of the world to be born into—but only as long as they, not He, hold the reins of power and decide who shall live, who die. He is content. He is born. He hopes on, in us—in our unselfishness, our courage, our love for one another. Merry Christmas to all.

December 21

This is to say thank you in the only way, or one of the only ways, left. I remember you, 6 feet 4, broad as a dray horse, a voice of black thunder, striding around the sordid yard, promoting theater, a few stock phrases out of some third-rate handbook on revolution: Right on; Power to . . . You were stuck in the common muck, like ourselves, but deeper than ourselves; five years for refusing military service. Turned in, as it happened, by your own father; you, a black man proud as a demon, refusing the white man's fare of violence, guts, and chauvinism. So you landed here.

Shortly to learn, as we all had to learn, there is nothing like the difference between rumor and reality—every hell contains a deeper hell. They threatened you the first week, threw you into solitary by the fourth. "Inter House Visiting." You languish there, as of the writing of these lines.

We apologize to you, your fellow prisoners, who lack the peerless restoring sight of you, the sonic boom of your voice, your saving arrogance, your electric spirit among damp souls; a light, a human face, in the field of the dead . . .

Some passage must be entitled: beginning again.

Every day requires it, shaking off the old blind staggers, the sense of defeat, of being borne under by the poisoned atmosphere . . .

Then others as well; every new arrival among us says, in

one way or another: I can't begin from where you are, catch on to the moving van. Slow down, or stop dead, to let me aboard . . . So be it. But that takes hard doing, a sense of another's needs as prior to our purring passage, our self-congratulation, sense of having arrived against all expectation . . . Maybe, at this point, we are meant to include you, as a body must carry along, as it is carried along by, all its limits and gains!

December 22

Reading Barth's *Credo*: thinking how persuasively and simply he puts the truth, in a rational frame; a mind intent on and rejoicing in its function. Regretting also, being old enough to regret not being in such an age when the faith may be quietly exfoliated, leaf on leaf, before the "wondering admiration" of the faithful.

No. Grimaces, hints, splotches, silhouettes dimly and clumsily apprehended, fits and starts, itching for novelty, stimulation, body-feel; all the instant rewards that have nothing to do with classic liturgy or response or indeed with the "itinerary of the soul toward God . . ."

The time may be good for art but is lousy for theology.

Or is this merely part of the regret that clouds an "aging intellect"? Am I to take comfort in happenings, tinny music, force-fed spontaneity? . . . Superstar?

The discovery of *limits*; one way of putting the prison experience. It took so little time for me; "normal" work, noise, the grinding of gears was too much; from stupefaction and appalling and forced labor. By June I was a heap of twitching bones on the floor of the hospital. Since then, *limits* of every kind, hour by hour; walls, days, irritation at people, the ebb tide of exhaustion.

ANOTHER MOTHER FOR PEACE:
a Christmas letter

This year my brother and I will observe Christmas as we did a year ago; in prison.

Our mother, eighty-five years old, will observe the holiday at home, waiting, pondering, hoping. She waits, not for our release alone, but for the release of all prisoners, here and everywhere. She awaits in her prayer the release of humanity from the iron, conscienceless prison of war.

We who are her sons see in her many aspects of women's place in America. Her life has spanned two world wars, the Korean and Vietnam wars, urban upheavals, depression, political assassination of those on whom our best hopes had rested, the agonies of our poor. She saw four of her sons off to the Second War, two of her sons ordained Catholic priests; she supported us during our "crime," our trial, and visited us in prison. She said on television when asked about our breaking the law: "But it was not God's law they violated."

She had gone, I feel, to the heart of the matter; not only for us, but for all Americans, and more especially, for American women. Modern war is by necessity total war; it mobilizes literally everyone and everything, resources, moneys, families, human lives, conscience itself, on its ugly behalf. It is absurd then that women could think they stand apart from the issue of war. It is doubly absurd that they would dream of liberation, apart from the common task; which is the liberation of all from the bloody yoke that weighs unbearably on all.

Certainly the trouble is not that we do not want peace. We have seen enough war, we are sick of it, unto death. The war has come home like a stalking corpse, trailing its blood, its tears, its losses, its despairs—seeking like an American ghost the soul of America. We want the peace; but most of us do not want to pay the price of peace. We still dream of a peace that has no cost attached. We want peace, but we live content with poverty and injustice and racism, with the murder of prisoners and students, the despair of the poor to whom justice is endlessly denied. We long for peace, but we wish also to keep undisturbed a social fabric of privilege and power that controls the economic misery of two thirds of the world's people.

Obviously there will be no genuine peace while such an inherently violent scheme of things continues. America will in time extricate herself from the bloody swamps, the ruined villages, the mutilated dead of Vietnam. But nothing will be settled there, nothing mitigated at home. Nothing changed, that is, until a change of heart leads to a change of social structures in every area of our lives. In this change women will of necessity play a great part. Only thus will they liberate themselves.

To do this they must see clearly the nature of their enslavement. The modern state is perpetually mobilized for war, a mobilization of conscience, appetite, cupidity, and fear. Such a dragnet necessarily takes captive the 50 per cent of Americans who are women.

Women are part of the war-making state. It is absurd to conclude from some high-blown idealism that keeps women mesmerized in their place that American women do not want what American men want. The fact that women are taught to "want for their men," to extend male aggression into the home, into the children, into the schools and churches, does not change the fact one whit. Women have learned their lesson well. They are irreplaceable, efficient cogs in a cyclic machinery of cupidity and consumerism; they produce the children who fight the hot wars and accept cold war as inevitable. They guard private property, demand lily-white schools, resist neighborhood integration, reinforce the corrupt "nine points of the law" politics of those in possession.

Liberation from all this will mean something quite simple. For some women liberation will mean casting off the role of preordained poverty and exploitation; they will refuse any longer to be victims. Women must also refuse to act as the exploiters of others, realizing how cruelly dispassionate the will to power is, knowing that those who enslave inevitably become the victims of their own violence, greed, and hate.

The season we celebrate is one of the liberation of peoples. In Jewish and Christian tradition the liberation is both the gift of God and the achievement of men and women. It costs: blood, tears, energy, imagination—above all and including all, love, the instrument and end of all human striving.

Greetings to you, from prison. Peace and liberation.

December 25—after midnight Mass

I was reading Platonov's short stories all evening. The assistant warden came around armed with gifts in mufti clothing, in a box; just like ourselves. We had midnight Mass. I sit here afterward writing this like a sparrow chirping against the wind . . . Second Christmas here, a great outpouring nationally of cards, letters, encouragement. Last night our class had its Christmas runaround. What is it to each of us, this

Christmas? I was struck that the resisters, not many of whom are religious in any conventional sense, were still able to hit the most positive note; they hope for something of mankind. The others fidget, sweat in the stocks, hit hard on the putrescent fallout, which of course can be smelled by anyone with a face; but so what.

It is a question, as in Vietnam or anywhere else, of where one's center of gravity lies . . .

A long walk round and round in the rain with Phil today; soaked. But good and invigorating. Earlier, visit from Bill Guindon. He is a superior sort of man. I have to confess anger, though, when visitors ask banteringly after my health as though I were a professional invalid who only needs—à la Mrs. Gamp—to be poked with sticks or have his thumbs turned back in order to be brought around. Fact is I have very low days quite often, gut troubles etc., and require quite a bit of auto-arse-kicking to keep functioning at all.

A wet, blustery day. September or March in December. Hardly any snow yet this winter, we walk bemused as though half willing, half submitting to this freaky spell in nature.

Usual funky Mass relieved by Phil's reading of the Gospel, good handshakes before communion and many embrazzos later.

Ann here. Also Kunstler, hair in prophetic profusion, straight from trial of Harlem Six, which he pronounces good as won. Which may the gods bring to pass; and himself, Kunstler, for our brothers in the great world.

A group of us will fast tomorrow.

At least a few of the men seemed to sense the love we have for them—that they are the reason we are here, that we in a sense represent the high stakes of being men; however dimly they sensed this, there were tears in their eyes and their whole being in their faces when they greeted us after Mass. Indeed a moment of truth.

December 25, 12 P.M.

End of this day, Lew Cox here A.M. Ann B., P.M. Honey Knopp visited. We fasted all day except for some cereal which my gut obliges me to take. A ridiculous "down" movie *Came a Crooked Man*; about prison while being in prison, a veritable mirror of violence and horror.

Priests are taking off more and more into bizarre directions. Think of Nick, that sane gentleman of the D.C. Nine, now pleading guilty to armed robbery. Madness! Ed S. of my year, fifty and fat, holed away out of the world during a sabbatical listening to fundamentalist Bible preachers. What's your line? Vulgar, depressed, outlandish, evidence of a deep despair. One could do worse than jail these days!

Said to Cox: don't these people know *we* have a tradition too? Thought often on the suggestion and example of Platonov to try writing something futuristic. But why? The present is weird and uncontrollable and unknowable enough, one can scarcely discern its outline as it rushes by, a wind from a furnace, consuming all. If the first year of the '70s finds me in jail, where will the '80s find me? Ten years ago I was peaceably (peaceably?) teaching theology, wrapped in a cassock like a knight in his iron suit, locked secure. Tonight I sit under a raw prison bulb in frayed khakis, listening to the plumbing gurgle, my feet pressed on a concrete floor, setting down these notes through a fog of bad eyesight. Health precarious, future dim. And happy habitually as a thrush in clover—though unwarranted silent, a hushed thrush. Ha!

GANDHI

1) He invites compassion, not only with the world political leaders but with the religious believers as well. He embodies a tradition rather than mechanically acting it out.

2) The West, caught in the throes of its own violent de-

cline, might well look to a man for whom truth surpassed every seduction of religious bigotry, nationalism, racist "untouchability," the question of animals and ecology, love and rage.

3) His experiment with truth reached simultaneously into the world and into his own life. He wagered himself in the world; and the world on himself. This was an act of trust of the highest order. It must be conceded that he could not have entered on such a covenant without faith in God as arbiter of history.

4) On self: dietary laws, chastity, truth; in the world: fair dealing, honor, loving tactics, the truth. The two arenas were themselves self-revealing. The more he experimented on himself, the more skilled, experienced he became in dealing with the world.

5) Two steps to an experiment: crisis and reconciliation. The first unmasks the untruth, violence, fear, injustice at the heart of a given situation. The second makes healing possible, palatable.

6) One is to prefer, with Jesus, to suffer violence rather than inflict it. With Gandhi, this takes the form of a willingness to take on himself the burden of social sin. He becomes in his own flesh a sign of both crisis and reconciliation. This is not to be conceived of as a mere "show," or worse, a weapon against others. He really believed in the unity of man, in crisis as in reconciliation. He believed he was his brother's second (therefore) better thought, and vice versa.

7) Charism can easily come to equal idolatry. How does the charismatic leader neither a) consent to deny his mission, nor b) be seduced into becoming the "movement idol," further alienating members from growth and self-initiated action . . . I think he dealt with this as well as might be. Obviously the thing is never entirely solved.

a) He shared the weakness of others: he was that strong. When he fasted because others failed, he wanted to convey his sense that *he* had failed, that his teaching was awry. He refused all personal honor, money, security—the rewards of "leadership" in the world—so he set himself apart from the world, rejected it passionately, and slowly built up a new way of regarding the style of initiating social change. His fasting, silence, etc. must also be seen in this light: a rejection, subjection of that part of himself which was in connivance with the world.

b) So he was able to appear before his own soul and the public as *friend of man*, i.e., the one who neither dissembled nor bullied.

c) He experimented with personal relationships as well; sensing that one-to-one was the world writ small. He must find new ways in education, commune, industry; a way of making the world comprehensible, manageable.

d) In fact, no area of his life escaped his determination to live as a "new man."

e) His appeal to the transcendent is at once a call to the human. He wanted only to be human, so he called on God. There was no religious "argument"—he wanted only to "include" the most diverse realities in his search.

In most, age is the triumph of the unconscious; in him, lucid self-understanding; choice of life.

December 26

He came in tonight, without a knock, opening the door, only half coherent, crying like a bull struck by a mallet, if in a bull's heart were a man's pain.

Two friends killed; murdered.

They had been here to visit him some weeks ago. I remembered them because they came into the visiting room wearing bright tam-o'-shanters, identical in knit and shape but of different loud color. And they had refused in spite of orders of the sour guard to take off their hats. They sat there clowning and mock-serious by turn, waiting for P. to come through the door. When he came the three of them set up a paisano whoop that stopped the room dead.

The two are dead today, a gangland killing. The con enters my cell like a dazed bull, the faces of his dead friends pasted to his red eyes. His thoughts are those of a stricken animal, violence and God . . . I suggest the occasion befits neither. He will have to live with these deaths, this double hammer blow, and recover from it, and come to some better mind, about himself, his life and its direction, the bullets which strangely enough a prison wall protected him from.

He may be on the road to manhood at last. May be; it is too early to tell.

To round this off, a few random stories

A man I know had a dead mouse strung around his neck. The little creature, fanciful and devout, had its two pink hands folded neatly at its breast. It had been hanged by the neck.

He used to say when questioned: it's my savior, my albatross; I carry it because I believe in the resurrection of the dead, as well as in rodent power.

He also had a sense of being strung around some greater neck. But he seldom spoke of this; it was a species of lightheadedness that came from always doing the same things at the same time, looking at the same sky, eating the same food. Was he dead on his feet (often he didn't seem to be making ground) or was this the way it felt to be saved?

The little dried mouse, its teeth half revealed in a knowing smile, said nothing. Neither did—

The liberator was pounding like a bull's head, like a fist, at the throng that had gathered for days in the plaza to hear the good news. His beard was aquiver with the electricity that continually shot out sparks of creation into the eyes of those below him. He was making free men, he shouted, his arms going like an industrious windmill. So many factories,

so many new houses. Such a dream! He was sweaty as a giant
in a nightmare, he gave off a smell of will, of bullish intelligent purpose, he set his shoulder to the impervious wall of
history and heaved and pushed—shoved the throng, on and
on and on, with him, like a man who makes a tunnel, miles
long, engineering, shoring up, creating as he goes.

One man under the platform stood there like all the others,
to all intent earnest, hanging closely on the theme, the dream
. . . mouth open, face lifted.

Only he kept to himself a secret face, under his jacket
maybe, next to his breastbone. His face was exposed neither
to the sun nor to the blare of the liberator's voice nor to the
bullish answering roar of the throng. A secret blind face; its
outline the shape of his breast, a caul covering a face, a face
whose eye was his heart, just under the skin.

Incongruous. How like a scaffold the great plank platform
was. The liberator surrounded by his guard; how like a condemned man, sweating through his last speech.

How the sun stood there like an angel's sword. How much
death was in the air, how stale the air was, for all the claims
of freshness, life, freedom.

That secret blind face, how much it saw! It would be the
death of that man, only wait till its mouth opened one
day . . .

A girl with different-colored eyes; the left was tangerine,
the right coal black.

With the left she saw by day and with the right saw equally
well by night.

"With the right eye," she told me, "I see the sun, which
is tangerine in color, and flowers, which are variously red,
white, or golden."

Oranges, tangerines, nectarines, and apricots, however, left
her helpless. She could neither see, smell, nor taste them.
I have seen her hand pass over the laden bough of an orange
tree, pausing only among the leaves, passing through the
fruit like a magician's blade, or pure spirit. She said noth-

ing was there, she was bewildered at our insistence, our bewilderment.

At night she saw everything like a cat or owl or bat. Everything except the night. For her sunset was a fiction; she lived like a disenfranchised Eskimo, among twenty-four-hour days.

Not to know the night! She was like a cruel and totally illumined flat moon, beaten flat by a rolling pin and elbows, condemned to be all light, no shadow, no mystery.

Even her death was a blinding noon, as though she fled, not under ground, but into the heart of the sun.

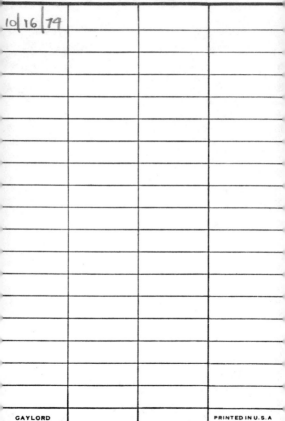

DATE DUE

10 16 79			
GAYLORD			PRINTED IN U.S.A